What Is
Buddhist
Enlightenment?

———◦(◦)◦———

DALE S. WRIGHT

OXFORD
UNIVERSITY PRESS

OXFORD
UNIVERSITY PRESS

Oxford University Press is a department of the University of Oxford. It furthers
the University's objective of excellence in research, scholarship, and education
by publishing worldwide. Oxford is a registered trade mark of Oxford University
Press in the UK and certain other countries.

Published in the United States of America by Oxford University Press
198 Madison Avenue, New York, NY 10016, United States of America.

CIP data is on file at the Library of Congress
ISBN 978–0–19–062259–6

3 5 7 9 8 6 4 2

Printed by Sheridan Books, Inc., United States of America

Contents

Acknowledgments

THOSE WHO STUDY Buddhist philosophy or engage in any of its practices of introspective mindfulness cannot help but develop an awareness of a paradox at the very center of human life—that our freedom or independence is correlative with its opposite, our dependence. This is to say that our capacity to stand on our own, independently, is roughly proportional to the guidance and help that we have been given from birth forward. Although these dependencies are so far-reaching in my case that I cannot possibly name them, it seems important to state openly that whatever has been accomplished in this book is deeply dependent on the roles played in my life by many people and many communities. Without their guidance and support, this would not have been possible.

I bow in deep appreciation to my parents and ancestors and extend that gratitude to many other members of my family too numerous to name, although in this instance, I cannot help but mention Brendan Wright, Lindsay Wright, and Diana Browning Wright. Gratitude goes to my teachers at all levels but especially in later stages: Allan Anderson, G. Ray Jordan, Issa Kahlil, Wang Pachow, Robert Baird, Robert Scharlemann, and Taizan Maezumi. Thanks to many students at Occidental College whose expectation that I teach something worthwhile has helped me to learn something worthwhile, and to everyone at Occidental College with whom I have long shared the pleasures and struggles of a diverse and complex intellectual community. Deep appreciation goes to friends and colleagues with whom ideas are shared and honed, among them Maria Antonaccio, Steven Barrie-Anthony, Stephen Batchelor, Sylvie Baumgartl, David Eckel, Steven Heine, David James, David Jasper, John Kelly, Karen King, David Klemm, Taigen Leighton, Sam Mowe, D. Keith Naylor, and Kristi Upson-Saia. Special appreciation to Malek Moazzam-Doulat with whom I have cultivated ideas in a course titled "What Is Enlightenment?" I extend my gratitude to Cynthia Read and her staff at Oxford University Press as a fortunate recipient of the professional expertise that this publisher has long exhibited at the highest level of excellence. I dedicate this book to the poet in my life, Martha Ronk, upon whom I depend daily for love and liberation.

The ideas presented in this book have been under development for much of my life. Several chapters and segments of chapters have appeared in publication in earlier stages of this development and are acknowledged here. A preliminary version of chapter 1 was published in *Ethics in the World's Religions*, edited by Joseph Runzo and Nancy M. Martin (Oxford: One World Press, 2001). Several of the key points in chapter 4 were published in an essay, "Critical Questions Toward a Naturalized Concept of Karma," in the *Journal of Buddhist Ethics* (Vol. 2, 2004). An earlier version of chapter 5, "*Satori* and the Moral Dimension of Enlightenment," was published in the *Journal of Buddhist Ethics* (Vol. 13, 2006). A version of 6 appeared as "Humanizing the Image of a Zen Master: Maezumi Roshi," in *Zen Masters,* edited by Steven Heine and Dale S. Wright (Oxford: Oxford University Press, 2010). A version of chapter 8 was published as "Re-thinking Transcendence: The Role of Language in Zen Experience," in *Philosophy East and West* (Vol. 42, No. 1, January 1992). A version of chapter 9 was previously published as "Empty Texts/ Sacred Meaning: Reading as Spiritual Practice in Chinese Buddhism," in *Dao: Journal of Comparative Philosophy* (Vol. 2, No. 2, Summer 2003). Chapter 10 is an expansion of ideas first published as "The 'Thought of Enlightenment' in Fa-tsang's Hua-yen Buddhism," in *The Eastern Buddhist* (Vol. 33, No. 2, 2001).

What Is Buddhist Enlightenment?

Introduction

WHY ASK WHAT ENLIGHTENMENT IS?

WHEN EUROPEAN INTELLECTUALS in the late eighteenth century engaged in high-profile, public debate on the question "What is enlightenment?,"[1] Buddhist answers to this question never came up for consideration, and it is safe to say that no participant in these debates would have or could have believed that this "oriental" religion had anything even remotely to do with "enlightenment." Although knowledge of Buddhism was already accumulating in Europe by that time through the merchants, missionaries, and soldiers that the various European empires had dispatched to Asia, what they "knew" about Buddhism was that this ascetic, monastic religion was curiously nihilistic in its central goal: *nirvāna* or "nothingness" as it was called in various European languages. "Enlightenment," by contrast, was—in Immanuel Kant's influential version—a state of "maturity" in individuals and communities that gave them the courage to think for themselves rather than turning the crucial decisions in their lives over to priests and lords. It seemed to them that the teachings of the Buddha were intended to negate and transcend human life whereas the "enlightenment" that modernity cultivated turned away from the ascetic world denial characteristic of traditional religions in preference for a liberating affirmation of human life in this world.

A little over a half century later, for an interesting set of reasons, Max Müller and other philosophically minded scholars curious about Asia began to use the word "enlightenment" in reference to the ultimate goal of Buddhism. What Buddhists sought and sometimes attained through their practices, these scholars claimed, was enlightenment. The prestige that the word "enlightenment" still carried in Europe initiated a radical reversal of views about Buddhism. This linguistic and cultural innovation was so successful that, by the end of the twentieth century, very few people in the West could hear the question "What is enlightenment?" without thinking of Buddhism. "Enlightenment" came to signify what Buddhism was all about, and nothing seemed to be about enlightenment as much as Buddhism.[2]

In spite of that historical development, however, very little discussion of the meaning or possibility of enlightenment takes place among contemporary Buddhists, East or West. The question "What is enlightenment?" is carefully avoided, acquiring, in effect, an almost taboo status among Buddhists. There are interesting and often persuasive reasons for this unspoken prohibition on inquiry into the meaning of enlightenment, including the following:

- In the early stages of the practice of Buddhism, whatever conception we might have of enlightenment would be misleading, even blatantly false, and in more advanced stages of practice there would be no point in asking the question.
- Any answer we might give to the question "What is enlightenment?" would inevitably reify the aim of the spiritual quest, and reification—considering something more substantial and definable than it could ever be—is in Buddhism the quintessential error of an unenlightened life.
- Any concept of enlightenment that we might hold as a goal will inevitably presuppose a troublesome temporal dichotomy between our unenlightened present and our hoped-for enlightened future, so the goal is always projected far out ahead of us in time and is, as a consequence, never present in the here and now.
- In any case, pondering a distant goal in theory is a waste of current energy—energy that would be much better applied to practice. Instead, quiet the flow of obsessive thinking, put yourself in a mindful state of presence, and let enlightenment take care of itself.

Although we could probably extend this list of reasons to avoid the question that guides this book, our aim is to provide persuasive reasons to the contrary. This book aspires to make the case that, if you are a serious practitioner of human life, whether Buddhist or not, the question "What is enlightenment?" (or any equivalent version of the question) is among the most important questions you can possibly ask. Although justification pg 3 questions:

Thich Nhat Hahn : The 3rd door pg. 154
OF Liberation = aimlessness

. There is nothing to do, nothing to
realize, no program, no agenda.

. Your purpose is to be Yourself.

. No need to run, strive, search or struggle

. our responsibility is to bring peace
+ joy into our own lives

. If I worry, am anxious - the
situation doesn't change. I
only add to the disharmony (negative
energy)

CONFIRMED CUSTOMER CONCERN. BUMPE
0PSI. SPRAYED ALL TIRES WITH SOAF
ITON. UPON INSPECTION FOUND NO SI
NCTURES. SET PSI BACK TO MANUFACT
RESET TIRE LIGHT. ROAD TEST.

- -

#4 - MATSOK: VEHICLE IS EQUIPPED WITH
             FLOOR MAT, AND IS INSTALLED
             FACTORY GUIDELINES.

- -

Please Note: CC CREATED 2018-08-24 09

for that claim is explored throughout the chapters of this book, the most significant initial points are as follows.

First, without some motivationally effective conception of an aim in life, there would never be a beginning to transformative practice. Engagement in practice always gets underway because there is a reason to do it, a motivating thought that inspires disciplined action. This reason is the realization that there may be insights into the meaning of our lives and ways to live our lives that are profoundly superior to the ones we currently exhibit. The point of Buddhist practice is that it might eventuate in some form of awakening, in some groundbreaking transformation: in enlightenment. Synonyms for the question "What is enlightenment?" would, among others, include

"What ideals should I pursue in my life?"
"What kinds of lives should we be living?"
"Who or what should I strive to become?"
"What kind of community should we aspire to create?"
"What would it mean for all of us to wake up to the realities and possibilities for human life now within our reach?"

Answers to any version of this overarching question provide an ideal image in view of which we activate our lives and get some form of transformative practice underway. In this sense we must have asked the question "What is enlightenment?," at least implicitly, in order to have found an answer compelling enough to put us on the path of practice.

Second, not only do we initiate a discipline or practice in the wake of motives provided by this fundamental questioning; it is also true that ongoing meditation on the ideal of enlightenment is essential all along the path once practice is underway. Enlightenment is not something that we understand adequately at the outset and then proceed to achieve by focusing entirely on the means to an already known goal. The image or conception of enlightenment and the practice of it are correlative. They belong together and function in reciprocity. The fact that anyone's initial image of an enlightened goal is invariably naïve coincides with the level of sophistication of the practice itself, which at the outset is always immature and underdeveloped. But when the understanding of what we seek changes, so does the way we seek it, and when our mode of practice changes, so does its rationale and aim. Conception of enlightenment as the aim of practice and the practice itself are both corrected and reimagined in light of each

other in ongoing reciprocity. If things go well, the initial interests of anyone seriously engaged in practice will be transformed through the practice
to the point that they no longer seek exactly what it was that brought them
to the practice in the first place.

Third, the foregoing points imply that a serious spiritual practice
includes an ongoing education in the character of what it is that we ought
to pursue in life. This is especially important since the most effective forms
of enlightenment are those that are well aligned with the individual characters of those who seek them—that is, aligned with their own particular
backgrounds, histories, capacities, strengths, weaknesses, inclinations,
loves, and orientations. Because there is thus no single "enlightened" state
to pursue, if we have not continued to meditate on what it is that we seek
to embody in our lives, we may very well be pursuing an inappropriate
and inadequate goal by means of practices that are out of sync with who
we are.

Vibrant spiritual communities recognize that their ideals and overall
aims will inevitably be reformulated from time to time as the tradition
evolves and as history presents new difficulties and opportunities. Such
communities encourage rather than fear critical reflection on their highest
ideals. The greatest figures in the Buddhist tradition from the Buddha and
Nāgārjuna to Tsong-kha-pa, Dōgen, and Shinran were individuals whose
answers to the question "What is enlightenment?" went beyond what
their traditions maintained in their time. They succeeded in reformulating both the image of enlightenment and the character of its practice so
persuasively that new subtraditions were formed. Their own experiments
in conceiving and practicing "the Buddha Way" expanded the number of
"ways" that Buddhism could encompass. Over time, large-scale traditions
like the major religions become repositories of these ideals—collections of
answers to the question "What is enlightenment?" that are made available
to practitioners in their own efforts to respond to this question in their
own lives. Since there is not just one kind of life that fulfills the criteria of
"enlightenment" for all people in all circumstances, the responsibility falls
to each of us to grapple seriously with that question and to live our lives in
light of our best answers.

These points suggest a fourth realization concerning the importance
of ongoing meditation on enlightenment—that there are at least two overarching kinds of practice. One is engagement in chosen practices that
are effective "means" for the transformation of our lives, and the other
is engagement in practices that seek to reconceive and deepen the "ends"

that our practices seek. The first proceeds by simply assuming the ideal to which it aspires—just taking it on faith in order to advance in the practice—and the second submits those ideal ends to critical scrutiny and imaginative extension. Spiritual traditions at their best incorporate both of these practices, but the open recognition that critical reflection and debate over ideals is an equally essential practice is rare. Although we will always live on the implicit or explicit foundations of some answer to the question "What is enlightenment?," keeping that question open and alive as a vibrant working inquiry and as a form of contemplative discipline helps avoid the dogmatic tendencies that emerge when traditions become inflexible, static, and no longer attentive to the conditions and possibilities alive in their time.

The chapters in this book are grouped into three larger categories of inquiry—Contemporary Images of Enlightenment, The Moral Dimension of Enlightenment, and Language and the Experience of Enlightenment—so readers can either begin with their areas of primary interest or read directly through from start to finish. The chapters address a wide range of issues that have a bearing on the contemporary meaning of enlightenment, each chapter adopting a different theme and each probing in its own direction.

Chapter 1, "The Bodhisattva's Practice of Enlightenment," interprets a *Los Angeles Times* newspaper opinion piece by Thich Nhat Hanh as a contemporary image of enlightenment with far-reaching implications. Written in response to the brutal police beating of Rodney King and not intended for a Buddhist audience, this small op-ed essay nevertheless provides glimpses into the contemporary meaning of enlightenment. The chapter considers Thich Nhat Hanh's comments in relation to the basic principles of Buddhist ethics before turning to the *Vimalakīrti sūtra*, a classical Mahayana Buddhist scripture, to extend an understanding of what it would mean to experience the world through an in-depth awareness of "no-self." Dwelling on the bodhisattva's effort to cultivate generosity of spirit, we consider the kinds of human relations that Thich Nhat Hanh's sense of enlightenment entails.

Chapter 2, "The Awakening of Character as an Image of Enlightenment," describes in some detail two unforgettable characters in the Korean Buddhist film *Mandala* in order to consider the range of diversity that enlightenment can encompass. Two very different Buddhist monks are presented in the film as deeply enveloped in ordinary human suffering and as breaking through that suffering to experience a transformation of character that we can only understand as enlightenment. While the kinds of character that emerge in each case are quite distinct, viewers are left to puzzle over how these entirely different paths through human life could both be legitimate instances of enlightenment. While each character in the film provides an image of the Buddhist path for us to contemplate, we are presented with the task of sorting out how our own paths align or contrast with the two provided.

Chapter 3, "Secular Buddhism and the Religious Dimension of Enlightenment," follows Stephen Batchelor's impressive effort to articulate what Buddhist awakening might mean in the current secular culture. Assessing the issues that have prompted the creation of a new nonsectarian "secular Buddhism," this chapter raises questions about whether this form of "secularity" nevertheless continues to carry religious meaning as its most fundamental motivation. Reflecting on the possibility of nontheistic forms of religious practice and experience, it links insights in contemporary Western religious thought to the a-theism that runs throughout the Buddhist tradition in order to further our inquiry into the qualities and character that Buddhist enlightenment might take under contemporary, secularized conditions. This chapter aspires to cultivate insight into the inevitable relationship between religiosity and any quest for enlightenment and hopes to stimulate reflection on what religion might be in our time.

Chapter 4, "Enlightenment and the Experience of Karma," analyzes this traditional Indian and Buddhist moral/ethical concept in order to assess the role that it might play in a contemporary culture of enlightenment. Elucidating five dimensions of this moral principle where questions can be raised by means of critical inquiry, the chapter strives to articulate a naturalized conception of karma that could conceivably play an important role in future global society. In order to do that, we reflect on the traditional connection between karma as a moral principle and rebirth as a religious concept and ask what it might mean to develop a karma-based morality without a necessary link to any traditional understanding of afterlife. The chapter aspires to develop elements implicit in the traditional Indian idea of karma that could provide a basic structure for the human moral practice that is essential to any society and any quest for enlightenment.

Chapter 5, "Enlightenment and the Moral Dimension of Zen Training," responds to a recent controversy about the character or moral quality of Zen enlightenment. The controversy has been ignited by critical accusations that the roles played by a significant number of Japanese Zen masters in the Second World War were morally deficient. The criticism extends to the allegation that their "enlightenment" did not prevent these Zen leaders from active participation in the nation's ruthless military aggression against neighboring countries and that after the war some Zen masters made public statements that expressed an inexcusable indifference to the pain and suffering that their actions in the war helped cause. This chapter seeks to address these criticisms by inquiry into the role of morality in Zen training. It finds that concern for morality does not play a substantial role in Zen training and that the outcomes of Zen practice have not traditionally been thought to include moral sensitivity. The chapter probes further to evaluate what that realization implies about the character of enlightenment in Zen and concludes with open suggestions about how Zen practice might expand to more effectively encompass the moral sphere of human life that has always been central to the Buddhist tradition as a whole.

Chapter 6, "Enlightenment and the Persistence of Human Fallibility," addresses our expectation that the enlightening insights of Zen masters render them invulnerable to the kinds of moral and ethical errors that we make in our lives and that therefore some form of infallibility has been achieved in their lives. The chapter traces this expectation to traditional Zen literature where the great Zen masters demonstrate supernatural powers and transhuman capacities. Realizing that these narrative descriptions of the great Zen masters were animated by the ongoing development of Zen mythology and the devotion of Zen chroniclers, we turn to a highly regarded twentieth-century Zen master whose life we can examine in full detail without the traditional projections of divine powers. The chapter describes the life of Taizan Maezumi Roshi, founder of the Zen Center of Los Angeles, whose life story was marred by tragic errors of judgment but who has nevertheless continued to be regarded as a profoundly enlightened Zen master. Maezumi's life, it concludes, helps us humanize and deepen our understanding of what Zen enlightenment could be.

Chapter 7, "The Thought of Enlightenment and the Dilemma of Human Achievement," undertakes a philosophical examination of the Buddhist concept of *bodhicitta*—the thought of or aspiration for enlightenment. Comparing this Buddhist concept to the Greek philosophical notion of the "idea of the good," we find both playing a similar role in articulating ideal ends—the ultimate goals of human life. If in actual human life, however, these ideals are never fully achieved, a dilemma emerges at the heart of human practice. Although the transformations cultivated through practice may be substantial and far-reaching, perfection remains always beyond our reach. This chapter examines several reasons for that inevitable unreachability and concludes that, rather than undermining the value or legitimacy of the quest, this dilemma of human achievement adds nuance and depth to the meaning of human enlightenment. Because human beings will always strive toward some form of excellence, humility and the capacity to release the tension of compulsive perfectionism become essential features of enlightenment.

Chapter 8, "Language in Zen Enlightenment," attempts to think philosophically about the role that language might play in the experience of enlightenment. Taking as its initial orientation the Zen claim that enlightenment is "not dependent on language and culture" and that enlightenment is understood as a "pure experience" of "things as they are" prior to the shaping effect of language, this chapter asks how we might assess that claim from the perspective of contemporary philosophy and linguistic psychology. That assessment begins by considering the two primary Western interpretations of the relation between language and Zen enlightenment. In order to articulate an alternative understanding of language and spiritual experience that goes beyond these earlier attempts, the chapter explores the kinds of language use found in the daily life of Zen communities, the role of the Zen master's cryptic rhetoric of instruction, and the predominance of silent meditation in Zen training. It concludes with reflection on the possibility that Zen enlightenment might entail awakening *to* the power and subtlety of language rather than *from* it.

Chapter 9, "Enlightenment and the Practice of Meditative Reading," examines the practices of reading and the critiques of reading that were common in the first few centuries of Chinese Chan Buddhist monasticism. Because Chan criticisms of earlier scholastic Buddhism in China were so important, it has been tempting to conclude that reading ceased to be a central practice in the institutions of Chan. But we find, in fact, that reading and writing were perhaps just as central to Chan practice as they had been in earlier forms of Chinese Buddhism. Since at the historical moment when Chan rose to prominence China was the most literate culture in the world, it would have been inevitable that the culture of literacy would extend through Chan practice. Indeed, we find that a highly unusual and sophisticated theory of reading was developed in Chan and that practices of reading aimed at enlightenment thrived. This historical realization raises questions about the relation between our own practices of meditation and reading, suggesting the possibility that our understanding of reading might be developed and deepened by learning to conceive of it as a form of meditative practice.

Chapter 10, "From the Thought of Enlightenment to the Event of Awakening," follows the philosophical reflections of Fazang of the Huayan school of Chinese Buddhism as he explores the progression along the Buddhist path from an initial concept or image of what enlightenment might be all the way through to the culminating experience of enlightenment. His paradoxical claim that complete enlightenment is already fully contained in the first legitimate thought of enlightenment is analyzed in this chapter by understanding it in relation to the basic components of the Huayan Buddhist worldview of thoroughgoing interdependence. In Fazang's Huayan Buddhist philosophy we find in an early philosophical form the basic conceptual elements of the historic debate in China concerning the experience of enlightenment—the widely cited controversy about whether enlightenment occurs gradually over time or through a sudden, momentous breakthrough. This chapter explores the enlightening consequences of meditation on the interdependent character of all realities.

Throughout the chapters of this book the question "What is enlightenment?" is raised in the present and future tenses. Although these meditations often take as their point of departure an interest in what enlightenment was or has been in past Buddhist traditions, the historical considerations in this book are subordinate to the question that our lives press upon us: What kinds of lives should *we* aspire to live here, now, and into the future? The overriding concern in this book, therefore, is for the meaning of enlightenment *for us*—for those of us living in the world right now.

The audacity entailed in any such attempt to write a book on enlightenment will justifiably prompt the question: "How do you know?" The answer in this case is simple: "I don't." This is a book of reflective inquiry; it makes no claim about "knowing" or "knowledge." It does, however, take the risk of probing into a fundamental and therefore sensitive area of Buddhist tradition by raising questions about the ideal of enlightenment and testing possible responses in relation to the lives we live. In doing so, the book seeks to provoke you the reader into your own inquiry on this matter on the hunch that, in the final analysis, there is no more important question to ask than this one. It challenges you to begin meditation on this simple question ("What is enlightenment?") and to pursue it further along paths of your own choosing wherever they lead. While there are few clearly marked directional signs along the way and many confusing crossroads, there is nevertheless considerable illumination provided by Buddhists pathfinders and others in wisdom traditions all over the world. These inspiring guides tell transformative adventure narratives and offer sound advice. But they also challenge us to realize that this is our own life's journey and that no matter how we align our quest with community and tradition, there are important choices to make that are ours and ours alone.

Finally, to get these meditations underway a guiding *kōan* for this book is drawn from a passage in *The Large Sutra on Perfect Wisdom* where a well-known disciple, Subhūti, puts the crucial question to the Buddha:

"How, then, is enlightenment attained?"

Although on this occasion the Buddha would not answer Subhūti's practical "how" question, he nevertheless provides something of enormous value—a vital clue to guide Subhūti's meditation and ours about *what enlightenment is*. He says: "Enlightenment is attained neither through a path nor a nonpath. Just enlightenment is the path and the path is enlightenment."[3]

Dale S. Wright
Eagle Rock
July 2015

PART I

Contemporary Images of Enlightenment

I
_____

The Bodhisattva's Practice
of Enlightenment

IMAGES OF BUDDHIST enlightenment can make their appearance in the least expected places. On April 15, 1991, an unusual op-ed article appeared in the *Los Angeles Times* titled "We Are the Beaters; We Are the Beaten." This brief piece by the well-known Vietnamese Buddhist monk Thich Nhat Hanh offers a startling response to the brutal beating of Rodney King by officers of the Los Angeles Police Department earlier that year, witnessed on television by millions of people all over the world. What is startling about this public response is that amidst all the finger-pointing, blaming, and criticizing that filled the press and the minds of the people of Los Angeles at that time, Thich Nhat Hanh was the only one to step forth and take the blame: "I accept responsibility for this travesty," he appeared to be saying, "and here is what will need to be done to address this severe problem." Since this Buddhist monk does not even live in Los Angeles, much less the United States, that is a surprising admission.

This admission can make sense, however, when understood in relation to traditional Buddhist ethics and an image of Buddhist enlightenment that was developed in the classical texts of Mahayana Buddhism. The point of this chapter is to engage in an extended meditation on several fundamental insights in Buddhist ethics in order to extend them into a clearer articulation of what "enlightenment" might mean in the domain of human relationships. To accomplish this we contemplate Thich Nhat Hanh's newspaper editorial as exemplary of the ethical aim, goal, or intention of Buddhism, interpreting it in relation to the classical principles of Buddhist thought generally and more specifically in relation to an articulation of ethical principles in the *Vimalakīrti sūtra*, an early Mahayana

Buddhist scripture from the second century BCE. The chapter concludes with reflections on what this kind of meditation entails and on the relationship between meditation, Buddhist ethics, and the ultimate aim of enlightenment. Since a specifically Buddhist ethics cannot be understood without reference to several basic principles of Buddhist thought, we begin there.

Fundamental Buddhist Principles

We begin with four early Buddhist ideas that, although certainly not unchanging in the history of Buddhism, do constitute the building blocks from which virtually all later Buddhist philosophical and ethical systems were built. The first is a premise, the reason why Buddhism came to be in the first place. This is that human life in all of its forms entails suffering, universally and inevitably, not just among the downtrodden like Rodney King but for every one of us. Buddhism arises as an answer to human suffering, as a response based upon a certain kind of understanding that reorients and in certain ways overcomes the suffering and awkward dissatisfaction that all of us feel throughout our lives. The next three ideas provide the essentials for that understanding, constituting as they do the starting point for Buddhist meditation.

After *dukkha,* the Buddhist insight into a universal suffering that *marks* all human existence, the second idea is impermanence, the Buddhist principle that nothing remains the same over time. Simply stated, the early Buddhists recognized that all things are in process, in flux, changing from one state or condition into another endlessly, and that failure to recognize this and to adjust one's life accordingly leads inevitably to poor judgment and to forms of clinging and attachment that are doomed to failure in a world of change. Unless we explicitly understand movement and transformation as inevitable in every dimension of the world, both planning on it and allowing for some degree of unpredictability, we will suffer the consequences of this refusal in addition to the pain that has emerged from the situation itself. The capacity to recognize, accept, and begin to understand patterns of change is one condition upon which an enlightened form of life rests.

Third, early Buddhists went further to maintain that change is not random and that at least one principle is visible within it: that all things arise and change over time dependent on relations to other things. Several important realizations follow from the Buddhist principle of "dependent arising": that all things depend on others as their cause or condition; that nothing, therefore, stands alone, independently; and that the extent of our inability to comprehend in a very practical way the "relationality" or "relativity" of everything is another source of misjudgment and hence additional suffering. Everything just depends. The cultivated ability to discern what human experiences like suffering, or kindness, or enlightenment depend upon is another condition for the achievement of both freedom and wisdom.

The fourth and final Buddhist idea that we employ in understanding Thich Nhat Hanh's Buddhist ethics is the counterintuitive and to some extent outrageous idea that there is "no-self"—no soul or no internal, fundamental ground to a human life. *Anātman* can be understood to mean that there is no single element or dimension to a human being that is permanent, stable, and that undergirds all the other less essential elements of life. What prompts this denial of the self in Buddhism are the implications of the doctrines of impermanence and dependent arising. If, like all things, I "arise dependent" on a variety of conditions and change continually throughout my life depending on which other conditioning factors appear—including my own choices—then it would follow that there simply is no dimension to my life that is unchanging and self-established. Buddhists claim that there is no self if by "self" we mean something identical and stable over time that constitutes the real me as opposed to other clearly changeable factors like my body, my thoughts, my feelings, and so on.

There is another motive for this denial of a permanent center to self, however. This is that, from a Buddhist point of view, nothing leads more directly to unwise decisions, emotional clinging, intellectual attachments, and to suffering than "selfish" or self-centered behavior and thinking. And nothing leads more directly to such behavior than the mistaken understanding that I am autonomous and fully independent from others and that this fundamental state of affairs requires me to focus my life and activities completely on my own interests in order to secure myself and to guarantee that only good things come my way. Thinking otherwise— that there is no such self or essential nature and that, like all things, I exist in relation to innumerable other elements in the world and change continually in correlation with changes in the world—and meditating consistently on this thought, I just might begin to behave to some extent otherwise.

This, in short, is why Thich Nhat Hanh feels that he must step forth to accept the blame for violent criminals and violent cops in a city halfway around the world from where he lives. His basic claim is that these police-men live and act the way they do because the rest of us live and act the way we do. Their violence is not independent of who we are and what we do. Therefore Thich Nhat Hanh hopes that, even if in some minute and infini-tesimal way, some new, perhaps less violent, situation in Los Angeles will arise dependent on his having taken such a stand. Having now introduced what we here propose as the fundamental principles of Buddhist ethics, let us return to Thich Nhat Hanh's position on violence in Los Angeles.

Thich Nhat Hanh: "I Am Those Policemen"

Thich Nhat Hanh begins the article by recalling the pain he felt watching the video clip of the beating—how, probably like all of us, he could almost feel the blows of the police clubs. But then, "looking more deeply," he says, "I was able to see that the policemen who were beating Rodney King were also myself." Why would a pacifist monk, and one of the gentlest human beings in the world, picture himself as an angry, club-wielding policeman intending to inflict pain and suffering upon a man prone on the ground with powerful blows from his club? Thich Nhat Hanh sees himself in this way because their anger and violence is not just the independent product of these individuals; it is also produced daily by our society and the larger world and inevitably absorbed into the minds and characters of all of us to varying degrees.

The individuals who enact this violence are extensions of the current levels of anger and hatred in the society at large; they are just as much products of it as they are its producers. It is not simply that the police are our employees—hired guns to do our dirty work. Although that is cer-tainly true, it is more important to recognize from Thich Nhat Hanh's Buddhist point of view that the violent way they live is a consequence of the larger patterns of life that we have all accepted. Their acts of brutal-ity and thoughtlessness are the outcomes of the forms of consciousness currently circulating in our time and place. Their acts arise dependent on our acts and vice versa, and there is simply no escaping this inextri-cable interdependence. Therefore, he writes, "We are co-responsible. That is why I saw myself as the policemen beating the driver. We all are these policemen."

Thich Nhat Hanh then proceeds to clarify the Buddhist point of view from which he writes:

> In the practice of awareness, which Buddhists call mindfulness, we nurture the ability to see deeply into the nature of things and of human beings. The fruit of this practice is insight and understanding, and out of this comes love. Without understanding, how can we love? Love is the intention and capacity to bring joy to others, and to remove and transform the pain that is in them.[1]

This practice of mindfulness is better known as meditation, and in everything he says in this essay the author demonstrates the outcome of his own practice of mindfulness meditation. Developing understanding and love for others through insight meditation, he quite naturally extends himself to include others within his domain of responsibility. He recognizes that he shares responsibility for what human beings are doing anywhere in the world. Therefore, he proceeds to write:

> From the Buddhist perspective, I have not practiced deeply enough to transform the situation with the policemen. I have allowed violence and misunderstanding to exist. Realizing that, I suffer with them, for if they do not suffer, *then* why would they do what they did? Only when you suffer much do you make other people suffer; if you are happy, if you are liberated, then there will not be suffering in you to spill over to others.[2]

This is what was meant earlier by Thich Nhat Hanh's willingness to take the blame. *He* did not practice meditation deeply enough to do what? To change these officers, human beings from another culture and city whom he has never even met? On an individualistic understanding of separate selves, this is clearly absurd. But on his Buddhist understanding, where there simply are no isolated and unaffected selves and where impermanence and dependent arising are thought to be fully in effect, it not only makes sense but begins to alter the way we look at everything taking place in our own societies. Obviously Thich Nhat Hanh has no magical control over the individual acts of other human beings. But he does have proportionate control over the kind of influence on the world that *he* exerts in his own actions and life, and he knows very well that each of us, in every one of our acts, leaves a deposit on the spirit of the world and that the world as it is in any given moment is simply the sum total of these imprints large, small, and of all shapes.

Picturing the problem with the Los Angeles Police Department and the violence in the world generally as *our* problem and not just a limited problem of a couple of bad cops, Thich Nhat Hanh goes on to say what needs to be done:

> Putting the policemen in prison or firing the chief of police will not solve our fundamental problems. We have all helped to create this situation with our forgetfulness and our way of living. Violence has become a substance of our life, and we are not very different from those who did the beating. Living in such a society, one can become like that quite easily. Daily, we are being trained like those who did the beating: to accept violence as a way of life, and as a way to solve problems. If we are not mindful—if we do not transform our shared suffering through compassion and deep understanding—then one day our child will be the one who is beaten, or the one doing the beating. It is our affair. We are not observers. We are participants.[3]

Thich Nhat Hanh is what Mahayana Buddhists call a *bodhisattva*, literally, an "awakened or awakening being," one who through extensive meditation on selflessness, dependent arising, impermanence, and suffering is transformed in such a way that one can meaningfully live as though the real problem is not just one's own suffering but suffering itself—all of it, as it is experienced all over the world. A bodhisattva is one who, having been transformed in this way, makes a commitment to seek enlightenment not just for his or her own benefit but for everyone equally. In this sense enlightenment is an awakening to and from the greed, hatred, and delusion that intensify and multiply human suffering and illusion. Ultimately, our separateness is relative and fleeting, and to focus all of our energies on it is the greatest of all illusions for human beings. Those whose lives are admirable, and most significant over time, are those who either by historical influences or by methodical practice have penetrated and overcome this illusion. Martin Luther King Jr. is clearly a modern example of this form of greatness, of selflessness on behalf of something far greater than his own pleasure, and it is no accident that he could also see this capacity in the then youthful Thich Nhat Hanh, whom King nominated for the Nobel Peace Prize for his work in response to the senseless violence of the Vietnam war.

Vimalakīrti and the Bodhisattva Ideal

We now examine a classical example of a bodhisattva, an exemplary human being as projected in the minds of early Mahayana writers who imagined in their time what true human greatness might be. The example chosen for this purpose is Vimalakīrti, who, whether he ever actually lived or not, is, as described in the sutra, clearly the projection of an ideal. Unlike Thich Nhat Hanh, Vimalakīrti was a layman and in that respect more like most of us. But he was also an extremely wealthy and prominent citizen of his city and therefore a good test case for the practices of selflessness we are examining. The question this sacred text asks us to consider is: If you are not a monk or nun and must therefore live in the world of worldly activities, how could you possibly actualize the kind of understanding that we see personified in the life of Thich Nhat Hanh? The second chapter of the sutra is devoted to describing the character of Vimalakīrti, and, to my mind, this is one of the great segments of classical Buddhist literature. This chapter is exceptional in the sacred literature of Buddhism in that it focuses with fine-tuned description on the persona and character of someone who has not taken monastic vows but who is nevertheless leading an exemplary Buddhist life.

Vimalakīrti is introduced in the second chapter of the sutra as a great man living as a wealthy and prominent citizen of the city of Vaiśālī in India. He was known for his superior understanding of Buddhist teachings, his compassion for all living beings, and his eloquence. It says that he was praised, honored, and commended by everyone, including the Buddha. The following are samples of the kinds of character traits that the sutra attributes to him:

> In order to be in harmony with people, Vimalakīrti associated with elderly people, with people of middle age, and with the youth, yet always spoke in harmony with the Dharma. He engaged in all sorts of businesses, yet had no interest in profit or possessions. To train living beings he would appear at crossroads and on street corners, and to protect them he participated in government.... To

develop children, he visited all the schools.... He was honored as the businessman among businessmen because he demonstrated the priority of the truth. He was honored as the landlord among landlords because he renounced the aggressiveness of ownership. He was honored as the warrior among warriors because he cultivated endurance, determination, and fortitude. He was honored as the aristocrat among aristocrats because he suppressed pride, vanity, and arrogance.... He was compatible with ordinary people because he appreciated the excellence of ordinary merits.[4]

These character traits, moreover, are just the beginning of what is attributed to Vimalakīrti. What the author of the sutra has done is, based upon his own training in the various disciplines of Buddhist thought and practice, to project an ideal layman to provide a clearly defined literary embodiment of the highest trajectory of Buddhist practice. Here the whole history of Buddhist practitioners has been given a clear glimpse of one powerful version of the ideal goal of enlightenment.

It is worth pointing out at this juncture that what we see in this example is not a norm or an achievement that we can expect to see among Buddhists but rather an ideal. It is another, and open, question whether any Buddhist monk, nun, or layperson has ever truly lived up to this ideal. That is an historical question about what in fact has happened in the history of Buddhist societies. Our question is not so much how people actually lived in Buddhist history as what in any given time and place was it possible for Buddhists to imagine as the highest ideal of human excellence. Ideals are always cultural projections, the highest aspirations imaginable by a group of people, and they are always undergoing modification through history. Moreover, ideals are, strictly speaking, unattainable; that is, whenever we find ourselves in a position to actualize what we set out to accomplish, at that point we will also find ourselves able to conceive more profound and more sophisticated goals to set out before us. Having an ideal is always understanding the gap between who we currently are and what at that particular point we could imagine ourselves being. As we move toward it, our imagination deepens and our target will be suitably altered or extended.

In Vimalakīrti's case, somewhat in contradistinction to much of the Buddhist tradition before him, what we have is an ideal of worldliness. Rather than following the contemplative, monastic track of Buddhist culture and withdrawing from the messiness and virtuelessness of the ordinary world, Vimalakīrti dives into the world and uses it as the basis of his own practice. He is pictured, contrary to much of the earlier Buddhist tradition, as spending time with gamblers, prostitutes, drunks, and shysters, in addition to children, government officials, policemen, and the homeless. In their midst, he maintains equanimity, poise, wisdom, and most of all compassion. When engaged in business, he shows what it would mean to conduct business in full awareness of the impermanence of all things and the emptiness of personal desire, self-interest, and possessiveness. When in contact with anyone the question before his mind is: How can I help this person open to greater insight and to a form of life in which he or she can flourish without self-imposed diminishment and suffering? The aspiration guiding his numerous activities is no less than a transformation of the world, and, in view of this lofty goal, he simply smiles in tenderness when the rest of us scurry past him in our various small-minded and selfish pursuits.

Vimalakīrti is imagined in the sutra as an aristocrat with no trace of arrogant self-importance. He is a wealthy and successful businessperson whose purpose in business and goal in wealth creation is to support others in his city who are unable to support themselves. He knows everyone from government officials to the homeless and holds as his primary aim their awakening to enlightened forms of life. As a model of enlightened life, Vimalakīrti is an astonishing character.

Practicing the Six Perfections

What, according to the sutra, does Vimalakīrti do or practice in order to develop and sustain this level of magnanimity? He practices the "six perfections," a set of ideals articulated in most early Mahayana Buddhist sutras as the basis for the bodhisattva's life and that emerge in the sutra over and over again for consideration. The *Vimalakīrti sūtra* introduces these six ideals in six sentences, one each for the perfection of generosity, the perfection of morality, the perfection of tolerance, the perfection of energy, the perfection of meditation, and the perfection of wisdom.

> His wealth was inexhaustible for the purpose of sustaining the poor and the helpless. He observed a pure morality in order to protect the immoral. He maintained tolerance and self-control in order to reconcile beings who were angry, cruel, violent, and brutal. He blazed with energy in order to inspire people who were lazy. He

maintained concentration, mindfulness, and meditation in order to sustain the mentally troubled. He attained decisive wisdom in order to sustain those who had little understanding.[5]

This same sequence of six appears throughout the sutra. Vimalakīrti strives to perfect his generosity, his morality, his tolerance, his energy, his meditation, and his wisdom, but notice that in each case the sutra gives his rationale: Why does he perfect himself in these ways? The sutra says, "In order to sustain the poor and helpless, in order to protect the immoral, to reconcile beings who are cruel, angry, violent, and brutal, to inspire those who were lazy, to sustain the mentally troubled and those who had little understanding." Why does he practice these forms of self-transformation? Clearly *not* on behalf of his own greatness. In fact, in each case, the word "his" that I have added is inappropriate. What Vimalakīrti seeks is not so much "his" generosity, morality, and so on but the development of generosity, morality, patience, energy, meditation, and wisdom in the society itself and among all human beings. That is his goal, almost as if there truly is no-self that should be or could be the focus of his attention. Thinking, as Buddhists should, that all things change, including people, and that all such changes arise dependent on various alterable conditions and causes, Vimalakīrti proceeds as if his own striving in this way can and will change others and the world even if only incrementally. Transforming himself and enlightening his society were so closely linked as to be virtually the same activity.

So, "blazing with energy," as the sutra describes him, Vimalakīrti shoots out of his house every morning on his way to the school to work with children, or to the city council meeting to weigh in on the quality of decisions that are being made on the people's behalf, or to the encampment of homeless people or the police station or the women's shelter. He honestly thinks that if he is deeply generous, impeccable in moral standing, always tolerant and patient, full of energy, profound in meditative mindfulness, and penetrating in wisdom, this will permeate the minds and behaviors of others, and through this process the whole society will be transformed. At least this is what the sutra encourages us to think about in our own lives, and Vimalakīrti is placed before us as a model.

Considerable concern is expressed in the sutra about the quality of our aspirations: What is it that we seek in life? Unless our aspirations demonstrate profound understanding of the impermanence of all things, the relatedness of all things, and our own lack of a predetermined essential nature, we will be vulnerable to poor judgment, feelings of insecurity, and the likelihood of seeking something ultimately unsatisfying and unworthy of our efforts. Therefore the sutra shows us the example of Vimalakīrti and has him instruct the other bodhisattvas in the importance of the quality of their own aspirations. The reason for this, again, is not just that they are *our* aspirations and that our lives can be improved, although that is certainly true. At least as important is that "living beings with inferior aspirations will be inspired by lofty goals";[6] that is, humanity as a whole would be enlightened in some way and to some degree, thus enabling the initiation of nobler aspirations guiding life in human society overall.

This cannot be accomplished, however, if the virtuous go about their business in the spirit of moral superiority. Vimalakīrti refuses to separate himself from the poorest and humblest of citizens, because, on the Buddhist principles we have introduced here, they simply are not separate. Vimalakīrti's most famous and most impressive deeds show the mastery of what the sutra calls "nonduality," the recognition that ultimately there are no separate and distinct selves and that what each of us becomes in life arises dependent on the lives and actions of others. In this bigger picture, our achievements are not just our individual accomplishments. From this point of view, what we attain in our lives cannot be comprehended through "dualistic" modes of conception that distinguish sharply between what we do and what others have done to make what we do possible.

Therefore when Vimalakīrti is out seeking to enlighten people whose aspirations are weak, deluded, or in some way harmful, the sutra makes a point of having him acknowledge his own complicity in the crimes of criminals. As it says, "Only those guilty of the five deadly sins can conceive the spirit of enlightenment and attain Buddhahood."[7] The sutra does not bother to explain this cryptic remark. We already know from what we have read up to that point that Vimalakīrti *himself* has not committed these sins. He has not murdered, stolen, and so on, and enlightenment is not a human state in which one would commit such atrocities. Indeed, enlightenment is a condition in which you will not do these things. But it *is* a condition in which you will see clearly the illusions and limitations of the conception of human beings as isolated individuals. To be awakened is to realize in a practical way that you are implicated in everything that happens. The interdependence of all beings ties us in one way or another to every act ever performed. Therefore when the sutra says, "Only those guilty of the five deadly sins can conceive the spirit of enlightenment and attain Buddhahood," we can take it to be saying, "Only those who realize the universality of suffering and the truth of 'no-self' and only those who profoundly grasp the ultimate interdependence of all beings can conceive the spirit of enlightenment and attain Buddhahood."

Some pages later, a bodhisattva friend of Vimalakīrti, in what would have been an excellent description of Vimalakīrti, says, "When there is thorough knowledge of defilement, there will be no conceit about purification."[8] Conceit about one's own state of purity is a sure sign of impurity. It implies a profound misunderstanding, from the Buddhist point of view, of what a "self" is. It fails to recognize that all attainments of greatness are best understood as the accomplishments of the culture, the society at large, a family, or an educational system and are not just *my* attainment. On the principles set forth in the sutra, the best way to overcome such pride is not just the practice of humility; it is rather the thoroughgoing effort to understand that all human "defilement," all human failure, is in some way *my* failure.

Hence, we see Thich Nhat Hanh in 1991 writing publicly in the *Los Angeles Times*, "I have not practiced deeply enough to transform the situation with the policemen. . . . We are these policemen." Mahayana Buddhist texts like the *Vimalakīrti sūtra* provide the six perfections as the training program for bodhisattvas. An unusually large and sophisticated literature on these six dimensions of human character, in both theory and practice, has developed in the two-millennium history since their emergence. But in order to offer a more concrete sense of what these might be, let us elaborate a bit on just one of them, the first perfection: the "perfection of generosity" or the "perfection of giving."

Enlightenment Through Generosity

The perfection of giving is a positive correlate to the negative prohibition on stealing—on taking what is not ours or demanding more than we deserve. As a positive ethical demand, beyond what we should refrain from doing, it asks the bodhisattva practitioner to set aside questions of personal gain and extend a compassionate hand in offering what may not even be deserved in any standard sense of justice. Just as biblical texts establish in no uncertain terms what "Thou shalt not do," they also suggest an ideal in its positive dimension: "Love your neighbor as yourself." "Loving your neighbor as yourself" would require an exceptional degree of selflessness, an ability from a Buddhist point of view to recognize that ultimately there is no such separation between us. Otherwise, although we might in fact be quite fond of our neighbor, it would never amount to the kind of concern and affection that we invariably show to ourselves.

Realizing this, when Vimalakīrti attempts to define "perfect generosity," he must articulate several dimensions of this perfection. His most succinct definition is:

> The giver who makes gifts to the lowliest poor of the city, considering them as worthy of offering as the Buddha himself, the giver who gives without any discrimination, impartially, with no expectation of reward, and with great love—this giver, I say, fulfills the perfection of giving.[9]

Two points in this initial definition warrant explication. Giving is perfected when we can do it impartially, without discrimination, and when we are just as eager to give to the poor who cannot reciprocate as to a friend, family member, or superior who can and may repay the gift. Vimalakīrti 's requirement, therefore, is that a pious Buddhist's offerings to the Buddha, from whom great reward might be anticipated, be extended to every sentient being without discrimination. To emphasize this Vimalakīrti adds the words "with no expectation of reward." Reward comes in many forms, and Vimalakīrti is clear in including them in his articulation of giving. We may give because the other might reciprocate by giving back in equal or greater proportion. We may give in order to be thought well of, to be loved, or to enhance our reputation for generosity. Or we may give in order simply to think well of ourselves, to clear our conscience, to accumulate good *karma,* or to enhance our self-help program of "perfection." But by Vimalakīrti 's account, all these versions of giving "in order to" fall short of perfect giving.

That does not mean, of course, that Vimalakīrti would suggest that giving with lesser motivation should not be done. Giving of almost any sort qualifies as a "practice" and as one step toward the perfection of giving even if the act itself does not fulfill the ideal. Vimalakīrti then goes on to add another dimension to the ideal: the giver whose act has been perfected gives "with great love." Love is the motive that most readily qualifies an act as perfect giving. Loving one's neighbor as oneself can easily be seen to lend itself to empowering the spirit of giving. When we give a gift to ourselves, our love is unquestionable. What would it mean to extend that same spirit of generosity to others, and how would we ever manage it?

The sutra's answer to this is that "equanimity" is the key and that equanimity is attained through the realization of the selflessness and relationality of all reality. Therefore when Mañjuśrī, the bodhisattva of wisdom, asks Vimalakīrti, "What is the equanimity of the Bodhisattva?" our hero responds, "It is what benefits both self and others."[10] Both self and others are benefited when the bodhisattva is able to treat all things equally, in just proportion, and does not favor his or her own self as the rest of us tend to do. Since equanimity and peacefulness are treated in the sutra as equivalents, the sutra can go on to claim that the perfection of generosity "is consummated in peacefulness."[11] And when Mañjuśrī asks, "What is the great joy of the Bodhisattva?" Vimalakīrti does not hesitate to turn the question back to the practice of giving: "It is to be joyful and without regret in giving."[12]

Making this same point in his book *Ethics for the New Millennium,* the Dalai Lama writes,

> Looking back over my life, I can say with full confidence that such things as the office of Dalai Lama, the political power it confers, even the comparative wealth it puts at my disposal, contribute not even a fraction to my feelings of happiness compared with the happiness I have felt on those occasions when I have been able to benefit others.[13]

Since, as the Dalai Lama writes elsewhere in the book, the "principle characteristic of genuine happiness is inner peace,"[14] that explains why the *Vimalakīrti sutra* would claim that the perfection of generosity is consummated in peacefulness, in an equanimity that is not out of accord with the equality and relatedness that both the Dalai Lama and the sutra recommend as the character of the world. In any case, all of us can sense, I think, what the Dalai Lama means when he links feelings of happiness to acts of generosity. For the rest of us, even a momentary act of pure giving—a truly unselfish moment—is invariably accompanied by a sense of exhilaration, a sense of expansion out beyond ourselves. The sense of warmth and joy that ensues, even if just momentary, contrasts sharply with our usual perception of narrowness, the sense of being inextricably confined to ourselves and nothing beyond. In the act of giving we expand, which is the very meaning of magnanimity.

Giving is perfected, then, when we give not because we must but because we want to. And wanting to give can become the norm in our lives only through a fundamental transformation of our self-understanding. This transformation in perspective reorients the point of life. Therefore when Vimalakīrti says that "the Bodhisattva should live for the liberation of all living beings,"[15] he makes clear that the perfection we pursue is not *our* perfection; it is just perfection as seen from the vantage point of equanimity.

Since all acts can be inspired by the perfection of giving, that includes acts of receiving as well. In breaking down all dualism, Vimalakīrti includes the dualism between an active giving and a passive receiving. Neither activity nor passivity can encompass either act successfully. Therefore, when receiving a gift, bodhisattvas like Vimalakīrti, Thich Nhat Hanh, and the Dalai Lama practice mindfulness; they *give* concentrated, thoughtful attention both to the gift itself and to the giver. They make sure to give the giver all that they can so that whatever love and selflessness has inspired the gift will be given back and multiplied several-fold. Giving the gift of genuine gratitude is enabled by a sense of deep, primal gratitude that accompanies the realization of no-self and dependent arising. In fact, since we are not self-created, our very lives are a gift. We do not have to be religious, much less Buddhist, to realize that we owe our very existence to forces and events beyond us. This level of gratitude is inspired by a readiness and an ability to understand everything that comes to us as a gift, rather than as our achievement. And if everything is a gift, no attitude will pervade our daily lives as thoroughly as a profound sense of thankfulness. Nothing less than this overarching sense of gratitude could adequately explain the fact that what bodhisattvas give, in the end, is themselves.

Ethics and the Perfection of Wisdom

Generosity and a willingness to give in large measure are never quite enough, however. We may have deep feelings for the suffering of others and be moved to help them and still end up acting in such a way as to be ineffectual or to make things worse. Even with the noblest of intentions, our actions might still have the effect of creating even more suffering for others. Wise ethical discernment is essential to any form of well-honed generosity. Without clear thinking and moral intelligence, our kindest acts may come to be resented, or inappropriately taken advantage of, thus doing harm to the recipient. A broad range of skills are required in addition to the requisite feelings in order to approach perfect giving. In addition to intelligence or wisdom, perceptual skills are important. It is not helpful, for example, to be generous in spirit if we are insensitive or oblivious to the needs of others. People who are so entrapped in themselves that they never notice when others are in serious need will not have developed the kinds of mindfulness that Vimalakīrti's practice of generosity demands. Attentive skillfulness, what bodhisattvas call *upāya*, or "skill-in-means," is important as a correlate to the kind of self-understanding that makes possible any intention to give selflessly.

The bodhisattva's *upāya* or "skillfulness" is typically the last word in matters of ethics in Mahayana Buddhism. This is true because *upāya* includes and is based upon a realization that no understanding we have of these matters, no matter how sophisticated, will be either true or effective in all circumstances. The bodhisattva's "skill," in other words, includes a deep sense of the relativity and impermanence of all modes of understanding and an agile flexibility in response to that sense. Although Vimalakīrti may be quite satisfied with his account of perfect giving, if he lacks a thorough sense of the limits of its applicability and the possibility that in some context he may turn out to have been wrong, then he will have failed in the sixth perfection, the perfection of wisdom, and in the skills of *upāya*. If all things are impermanent and arise to be what they are dependent on changing circumstances, that would imply that there is no fixed goal for all times and places or for all human beings. And, if in response to the question "What is our true nature?" Buddhists posit "no-self nature" because all natures are dependent and change over time, that leaves open the question of what an adequate goal might be.

If the character of human enlightenment is not defined in advance by a fixed human nature, then a range of possibilities for self-transformation are opened. In fact, this is a good way to understand the history of Buddhism, or any tradition for that matter, as a precious repertoire of images of human excellence set before us as an inheritance for our use in creative, critical imagination. If no-self means that who we are is not a static and predetermined given, then it must be a product, a work of art, which each of us can either take upon ourselves or fail to do so. And since perfection is never attained before death intrudes—that is, the task is always open and never complete—it is never too late to begin anew. As a Tibetan monk once said to me: resting on our past accomplishments is as dangerous as lying down to rest while out walking in a snowstorm. The result is that we freeze up and never move again. Therefore, the bodhisattvas consulted here posit persistence and adaptability as the requisite virtues for an ethics based upon impermanence and lack of self-nature.

These points and others help us understand why a Vietnamese Buddhist monk living in France would respond to police violence in Los Angeles the way Thich Nhat Hanh did in 1991. As a bodhisattva, he cannot help but consider all human problems to be *his* problems.

2

The Awakening of Character as an Image of Contemporary Enlightenment

IN GENERALIZED PHILOSOPHICAL accounts of enlightenment and in much classical Buddhist literature, it is difficult to picture how enlightenment would become manifest among actual human beings in specific situations facing particular problems of the kinds that we encounter in our own lives. This concern for the distinctive *human* character of enlightenment appears occasionally in the earliest layers of Buddhist literature and then sporadically throughout the tradition, as for example in stories that describe the particular personalities of early Zen masters in East Asia. This focus on the distinctively human character of enlightened beings is rare, however, since as Buddhism developed into the Mahayana period, characters represented in the sutras tended to take on transhuman powers.

In these Mahayana texts, bodhisattvas are typically described in ways that are unencumbered by human limitations. They are often pictured as though they reside altogether beyond the human sphere even if still in compassionate contact with ordinary, fallible human beings. Although there are extremely interesting narratives of enlightened comportment that emerge in these sutras, they lose their capacity to serve as human models for us because they simply don't share our human finitude. Even the layman Vimalakīrti, described so brilliantly in his sutra, stands so far out beyond the human domain that we can't see his limitations at all and therefore can't identify with his humanity. The sutra authors who created Vimalakīrti as a character imagine his personal powers to transcend human limitations altogether. Vimalakīrti suffers no perplexity. He has no questions, no yearning, no needs at all. He does not suffer confusion, or pain, or loneliness like we do, and that is both the point and the brilliance of the text.

This Mahayana tendency is taken to its full potential in other sacred texts that imagine the exalted divinity of bodhisattvas who have unlimited powers and who attend to human suffering out of deep compassion. Indeed, when the *Sutra on Ten Stages* (*Daśabhūmika sūtra*) sets out to describe the life trajectory of the bodhisattva, it begins the very first stage at so inconceivably exalted a level that even for the bodhisattva at the first and lowest level, what we take to be limited human capacities have been expanded into enormous cosmic powers. Given this otherworldly and transhuman orientation, the reader knows immediately that this text will not provide practical guidance to those whose quest faces the full range of problems related to human finitude. Fascination and perhaps devotion to such characters seems appropriate but not the kind of learning that is inspired by contact with a plausible role model.

In the twentieth and twenty-first centuries, this thirst for fully human models reasserts itself, and through no accident at all, this occurs at precisely the historical moment when media have emerged to provide detailed accounts of human beings struggling to live lives of excellence and in Buddhism to pursue enlightenment in both authentic and realistic ways. These media include novels, historical biography, and film, both fiction and documentary. Through these modern media, we now have at our disposal what traditional Buddhists could not have had—fictional and historically descriptive narratives that attempt to articulate in vivid detail what a quest for awakening would mean for actual human beings in earlier histories and in our times and places. One brilliant cultural production that makes significant moves in this direction is the Buddhist film *Mandala*.

The Awakening of Character in the Buddhist Film Mandala

Mandala is a 1981 Korean film by the award-winning director Im Kwon-taek that boldly and effectively takes up questions that have both central importance in traditional Buddhism and far-reaching contemporary resonance.[1] Narrating the spiritual quests of two twentieth-century Buddhist monks, the film probes the forms and qualities of human suffering and provides visual images of what it might mean to break through the undertow of suffering into visionary forms of redemptive consciousness. In the process, *Mandala* poses challenging questions to the Buddhist establishment in Korea about the tension between responsibilities for self-cultivation that one owes to oneself and responsibilities for selfless work in the world that one owes to others.[2]

The film follows the careers of two Buddhist monks over a span of several years as they grapple with questions about the meaning of Buddhist enlightenment and the forms of practice appropriate to that ideal in contemporary circumstances. One monk, Bupwon, abandoned by his mother as a child, has dropped out of college and left his true love in order to live a monastic life. A question burns in his mind—that of suffering, death, and the meaning of life in view of those destructive forces. Bupwon takes his quest and his meditative practice with great seriousness but succumbs regularly to remorse and depression about his failure to achieve awakening in his six years of ardent study. He is calm and introspective, occasionally brooding, and in all these senses well suited to monastic life.

The other monk is Jisan, perhaps a decade older and in almost every way the opposite of Bupwon. Jisan is what in East Asia is known as a "wild monk," a monk whose practice includes iconoclastic and antinomian deviations from traditional monastic comportment. Jisan consumes alcohol in violation of the monastic precepts and does it flagrantly and to shocking excess. He also breaks the monastic prohibition on sexual intercourse and does this both as a critique of the Buddhist tradition and as a form of transgressive spiritual practice. Jisan hopes that through a life of sublime excess he can break through the chains of psychological repression and open himself to forms of freedom that lie on the other side of moral and ritual constraint. In some moods Jisan flaunts his practice, laughing at the Buddhist establishment and challenging other monks to follow him to nirvana, while in other moods he yields to extreme self-contempt, confessing that his practice is a shameful delusion and that, as a result, he is unworthy of his opportunity to live a human life.

Filmmaker Im Kwon-taek gives both monks equal standing as well as equal camera time. Viewers are given reason to identify with both at various times and to take their divergent quests as legitimate human possibilities. Both monks attract our sympathies, providing for us images of suffering and responses to it in two quite distinct forms. Following opening shots of monastic meditation and chanting, the story begins with the meeting of the two monks as they wander the dirt roads of rural Korea during the interim period between winter and summer meditation retreats. Although deeply impressed with the fearlessness and insight of his new acquaintance, Bupwon is shocked by Jisan's irreverence and scolds him severely. Jisan simply retorts in laughter and further transgression as he opens another bottle of rice wine. As they wander, each tells the story of his life, how they have come to be who they are. Jisan reports being eagerly seduced by his lover, Oksun, while she toured the temple where he had been studying as a young monk. Unable to justify the monastic practice of sexual repression, he decides to overcome his lust and fear by confronting it directly. Leaving the monastery for a life of self-indulgence in the city with Oksun, he pushes to an extreme his effort to achieve liberation through drinking and sex.

Bupwon tells the equally heart-wrenching story of abandoning his college lover, just as his mother had abandoned him, and of the torturous quest for the meaning of his existence. When the two monks part company, Bupwon enters a monastery for a period of meditation and practice. There he meets an old friend, Sugwam, whose Buddhist ascetic practice includes burning his fingers down to stubs by holding them in a candle flame while in meditation—all of this against the adamant protest of the abbot of the monastery who Sugwam cannot respect due to the conservative and orthodox character of his Buddhist practice. The film forces our participation in his personal agony by making us watch bodily mutilation in the excruciating detail of lengthy, close-range shots of melting flesh and muscle.

After this ordeal, perhaps months later, Bupwon meets Sugwam again, this time out on the road. Sugwam now criticizes himself for the foolishness of thinking that mortification of the flesh would produce enlightening insight. Still unable to accept orthodox monastic practice, however, Sugwam espouses "discovering oneself through others" by which he means the selfless devotion of one's energies to the practice of alleviating the suffering of those unable to protect themselves in a world of violence and exploitation. Identifying with Guanyin, the bodhisattva goddess of compassion, he vows to make no distinction between himself and others. Moreover, he reports to Bupwon that he has seen with his own eyes an actual model of this selfless ideal, a "true monk" as he puts it. On Jook Island, he reports, a terrible plague had swept through the village, killing many and rendering the majority of the population so sick as to be unable to care for themselves. While the few healthy retreated to maintain their slim chances of survival, a monk arrived who tended to the sick without the least regard for his own life, gently washing the festering sores of the plague victims in the sea. When the plague finally subsided, the remaining villagers sought to honor the monk by dedicating a temple to his enlightened efforts, but by then the monk had already disappeared, his selfless task now complete. The significance of the story is made even more real for Bupwon when he is told that the heroic monk's name is Jisan.

At that junction the camera shifts to Jisan meditating in a temple, a flock of birds rising into the air symbolizing his having solved the "bird in the bottle" *kōan*, thus designating his achievement of enlightenment. Bupwon, relentlessly searching for Jisan after having heard the story of his saintly activity on Jook Island, finally locates him drinking in a village pub, and the two are reunited for the climax of the film. They wander into the mountains, shown in breathtaking cinematography, where they settle in a recluse's abandoned hut. Soon thereafter an elderly woman approaches, requesting that the monks come into town to conduct an opening ceremony for the Buddhist temple that she has funded for construction. They agree, needing money for supplies, and there Jisan delivers a sermon worthy of his enlightened state, a talk of transformative power that demythologizes the customary ritual while respecting its mythic status. Although skeptical at first, the women at the temple—shown bowing and scraping—finally get the point of the sermon and recognize both the liberating quality of the message and the masterful status of the monks before them. Money in his pocket, however, Jisan seeks a drink and takes leave of Bupwon in order to indulge in the local tavern. Ousted by the proprietor at 1 o'clock in the morning, Jisan is found the next morning in full lotus meditation posture frozen solid in the snow.

Cremating Jisan in a Buddhist ceremony by burning his body in the mountain hut, Bupwon goes immediately to the city where he seeks the one reconciliation that has blocked his own awakening. He visits his mother, who has not seem him since she abandoned him as a child in order to seek a better life for herself in the city. She begs forgiveness, showing the suffering that her unconscionable act has caused her, and Bupwon gives it, not verbally but with a profound smile of compassion that is perhaps the finest visual sign of Buddhist enlightenment possible in cinematic medium. *Mandala* ends as he takes leave of his mother and sets out down the road for a life that viewers must project or imagine on their own.

Primary Themes: Karma, Suffering, and Enlightenment

Clearly one of the primary themes in the film is human suffering, and it is surely no accident that this is one of the central themes in

Buddhism—indeed, the first of the four noble truths. But in highlighting this theme, filmmaker Im Kwon-taek is not as interested in being Buddhist as he is in being Korean. Although the twentieth century was an epoch of unrelenting suffering in much of the world, it would be hard to find a nation more steeped in suffering than Korea during that time. The century opened on the Korean peninsula with the Japanese invasion, and by 1910 Korea had been wholly annexed into the Japanese empire. The Korean experience of the first half of the century was one of severe exploitation and oppression under a Japanese rule that allowed as little indigenous expression as possible. Although World War II ended Korean humiliation under the Japanese, it initiated further colonial rule, in the north by the Soviet Union and the People's Republic of China and in the south by an American oversight that was guided more by fear of communism than by interest in its alternatives. The Korean civil war that resulted from the division of the nation brought untold suffering and lineages of military dictatorships to follow in both north and south. Finally, the economic collapse of 1998 ended the century in Korea much as it had begun.

I retell this familiar story of the fate of modern Korea to highlight what I take to be the motives behind the making of *Mandala*. Born in 1936, Im Kwon-taek lived through much of the degradation of his country. Raised in poverty like most Koreans of that era, he had yet to even see a movie when at age 20 he took his first job in the Korean film industry out of the motivation of hunger rather than curiosity or cultural creativity as we might assume today. He was desperate for a job and basic sustenance in difficult times. As might be expected, then, many of Im Kwon-taek's films address questions of human suffering by focusing on the destiny of individual Koreans within the historical emergence of the modern era.

In *Mandala* no character avoids suffering, just as the Buddhist noble truth claims. The inescapable question that it evokes for us as thoughtful spectators is what posture, or personal stand, should one take in relation to human pain, both one's own and that of others? Although some suffering—especially large-scale historical suffering—is brought about by forces far beyond our control, other kinds of suffering—both one's own and others—is the direct result of our own decisions. This is the domain of the Buddhist concept of karma, and its impact on the film is substantial. Both monks seek desperately to shape their lives and characters by attending to the workings of karma and yet suffer relentlessly as a result of their own actions and decisions. Jisan, for example, seeks his own enlightenment by means of transgressive sexuality, and in choosing this tactic he fails to envision in advance the devastating impact that this will have on his lover, who he uses for his own enlightening purposes. Oksun ends up a prostitute in Seoul's brothels and is psychologically destroyed by the impact of this life.

At that point Jisan can only bemoan his thoughtless inability to take responsibility for the consequences of his own actions, and this matures eventually into a deep self-loathing. The cruel irony of ethical/moral consciousness is that one can only begin to be aware of it and develop it when the horror of one's own choosing badly has already shown its consequences. Wizened by the powerful effects of this suffering, Jisan begins to sense the far-reaching effects of the principle of karma and to rethink the meaning of his actions in accordance with it. The monk has what amounts to an "awakening of character," and this is what comes to dominate the filmmaker's concerns in shaping the narrative and characters of this film. Jisan awakens to the truth of his own role in the world—his responsibility—and realizes that the character he has been relentlessly constructing through his own choices has set destructive forces in motion that are now ineluctable.

In Buddhist theory, choice and character are mutually determining—each arises dependent on the other. The choices we make one by one shape our character, and the character that we have constructed, choice by choice, sets limits on the range of possibilities for choice that we can then consider in each future decision. Karma implies that once we have made a choice, it becomes a part of us in proportion to its magnitude. Having made a choice and acted upon it, we will always be the ones who at that moment and under those conditions did in fact engage in that particular action. The past, on this view, is not something that once happened to us and is now gone. From that moment on, we are that choice, which has been appropriated into our being along with countless other elements. In this light, human freedom can be terrifying—awesome in its gravity—but is noticeable only to one who has realized the far-reaching and irreversible impact on oneself and others of choices made. But if solitary acts of will have this considerable weight, how much more so do the unconscious "non-choices" that we make every day in the form of habits and customs that deepen over time, engraving their mark into our character?[3] *Mandala* gives us graphic explications of each of these dimensions of karmic impact.

In traditional forms of Buddhism, the practices of character development take account of the enormous importance of ordinary daily practice or customs, or what we habitually do during the day often without reflection—the ways we interact with the world, daydream, lose ourselves in distractions or resentment, down to the very way we eat, sleep, and breathe. On this understanding, ethics is largely a matter of daily practice, understood as a self-conscious cultivation of ordinary life and mentality. In Mahayana Buddhism, one such scheme of practice is called the "six perfections," which are six dimensions of character that are both crucial to the possibility of enlightened life and also amenable to development and transformation. These are the cultivation of generosity, morality, patience, energy, concentration, and wisdom.

Although Jisan and Bupwon are deeply ensconced in the traditions of Mahayana, the Son/Zen style that they practice places more weight on the experience of awakening interpreted as a monumental breakthrough of deeper forms of experience. Although some Son monasteries would not, on that account, have ignored traditional forms of self-cultivation in Mahayana Buddhism, the weight placed on the moment of break-through often pushed other more gradual practices of self-cultivation to the periphery where they might not have received the attention that was fundamental to other traditions. The film shows this emphasis in the Son monasteries and masters that we see, and the implied legitimacy of Jisan's transgressive practice is one expression of the shift of emphasis away from earlier forms of self-cultivation toward radical images of sudden breakthrough.

In a 1996 interview, Im Kwon-taek made clear that part of his intention in making *Mandala* was a critique of Korean Buddhism, especially the Son or Zen tradition featured in the film. As he put it,

> I shot *Mandala* thinking how beautiful it is to live with intensity. In filming it, I found a little more about the worldview of the monks. ... The Buddhism Korea accepted was the Mahayana sect, whose objective is to bring ordinary people to enlightenment. Many monks, however, do not follow the precepts of Mahayana Buddhism and communicate it to ordinary people. If reality is painful for most people, then it is necessary to share ordinary people's pain and struggle by following Mahayana Buddhism.[4]

Although Im's presentation of Buddhism shows a great deal of respect, even awe, for the traditional religion, there is no doubt that a critical undercurrent accompanies the film.

Mandala's *Critique of Son Buddhism*

Two strains of critique surface in the film. The first is an obvious suspicion of religious asceticism. Recall that Bupwon meets an old friend, Sugwan, who has turned his attention from meditation to mortification of the flesh. Sugwan has already burned two of his fingers off when the film introduces him in order to feature a third act of mutilation. It is important to recognize that these acts are performed by Sugwan against the admonition of the abbot of the temple, shown lecturing Sugwan sternly. This is to say that Im Kwon-taek was aware both that the official policy of Son Buddhism strongly opposes such acts of self-torture and that there has been a tendency for them to occur "unofficially" in the background of the religion in spite of this policy because the iconoclastic and apophatic ideology of Son Buddhism makes extreme asceticism a plausible attraction. Through close-up shots, the film features the depth of concentration, the agony, and the pointlessness of this ascetic practice. Sugwan is made to admit, shortly after his third burning, that "it was stupid of me" and "sheer nonsense." As the abbot had told him very clearly, "You need your body to become a Buddha." The abbot's advice to overcome mind/body dualism was initially lost on Sugwan until finally the point reaches its persuasive potential—not altogether too late but later than Sugwan would have wished in retrospect now that his hands are disabled.

Although an uncomfortably graphic part of the film, this criticism of Son asceticism is not central since the critique is already articulated in the Son sect's own policies. Much more important is the second criticism offered, that, as Im Kwon-taek put it in the interview, Korean Buddhists appear to be practicing "Hinayana" while they profess to be Mahayanists. By Hinayana Im means not the earliest traditions of Buddhism nor the kind of Buddhism practiced in Southeast Asia. Neither Im nor other East Asian Buddhists would have known very much about these. Instead Hinayana had become a symbol for self-serving practice, religious practice directed toward one's own well-being, coupled with inattention to the suffering of others. This is the point of *Mandala's* questioning: it wonders how Son Buddhism could have become so self-involved that it would fail to heed the suffering so prevalent in the nation at large. From their monastic location high in the mountains, it would be a continual historical temptation for Son monks to feel an enormous separation from ordinary life, contemplating the seemingly self-imposed suffering of others in the nation from a bemused distance. From Im's point of view, and from the perspective of Mahayana Buddhist thought, a truly enlightened life is one fully exposed to the world rather than sealed off from it, fully involved in it rather than in retreat from it.

To make this point, midway through *Mandala* Im Kwon-taek has Jisan carving a wooden image of the Buddha. Inspecting it, Bupwon asks why its facial expression is so grim and contorted. The question provides Jisan an opportunity to say what the filmmaker has on his mind: "The Buddha is not a god but a human. How could he remain so calm and unruffled?" As the camera scans traditional Buddha images characterized by a serene, removed bliss, Jisan goes on, "How could he keep smiling when the poor and the weak are suffering under oppression by the privileged? If Gautama was human, some Buddha images should bear expressions of agony, grief, sorrow, and rage. I want to create a real image of the Buddha."[5]

If current Buddhist practice can be reduced to learning not to care as a means of living an untroubled and suffering-free existence, then that degeneration would deserve the full brunt of Im's critique. It is in this sense that early Mahayana thinkers articulated the dangers of detachment. Indifference may indeed be a way to avoid feeling badly, but if the price of that avoidance is not feeling at all, then the cost is far too dear. Invulnerability to suffering is not the admirable ideal of Mahayana set forth in the image of the bodhisattva, the one who freely takes on the suffering of others and who vows not to seek nirvana for him- or herself alone but rather at all times on behalf of all beings. From this point of view, the only admirable response to widespread suffering is one of resolution and commitment to as large and all-encompassing a goal as was conceivable at that time, a goal that was both fully personal and deeply communal.

In the appraisal of Mahayana religious thought, a dualistic conception of the Buddhist goal that presses nirvana into another world beyond history and human society only breeds resignation and fatalism with respect to the world in which we must inevitably live. It encourages practitioners to renounce the human world in which suffering takes place. Such a conception makes nirvana a possession of the self rather than a shattering of the self or a form of self-transcendence. The transcendence of the self that Im Kwon-taek has in mind in the film *Mandala* is an expansion of the range of who we are, an expansion of personal identity that reaches out to include the community within which we live. And that, appropriately enough, is also one form of the transformation envisioned in Buddhist sutras in the image of the bodhisattva.

The process of cultivating a bodhisattva-like character is the process of reconstituting one's life so as to enlarge the range and variety of relationships that are encompassed by the self. The limit of this process of enlargement is the most expansive image of the bodhisattva conceivable, the furthest stretch of compassionate identity with the other that we can imagine.[6] The education of bodhisattvas, therefore, teaches them that their well-being as human beings is inseparable from the well-being of all those others with whom they share a community. Education into the expansive image of the bodhisattva involves the mastery and disciplining of desires and feelings, as well as their transformation, altering the self by opening up and expanding its boundaries.

Without this religious learning through rigorous practice, the monopoly of personal interests and a constricted conception of one's own person could not be overcome. The best image of this bodhisattva-like expansion that we see in the film is Jisan's selfless act of tending the plague victims on Jook Island.[7] Caring for unknown others as though they were as close to him as family members, Jisan demonstrates the logical extent to which the image of enlargement can be taken. At the heart of this training to expand one's self-conception is an apparent paradox. The paradox is that although the religious training that enables this form of self-transformation requires enormous concentration on the spiritual project of self-cultivation, focusing one's energies and thoughts too narrowly on these practices will obscure the wider sympathies needed to transform the self through communal identification. This is simply to say that thinking too much about "our own" self-creation or enlightenment will prevent the kind of compassionate identity with others that in fact provides the richest source of transformative power.

Two opposing images in Mahayana Buddhism are employed to envision the quest for self-transformation, but the opposition does not necessarily prevent their orchestrated, simultaneous use. One of these figures the quest in terms of self-purification, and this is the defining monastic image. On this first image, practitioners join the monastery in order to purify their lives of everything that is inessential, everything that stands in the way of intensely focused concentration of the central point of the practice. This purification includes simplification, the inclination to carefully pare down the immediate environment and one's life of extraneous concerns. Asceticism quite naturally accords with this image, where luxuries and distractions are eliminated in order to structure one's life around the crucial questions of the meaning of one's life.

The opposite image is one of self-enlargement, the bodhisattva's reaching out to the world rather than turning away from it. The quest to enlarge oneself focuses on the desire to include and embrace more of the world than one had encompassed previously. This necessarily "worldly" life seeks to extend its boundaries rather than to narrow them around a single central point. The risks of self-purification that are visible from the opposite perspective of self-enlargement are the dangers of Puritanism, where the admirable concern for self-cultivation becomes so self-absorbed that it distorts the selfless culmination of the practice. The risks of self-enlargement that are visible from the opposing perspective are the dangers of distraction, where a laudable concern to expand the self by encompassing more and more eventually undermines the concentrated ability to be clear, effective, and well focused on anything, much less a quest for individual and communal excellence.

Mandala *and the Task of Buddhist Ethics*

In *Mandala*, the tension between responsibilities we owe to others and responsibilities we owe to ourselves stands out thematically. The extent to which they are resolved in the end is an open question. But the suggestion is made by Sugwam, the ascetic, finger-burning monk, that the way to self-realization is through others, and the exemplar of this practice whom he cites as an embodiment of practical realization is Jisan. This suggestion, however, simply opens the question, and the rest is for us to ponder: What are these two domains of responsibility—self and other—and how do they connect with one another?

One way to begin to sort them out is to make a distinction, as does Paul Ricoeur, between ethics and morality. Although Ricoeur admits that there is nothing in the etymology or history of these two words that would mandate this distinction, we can appreciate the clarity that it brings to the issue. By ethics he means concern for the "aim of an accomplished life" and by morality "the articulation of this aim in norms characterized at once by the claim to universality and by an effect of constraint."[8] To put the distinction in different language, ethics is the self's striving for the good, however defined, in all spheres of life, and morality is the constraint upon that striving imposed by the demand of others for justice. As Ricoeur notes, dividing ethics and morality in this way entails that ethics encompasses morality, that morality is situated within ethics as one dimension of the aim for an accomplished life. I commit to training myself ethically in many ways, but one fundamental form of ethical training is morality—the moral demand that I do onto others as I would have them do onto me.

To put this in Buddhist terms, ethics is the quest for awakening, the intention to aim at an accomplished life of insight and awareness. Morality, on the other hand, is one domain of that striving, the justice and compassion that we owe to others both not to allow our own quest to obstruct theirs and, beyond justice, to reach out to them in compassionate awareness of their suffering. Failure to live morally would constitute an ethical failure, a failure to fulfill the promise of an accomplished life. Moral success, however, would not by itself amount to ethical success, although it would constitute one dimension of it. Notice that in the Mahayana Buddhist six perfections morality is one of the dimensions of training to which a bodhisattva submits. The six altogether would constitute the full domain of ethics, training toward the possibility of an accomplished or admirable life, which is simply another way of saying that ethics encompasses morality. While morality is a debt we owe to others, ethics is a relationship we have to ourselves and to the ideals that always stand out ahead of us—who we aim to become, including who we aim to become in moral relation to others.

Implicit in the film *Mandala* is a sense of variety that undergirds the goal of Buddhism. While one monk practices meditation with the utmost sincerity, another focuses on intellectual study, another on the moral precepts, and yet another on how to respond authentically to the suffering of ordinary people. If, in accordance with the Buddhist doctrine of karma, different results arise out of different causes and conditions, we would have to surmise that these are not simply diverse means to an identical goal of "enlightenment" but rather somewhat different states of character that naturally function in the world in somewhat diverse ways.

There are times, of course, when Son Buddhists would have been reluctant to admit this diversification of outcomes, succumbing instead to the reductionist desire to delimit and define the goal by narrowing the range of criteria for what would count as an accomplished life. But this reductionism fits poorly with Buddhist philosophy and does damage over time to the flexibility of Buddhists by rendering them less capable of responding to changes in historical contingency. In this way it risks potential obsolescence. At the heart of ethical reasoning is a capacity to formulate and to compare ends or goals—forms of enlightenment that are truly admirable under current conditions. This reasoning forces open the question that institutions in their inevitable conservatism often prefer remained closed, and the results of this openness would be variation in what we are able to admire in human comportment. Where institutions tend to prefer obedience to norms and practices already established, creative practitioners tend to reserve admiration for what emerges in the interplay between the tradition's resources and current historical conditions. Tension between the old and the new is hardly new but so perennial a problem as to be worthy of careful attention.

The resources of Buddhism are in some sense inherently weighted against the institution's own conservatism, in that the basic doctrines of impermanence, relational causality, and no-self tend to mandate an openness to change. The last of these doctrines—the claim that there is no permanent and fixed self—helps to open the question of enlightenment since it works against the thought that enlightenment is defined in relation to a fixed human essence. Given that lack of fixity, self-transformation takes on the character of self-creation, even when "the self" in that expression is constrained and constructed by larger historical and social processes from whence we inherit the models that shape our own individual acts of self-creation. The complexity, indeterminacy, and sheer difficulty of human reality simply add to the challenge and reinforce the importance of judgment, courage, and character. No amount of good judgment and character, however, will yield moral or ethical certainty. In a changing and unpredictable world where each moral/ethical situation is to some extent unique, risk is unassailable and the future always open.

The film *Mandala* asks, and entices us to ask, not just what means are appropriate to a far-reaching awakening of character but, more important, how could such an awakening be envisioned today? In a multicultural and widely diverse world, what range of variation might be encompassed within the sphere of human ideals, and what forms of personal practice are best suited to these ideals under current world conditions? Im Kwon-taek's *Mandala* does not answer these questions directly in any way. Instead, the film offers a variety of models, each with their own virtues and limitations, and the viewer is left with the dilemma of negotiating between them. Although the choice is initially hypothetical and projected onto the characters in the film, it also resonates with the choices that we must make in our own lives and provides us with language and images to assist in that process of reflective deliberation.

This is indeed the conclusion that Im Kwon-taek draws—that cinema should contribute to social and personal transformation by, as he puts it, "helping people to make better lives."[9] In order to do this, he claims, "one needs ... to feature a way to live a better life in film, and record better lives."[10] And in dozens of films from *Mandala* in 1981 all the way up to his most recent film, Im has attempted to do just that, and to impressive effect.[11] Cinema, like certain forms of literature, possesses the cultural power to broaden and make more vivid the language of ethical deliberation and, in doing so, extend the range of possibilities both in what we admire in others and in what we might seek to embody in our own practical lives. And, like theatre, film has the power to make transcendence in the ethical dimension *visible* in ways that other domains of human culture do not. Contemporary studies of ethics and culture can ill afford to ignore the capacities and potential of this medium.

3

Secular Buddhism and the Religious Dimension of Enlightenment

THE EMERGENCE OF "secularized" forms of Buddhism is one of the most important and interesting developments in the history of Western Buddhism. Although there is obviously a close relation between what is now being called "secular Buddhism" and the Buddhist-inspired meditation practices that are becoming ubiquitous in the secular world—mindfulness practices in hospitals, schools, businesses, and the military—these are not synonymous. The practice of meditative mindfulness that we now find in all of these venues is fully secular and therefore officially "not Buddhist." Were it to be called Buddhist, laws separating church and state found in most Western nations would prohibit its practice. In these cases, meditation is becoming secularized, but not Buddhism, even if, as we all know, the origins of these mindfulness practices are clearly Buddhist.

What then is secular Buddhism? This title has been adopted by Western Buddhists who consider themselves fully secular in their beliefs and practices while nevertheless enthusiastically adopting certain ideas and practices that derive from some dimension of the Buddhist tradition. Although it has taken time in the history of Western Buddhism to arrive at this name and particular orientation, we can see that it was there from the very beginning. Some practitioners of Buddhism in several of the early Buddhist lineages in the West, but especially Zen, felt uncomfortable with and critical of certain beliefs and practices that just seemed too close to the religious traditions that they believed themselves to be abandoning when they turned to Buddhism. Inspired by the rebellious, antinomian stories in Zen, they claimed to be uninterested in ritual, skeptical of authoritarian hierarchy, and unashamedly critical of traditional beliefs such as those referring to "hungry ghosts" or "cycles of rebirth," which just seemed irredeemably archaic or foreign. These elements seemed clearly "religious" or even "superstitious" and were not what attracted these Western practitioners to Buddhism in the first place. Although some of these experimenters simply abandoned the practice of Buddhism when they began to recognize its religious character, others remained and held their ground as secularists who were nonetheless profoundly engaged with Buddhist meditation practice and philosophy of life.

Other Western Buddhists were intrigued with the religious character of Buddhism—some because of its difference from their own religious heritage and others because they were raised without religious instruction of any kind and were therefore experimenting with religious life for the first time. Stephen Batchelor, the most prominent advocate of secular Buddhism, fits this latter description. Although Batchelor grew up without overt religious instruction from his own heritage or any other, upon encountering Tibetan Buddhism as a young man in Dharamsala he found himself engrossed in every aspect of the tradition. His autobiographical reflections show, however, that even as a monk committed to this tradition, modern Western skepticism was never far in the background.[1] Batchelor practiced in the Tibetan tradition for a decade, followed by several years in a Son Buddhist monastery in Korea before finally leaving monastic life in order to experiment with a form of Buddhism that was not tied to any existing tradition and therefore did not require adherence to beliefs and practices that from his contemporary Western point of view seemed outmoded or irrelevant. Through his extensive writing and lecture tours, Batchelor has honed this orientation to Buddhism into a highly refined and sophisticated conception of how Buddhism might be reimagined to more adequately address the lives of contemporary secular people East or West who are nonetheless attracted to the heart of the Buddhist teachings and to some of its practices. In Batchelor's hands, secular Buddhism has come into its own as an attractive alternative to the traditional sectarian forms of Buddhism that have continued to exert influence in Asia and around the world.

Secular Buddhists have worked through the tradition in order to locate those elements of Buddhism that are attractive and relevant today but that are not based upon and do not require overtly religious beliefs and practices. All forms of supernaturalism, beliefs about after death destinies, rituals, institutional religious hierarchies, and the religious aversion to science have been the focus of their criticisms. Although some secular

Buddhists align themselves with the kinds of hostility to religion that we have become accustomed to seeing behind the banner of contemporary "atheism," this has not been true of Stephen Batchelor. Although he does not mince words when it comes to critical judgment, Batchelor has written that his "secular Buddhism has a religious quality."[2] But because the word "secular" primarily means "not religious," it is not immediately clear how we should understand this claim. What could it mean to say that practices or ideas are both secular and religious? The aim of this chapter is to seek clarity concerning the secularity and/or religious character of Batchelor's secular Buddhism and to evaluate its prospects for the development of Buddhism in our time. We pursue this aim in four parts:

- The Sacred, the Mystical, and the Sublime
- Religion, Secularity, and Community
- Belief, Practice, and the Religious Dimension of Life
- Secularity and Posttheistic Religion

The Sacred, the Mystical, and the Sublime

One important theme that gives energy and coherence to Batchelor's writing is his adamant rejection of "otherworldly" religion. Wherever religious ideas appear to valorize a realm of reality that is beyond or above the world in which we live, he notices the extent to which we lose our focus on the here and now, the lives that right now press upon us. Whether the "beyond" is imagined as heavenly afterworlds, as transcendent divine beings, or simply as "the Unconditioned" beyond our conditioned world, Batchelor recognizes how the elevation of another ultimately "true world" out beyond our reach constitutes a diminishment of the sanctity of our current lives. When "the highest good is a transcendent state of nirvana located beyond the conditioned world,"[3] Batchelor sees the danger as a tendency to ignore the immediately present human tasks through which we might cultivate a path of awakening. In many passages Batchelor identifies this concern for the "beyond" with "religion," setting it in contrast to a new secular Buddhism that maintains its focus on human issues in the here and now. No doubt in many cases he is correct in that identification. But must religion in general and traditional Asian Buddhism in particular always be defined by a shift of concern to a transcendental world beyond our own? Is religion essentially concerned with a reality beyond this one rather than our lives in this world? If it is, then we should join Stephen Batchelor in his skepticism about religion and preference for secularity. But I doubt that this way of identifying religion covers the range of human phenomena that we typically include as religious.

Batchelor's critique is potent, however, and helps us notice our own escapist tendencies. We all have them. This is what Nietzsche meant by "nihilism," the tendency, while in the throes of human suffering, anxiety, and fear, not to face up to the reality that stands right before us but instead to turn attention toward imagined worlds in which the troubling conditions of human finitude do not apply. Living in make-believe worlds doesn't help us to live well in this world; indeed, it is conducive to lives of even more suffering because, drifting off into daydreamt worlds, we give up on realistic efforts to solve our problems right here. The question still stands, however, whether religion is primarily oriented to escape into other worlds or whether in important instances it is precisely the medicine that cures us of self-destructive escapism by teaching us how to come face to face with reality. If in the full range of our experience we find that religion sometimes does one and sometimes the other, then otherworldliness cannot be the defining essence of religion and what we find instead is a contrast between religion that challenges us to face reality directly and religion that consoles us in our suffering by offering images of alternative worlds.

But what is the reality that religions in this first mode encourage us to face in order to flourish in life? Is it simply the empirical, physical substance of our lives, the struggle to procure adequate food and shelter? Although sometimes focus on the most basic conditions of life is the most pressing issue for human beings, that is typically not the domain of religion. Religion comes into play when attention shifts to more abstract concerns than food and shelter, concerns for the meaning of our lives, a set of concerns that are in fact "beyond" ordinary human concerns. Batchelor is so clear about the otherworldly dangers lurking in this beyond, however, that it can often sound like he rejects any form of transcendence altogether. He finds these "religious" tendencies even in the earliest texts of Buddhism but especially in highly evolved forms of Mahayana. There, evoking Batchelor's critique, we find meditations on the Unborn, the Unconditioned, Ultimate Truth, and the Buddha Nature hidden behind the experienced world.

But in many of the most prominent Mahayana Buddhist texts, what is "unconditioned" is just the state of endless conditioning—ubiquitous dependent arising—and what is "permanent" is just the infinite movement of impermanence that the Buddha discovered. The Buddha Nature is frequently specified as the true nature of all seemingly un-Buddha-like things. Later Buddhists meditated on the irony of this insight for centuries without positing an "unmoved mover," a "first or primal cause" of all other subsequent causes. Wherever the Unconditioned comes to be reified in the minds of Buddhist practitioners, however, the "two-world" metaphysics that Batchelor denounces has indeed appeared. The problem, therefore, is the all-too-human tendency to reify or objectify religious concepts, and the brilliance of many Buddhist teachings and meditations is that they function as antireification therapies.

In order to counter this otherworldly tendency in Buddhism, Batchelor turns to two Son/Zen *kōan* stories that address this issue of the Unconditioned with famously potent Zen nondualism:

> A student once asked the Chan master Dongshan ... "What is the Buddha?" Dongshan replied: "Three pounds of flax."
> A monk asked the teacher Zhaozhou ... "Why did Bodhidharma come from the West?" Zhaozhou answered: "The cypress tree in the courtyard."[4]

For Batchelor, these Zen stories feature a rejection of the "abstract speculation" that the students' questions imply. As Batchelor puts it, the masters "pressed their students to consider the far more baffling and urgent questions posed by ordinary things."[5] The Zen master's reply, then, amounts to "bad question." But let us consider an alternative to this interpretation. Rather than understanding these Zen responses as rejections of the monks' abstract religious questions, we can also consider them not as direct self-sufficient answers but as pointed hints about the direction in which the students' minds must turn to find answers to their questions.

Remember that the question-askers are monks who spend years, even decades, pressing into questions about the nature of their quest. What is the Buddha? What is the point of Zen that brought Bodhidharma to teach in China? Rather than rejecting the questions, we can consider the masters to be bringing their students down out of a reified transcendence to consider how both "the Buddha" and "the point of Zen" pervade ordinary reality. The masters are not saying that if the monks stopped asking about "the Buddha," left the monastery, and just focused on flax farming they would find the appropriate answers. The questions that occupy the minds of flax farmers concern how to grow it successfully and how much it will yield on market day. The religious abstraction that the monks practice is essential to their quest, but it must simultaneously be concretized. Although farmers are not likely to find awakening in flax or cypress trees, that is where the monks will need to find it. For the farmers to consider the religious meaning of ordinary things rather than their everyday "food and shelter" meanings, they too would need to employ unconventional, non-farm concepts like "Buddha" and "nirvana."

The Zen point here is that even though the Buddha is not just one of the many things present in ordinary reality, there is nowhere to find the Buddha completely "beyond" ordinary reality. It must be found within *this* reality, even though finding the Buddha is not like finding other things. The Buddha is not one empirical thing among others, and questions about the Buddha are not located in the same region of brain functioning as other flax-like concerns. On this interpretation, it is not that the questions are wrong; it is that the monks will never find suitable answers by gazing off into other worlds. The Buddha and the point of Zen are to be found within ordinary reality, although hidden from ordinary view.

Extending that to our issue, the point is not that religious questions are inappropriate and that our questioning should stay focused on particular empirical entities in the world; it is rather that seemingly abstract religious questions must be addressed in direct relation to the world in which we live. Authentic religious questions are existentially grounded in order to affect the deepest concerns of our here-and-now existence. That, however, has been Batchelor's point throughout his writings. But from my point of view, there is an important distinction to be made between two forms of nondualism at stake here, one secular and one religious. Secular nondualism tends to favor the strong scientific claim that all there is to consider is empirical, physical reality; that there is nothing deeper that transcends this concrete world; and that questions of meaning and significance in life are unworthy human preoccupations. Religious nondualism, on the other hand, claims that what is transcendent or profound is not another reality far out beyond this one but rather the depth dimension of this one world in which we live, a dimension that can be encountered through spiritual practice that pushes us beyond ordinary human concerns like food and shelter.

Batchelor's version of the Unconditioned is one of the most potent elements of his dharma, and it too takes us beyond our natural or instinctual concerns. Working carefully through the early Buddhist *Nikayas*, he focuses on the possibility that human beings might learn not to be conditioned by "desire, hatred, and delusion." Here his theme is nirvana as freedom, the freedom to practice an intentional discipline that aims to undermine enslavement to habitual reactions that inevitably yield increased suffering for ourselves and others. This path through meditative reflection and practice teaches us to choose how we will react to a particular stimulus and to train ourselves to do that as a form of practiced second nature taking over from our initial, instinctual natures. This is not, strictly speaking, a state of being unconditioned but instead an evolved state of intentional reconditioning through practices we have chosen rather than by those we have inherited without choosing. In neuroscientific terms, the only way to undo a pattern of past mental habituation is to overwrite that ingrained neural pattern with another one that eventually takes over as our default move. While our brain structure is conditioning all the way down, our minds aspire to the freedom to choose what will condition our future acts. As Batchelor realizes, "The very idea of emancipation here in this world can only make sense only if it is possible for people to free themselves from the conditioning powers of their desire, hatred, and delusion."[6]

Even though he seeks to develop a secular form of Buddhism, Stephen Batchelor makes a point of acknowledging a "sacred" dimension to human experience that gives rise to the possibility of "mystical" experience. He writes: "I do not reject the experience of the mystical. I reject only the view that the mystical is concealed behind what is merely apparent, that it is anything other than what is occurring in time and space right now."[7] Similarly: "The sacred is not found in a transcendent realm beyond oneself or the world; it is disclosed here and now once your mind relaxes, quietens, and becomes clearer and sharper as attention stabilizes on the breath."[8] The contrast, then, is between a form of Buddhism that opens a sacred and mystical dimension of human life through the meditative cultivation of a path in life and those that refer instead to distant worlds of religious imagination beyond the here and now. While such a contrast is certainly important, it can also be found throughout the history of the Buddhist tradition. Because serious practicing Buddhists throughout this long history have leaned more or less in one of these directions or the other, it is not clear why one of these inclinations would now need to be called secular.

Regardless of what we call it, Batchelor has articulated something that is fundamental to the religious instincts that have been emerging in our time. When he writes that "there is no such thing as the unconditioned, only the possibility of not being conditioned *by* something,"[9] he is onto something important. Unreifying our religious concepts opens their power to transform our practices and subsequently our lives. What Batchelor has said here about the Unconditioned, however, should also be said about "the mystical" and "the sacred" that he employs elsewhere. Nominalizing these—making them nouns that refer us to things—can undermine our capacity to experience sacredness as a quality within things that is often hidden from our view. Batchelor's phrase for this is "the everyday sublime," which, although still in nominal form, directs us to a subliminal quality all around and within us.

Recognizing serious limitations inherent in contemporary secularity, Batchelor writes frankly about the dangers of referring to this contemporary form of Buddhism as secular. He admits:

> A secular approach to Buddhism could unwittingly encourage the tendency to regard meditation as simply a method for solving problems. By instrumentalizing mindfulness ... one could end up rejecting any sense of sublimity, mystery, awe or wonder from the practice. This tendency is reinforced when meditation is presented by its enthusiasts as a "science of the mind."[10]

Aware that secularity is often charged with the "disenchantment" of the world, a world stripped of wonder and mystery and reduced to rationality, utility, and progress, Batchelor hopes that secular Buddhism will "work toward the re-enchantment of the world."[11]

Religion, Secularity, and Community

With Batchelor's own hesitation about secularity in mind, we now consider his effort to define "religion." He proposes to use the word "religious" in

> at least two related but distinct senses. In the first sense, I understand "religious" to denote our wish to come to terms with or reconcile ourselves to our own birth and death. For many people, religious thoughts and acts are those that engage their deepest, core relationship to the totality of their life and what it means for them. This is what the theologian Paul Tillich called "ultimate concerns." ... In the second sense, I take "religious" to denote whatever formal

means are employed ... to articulate, frame, and enact one's ulti-mate concerns.[12]

Separating these two meanings of religion, then, Batchelor can under-stand himself and others as religious in one sense but not in another. Therefore, he writes that "my secular Buddhism has a *religious* quality because it is rooted in 'ultimate concerns.' "[13] Similarly, "one can be reli-gious in the sense of being motivated by ultimate concerns, without ever engaging in any overtly religious behavior."[14] But I wonder how well that distinction holds up once we see how much weight has been placed on the word "overtly," since by the first definition *any* behavior that expresses ultimate concern would be religious. Overt "religious behavior" seems to coincide with Batchelor's second definition of religious as "whatever for-mal means are employed ... to enact ultimate concerns."[15] Here he lists overt, formal religious means—"adherence to sacred texts, submission to the authority of monastics and priests, performance of rites and rituals, participation in spiritual retreats." Overt, formal religious means appear to be those that are readily recognizable out of our religious pasts. But how are these "means" different from those in the first definition—"reli-gious thoughts and acts ... that engage their deepest core relationship to the totality of their life"[16]—except perhaps in their being readily recogniz-able because they are familiar? On the first definition of religion, what-ever we do in response to our deepest level of concern *is* our "means" of being religious—whether that is prayer, meditation, engagement in social justice, hospice care, music, poetry, or wilderness immersion. Both defi-nitions end up being about *how* we "come to terms with or reconcile our-selves to our own birth and death."[17]

Two other criteria appear in various places in Batchelor's work that dis-tinguish two senses of religion and support a way of thinking about secu-larity that does not conflict with the first meaning of religion. He writes:

I also use the term "secular" in full consciousness of its etymologi-cal roots in the Latin *saeculum*, which means "this age," "this *siècle* (century)," "this generation." If we are secular, then, our primary concerns are those we have about *this* world—about everything that has to do with the quality of the personal, social and environ-mental experience of being alive on this planet. A secular approach to Buddhism is thus concerned with how the dharma can enable human beings and other living beings to flourish in this biosphere, not in a hypothetical afterlife.[18]

Although this definition of secular changes mid-paragraph from being about time (this age, this century, this generation) to being about location (this world, this planet, this biosphere), we can see that Batchelor is directing us to traditional religious beliefs in afterlife, life after death in some other world. So on this criterion, we are "religious" if our primary concerns are about afterlives in other worlds and secular if our primary concerns are about the lifetime or world in which we currently dwell. Translated into Buddhist terms, we are religious Buddhists if our primary concerns are for rebirth after this life or if we are on a quest for a form of nirvana that extinguishes life in this world. And we are secular Buddhists if our primary concerns entail awakening in this life—the pursuit of a path of human transformation; the diminishment of greed, hatred, and delusion in ourselves and others; the development of compassionate involvement with others; and so on. That distinction between religion and secularity is potentially confusing, however, because throughout the long history of Buddhism there have always been people engaged in both approaches to the dharma. In this sense, then, secular Buddhism is not a new development. Indeed, it may be that the point of Batchelor's insightful interpretations of the earliest Buddhist teachings is to highlight the extent to which Gotama was the first secular Buddhist.

Another way to understand what Batchelor is getting at in this definition of secularity is the difference between being a Buddhist who holds traditional beliefs such as "rebirth" and *parinirvana* that cannot easily be reconciled with the worldview of our time and place and being a Buddhist who participates fully in contemporary modes of thinking, including science, thereby eliminating beliefs from premodern Buddhist cultures that conflict with our contemporary worldview. A secular Buddhist is someone like Stephen Batchelor, who does not believe that the contemporary practice of Buddhism requires one to maintain the now-outmoded worldviews of earlier South and East Asian cultures.

While one can be inspired by Batchelor's understanding of what an authentic form of Buddhism would be for us today, it still is not clear why we would want to call that secular. Can't the word "contemporary" accomplish that same purpose? "Contemporary Buddhists"—like many of those right now reading this—would be those who live fully in the contemporary world and adapt admirable Buddhist ideas and practices to our lives in this world. A contemporary Buddhist would still be religious, in Batchelor's first definition or on any other updated definition of that term, but in contemporary ways so that being religious would not require that one hold onto the worldview of other times and places or "submit to the authority of monastics and priests," and so on. This alternative interpretation will make sense so long as we remember that, like everything else, both Buddhism and religion are impermanent; they change along with everything else.

Perhaps the difference for Batchelor between formal and informal means of religious engagement is really the difference between communal and individual religion, the difference between the "ultimate concerns" that empower a personal quest to come to terms with our own life and death and the already established institutions of ultimate concern that we find in religious organizations of all kinds. Here Batchelor is right that when we say the word "religion" or "religious," we often mean these institutions rather than the spiritual sensibilities and quests for meaning that give rise to these institutions. One of the themes that has driven Batchelor's call for a new secular Buddhism is his sense that although Buddhism originated as an authentic encounter with the meaning of life and death, it quickly thereafter "mutated into another organized Indian religion."[19] In this way Batchelor can affirm the religious quality of his Buddhist practice in the broad sense of ultimate concern while distancing himself from the institutional forms of Buddhism that he suspects may have diluted and in some cases neglected or abandoned its authentic origins as existential engagement with life and death.

Aware of the historic weaknesses of institutions, or in the common pejorative phrase "organized religions," it is tempting to valorize egalitarian, secular individualism, as is our tendency in Anglo-American culture. For very good Anglo-American reasons deriving from Ralph Waldo Emerson and early European modernism, Batchelor includes self-reliance as one of the chief virtues of secular Buddhism. Rather than turn to institutional religions that are organized hierarchically for spiritual guidance, we are encouraged to rely on our own instincts when pursuing matters of ultimate concern. Recall that this was Kant's definition of enlightenment as the mature capacity to stand on one's own and think for oneself. As heirs of modern Western culture, this makes perfect sense to us. It helps us individualize how we pursue spiritual matters so that they accord with our particular lives rather than trying to force our encounter with the meaning of life and death to fit larger social/cultural norms.

One potential consequence of this orientation to both Buddhism and secularity, however, is the further erosion of our sense of community, the longstanding Western preference for individualism over communal participation that has been the mark of modernity for several centuries now. Sometimes we fail to recognize that our criticisms of "organized religion" are really just criticisms of communities that share religious bonds. There are no communities without some form of organization—without certain ideas or practices or norms instituted—and there are no institutions without leadership emerging to help bring people together. Although it is very easy to find corruption and other forms of fault with "organized religious institutions," if we ponder the alternatives of "unorganized" or "disorganized" religion, or fully individualized religion, I suspect that the outcome would be considerably worse.

As we might expect, Stephen Batchelor is aware of this potential problem with secular Buddhism and with secular modernity generally. He shares the widespread view that modern society is overly individualistic and self-indulgent and is concerned about the rapidly eroding human sense of being part of a community. Although this dimension of his experiment with secular Buddhism is in its early stages, Batchelor strives to imagine what a secular sangha might look like that would alleviate or at least ameliorate the problems of estrangement that self-reliant individualism creates. He writes: "A secular sangha is a community of like-minded, self-reliant individuals, united by friendship, who work to mutually support each other in their own flourishing."[20] But what exactly such a community would look like is still an open question: He asks: How are we to "find a middle way between autocratic and hierarchical religious institutions, on the one hand, and isolated, alienated individualism, on the other? This is the challenge."[21] There are, no doubt, many options between the two extremes that Batchelor names, and he is certainly right that an authentic form of contemporary Buddhism will need to bring these two poles together.

One issue that emerges when Batchelor addresses the question of religion and community is that of "authority." He writes:

To imagine a secular sangha begins by posing the fundamental question of where authority lies. If we follow the earliest sources, we learn that such authority lies in the dharma. By restoring this key but often forgotten principle, monastics and householders, men and women alike, are seen to be beholden to a law that supersedes whatever institutional power someone might have acquired in the course of a career in a Buddhist hierarchy.[22]

This important political question is one that has and will resurface over and over again, one that requires imagination and rethinking in every new epoch. Buddhists have done that throughout the long history of the tradition, as have other religious communities. Batchelor's principle that "the dharma" is the authority that supersedes all individual human authorities is matched in Christianity by the priority of "the Gospel" over "the church" that was articulated in the Protestant Reformation. All authority would reside in the Bible, God's word, and the ultimate authority, not in the institution of the church. The problem that Christians quickly discovered, however, was that the issue of authority returned immediately thereafter whenever a controversy arose about what the Bible really meant to say. The splintering of Protestant Christianity is a reflection of the diversity of opinions about how to understand what the Gospel actually means. Likewise, the question returns for Buddhists: Whose understanding of the dharma should hold sway over the issue under discussion? How would that be determined? Analogous to this question of religious institutions, we can see the same pattern in legal matters. All authority lies in "the law" that has been democratically instituted, but that principle increases the need for trained judges to make decisions far more than it decreases it. Someone or some human institution is inevitably given the authority to decide what the law requires when debates must end and a decision made.

Batchelor is right to worry about the abuse of religious authority—we should all be concerned about this problem, since we see it in every human institution. But it is not at all clear how this concern enables any community to consider the abolition of authority. Here is one way Batchelor describes the problem:

Religious authority could now be understood as the privilege of those who had gained personal insight into the nature of ultimate truth. As the understanding of what constituted ultimate truth became subject to increasingly subtle philosophical and epistemological consideration, it could only be conveyed in the sort of highly technical language employed, for example, by Geluk lamas. Ordinary adherents find themselves excluded from participation in this discourse and thereby cut off from the possibility ... of gaining the kind of rarified understanding required to have authority within

the community. ... The result is that Buddhist institutions today
tend to be dominated by a professional and often deeply conservative clergy.[23]

This problem is actually much larger. Increasing sophistication of
the terms of debate is a serious issue in every area of human culture,
not just religion. It is the same problem in law, government, medicine,
and science—anything that is subject to ever-deepening refinement.
Unless we have educated ourselves to a very high degree of sophistication, we will be unable to participate in debates in any of these areas.
"More sophisticated," "more subtle," and "more nuanced" understanding has been a requirement for participation in every area of human
enterprise from athletics to music to science and the law. It is not just
that those who have not attained this expertise will be institutionally
excluded from participation; it is also that those who have not undergone the required level of training won't even be able to understand the
questions being posed.

This is certainly my dilemma in many areas of culture, from astrophys-
ics to music theory. Until I attain the necessary level of cultivation, I will
continue to be excluded from these discussions. Moreover, the expectation
that others step down to my level of understanding in order to include me
in their discussions can only be maintained on occasion when education
rather than decision-making becomes the primary concern. I am apprecia-
tive when the legal experts, for example, attempt to explain in simplified
terms what they think the law requires and what is at stake in their current
discussions. But I also need to understand that, when they are really in the
midst of serious debate, I will be unintentionally excluded from the discussions simply because I will not have the skills and refined understanding that active participation requires.

So how are we to deal with this increasingly common problem when
it comes to religious authority? Not, I think, by the rejection of religious
authority and a universal commitment to individual "self-reliance,"
because there is no escaping the fact that there are a range of different levels of sophistication in understanding and we will naturally give
authority to those whose understanding we find most able to address
the problems before us. Stephen Batchelor is himself one such "authority." Buddhist communities around the world read his books and invite
him to give talks and lead retreats on the realization that his grasp of

the issues is frequently more profound, more comprehensive than their own. Far from being an intrusive imposition, Batchelor's sophisticated understanding of the issues is appreciated and welcomed. Batchelor's authority, of course, is freely given to him by individuals and communities who believe that his knowledge warrants trust, rather than entitled by authority of position (in politics the distinction between *de facto* and *de jure* authority). But that difference is only occasionally significant since many institutional authorities are also freely authorized, *de facto* leaders, as is the case with a Zen master who has both the institutional position and the full respect of a Zen community or the head of institutional technology who has both the title and the sophisticated knowledge to back it up.

Most Buddhists do not make their living studying Buddhism, and, like all of us, in some domain they rely on advice from those who are more highly cultivated in the area of particular concern. That form of authority is not different from the authority that I willingly give to my auto mechanic and my computer technician who, by virtue of long study and full-time work, understand the issues far more comprehensively than I do. Although modern individualism tempts us to think otherwise—that in matters of "ultimate concern" everyone is equal and on their own—we can also see that careful examination of the social reality raises serious questions about that view.

Although we can still feel the empowerment of spirited and democratic assertions of self-reliance—and should appropriate the spirit of that message as fully as possible—we can also see the limitations that this position encounters. It is possible that Batchelor's rejection of organized religion and institutional authority might inadvertently work to undermine the rationale for spiritual community by highlighting the failures and weaknesses of authorities while overestimating the capacity of people to develop an effective life of spiritual practice on their own. The larger question of community is a significant challenge for Batchelor's rearticulation of the dharma for our time. I am quite confident, however, that he is up to the challenge. Few Buddhists today have had as much experience in religious communities, in his case, including the many Buddhist groups that he visits each year. Given this exposure, I suspect that he will help bring insight to bear on the shape that Buddhist communities might take in the future and on how they might flourish in the new era that is upon us.

Belief, Practice, and the Religious Dimension of Life

As we have seen, Stephen Batchelor brings two different and important orientations to bear when he attempts to define religion. One of these is the social, institutional, or behavioral orientation that defines religion as we encounter it outwardly in the social world around us, and the other is the philosophical effort to understand what human concerns motivate these religious institutions and behaviors in the first place. Philosophically, Batchelor takes his bearings from Protestant theologian Paul Tillich's image of being grasped by an ultimate concern, the deepest dimension of concern that connects us directly to the very meaning of life.[24] In that philosophical sense, religion is defined in terms of a spiritual dimension of human life and culture, a dimension that will always be present to some extent and in some way whenever human beings confront what in the Chan/Son/Zen tradition came to be called the "great matter of life and death."

On this basis we could say that there is a political dimension to culture, as well as an economic dimension, a religious one, and others, and although individuals might not be particularly astute or competent in any one of these—that is, they might participate unskillfully and ignorantly—that does not mean that this dimension of culture is not there or is not important. We can be politically agnostic, unengaged, clueless, or incompetent, but that does not mean that politics does not affect our lives, or that this dimension is not always in play in our lives in spite of our disengagement. We can be tone deaf in music, to use Richard Rorty's image, and simply not understand music at all, just as we can be spiritually "tone deaf" and not understand what motivates people to engage the "great matter of birth and death" as a religious concern. But that deficit is simply an individual's own lack of awareness, not the absence of the domain of human life in which the larger meaning of life is addressed.

On this account, the religious dimension of human culture is no more optional than politics or an economy. That was Tillich's point, and even if all religious institutions are currently inadequate for dealing with these issues, the human questions themselves do not go away, just as widespread political corruption does not get us out of politics or that severe economic depression would not allow us to claim that we will no longer have an economy. It is just there, no matter how inattentive we might be to it. Contemporary Buddhists are well positioned to contribute to this discussion in that, first, they can help us find innovative ways to identify and characterize that dimension, and second, they can help us articulate ways to cultivate and develop it so that in our time the religious dimension of human life can be rediscovered and reenvisioned. This would entail broadening our understanding of religion to include not just the past practices of spiritual meaning that we inherit from our ancestors but our own current practices as well. That, it seems to me, has been the life work of Stephen Batchelor, and from my point of view his success in this regard is unprecedented.

But on the terms of Batchelor's philosophical definition that is a religious concern, even if what it demands is religious reform. Putting the matter this way, we would think of Batchelor himself as a religious reformer, not someone who argues against acknowledging and cultivating this dimension of human life. Batchelor nods with tongue-in-cheek irony to this realization when, following his name on an essay, he gives himself the title "itinerant preacher."[25] Although not now identified with any particular Buddhist institution, hence "itinerant," Batchelor "preaches" the Buddhist dharma with insight and transformational power. Given that, I find it difficult to think of the dharma that Batchelor articulates as secular in any substantial sense.

Batchelor seems to justify this identification by referring to the Buddhism of the past practiced in conservative sanghas as religious and the innovative Buddhism of the present and future as secular. But if we allow "religion" to be identified with a particular form that it took in the past, which will by definition always be inadequate, we fail to see how our grappling with the meaning of our contemporary lives is analogous to the efforts of our ancestors to come to terms with their own. That our religious inclinations will differ substantially from those in the past does not lift us out of the domain of religion, given an appropriately comprehensive and historically astute understanding of religion. Things change, and that must include the religious dimension in which we face up to the "great matter" of the meaning of our own life and death.

This way of thinking of religion as a dimension of human life and culture does not focus primarily on doctrinal belief. One reason for this reorientation is the realization that the Anglo-American tendency to define religion as a "belief system" is misleading and very recent in the history of religious understanding. Belief is only one dimension of religion and is often not particularly noticeable. Only when significant differences of understanding become troublesome do participants notice that they hold beliefs on certain matters and begin to investigate them, cling to them, or insist on belief in them. "Belief" is a remnant of an earlier religious coherence, a belated tip of the religious iceberg. When we come to worry about our belief in God or in rebirth, the worldview that supports that belief is already under conscious review, or disintegrating, and the movement of history is already bringing cultural transformation to bear.

Religion in this derivative sense, as the willful effort to believe what is no longer believable, is neither fundamental to religion nor admirable. As contemporary people, we can only believe what we honestly think to be true, and some ideas that we have inherited from traditional cultures, like a theistic supreme being or the reincarnation of the soul, may be largely implausible in our time. For many of us, these ideas are not even serious candidates for belief. We do not need to debate them, or we could say that the debates that do forge ahead are for many of us simply irrelevant to the practices that structure our daily lives. At this point in human cultural history, our imaginations face in other directions when we ponder the basic structures and meaning of our existence. The "great matter of life and death" still presses upon us, but the modes of understanding that we bring to these issues and the kinds of issues that matter for us have changed.

Authentic religious thinking, traditionally called "theology" in the West, is a form of second-level critical reflection on religious belief and practice that historically follows after the founding of traditional religions in mythical narrative and ritual practice. Theology aims to propose ideals for thought and practice that inspire full engagement with "the great matter." When vibrant and healthy, this mode of reflection engages critically with religious ideas and practices so that they enhance life rather than impede it. It is in this sense, I assume, that Batchelor ponders whether he should refer to himself as a theologian, "albeit theology without *theos*.[26] So when Batchelor redefines the "four noble truths" as "four noble tasks," displacing them as propositions to be believed or disbelieved, thus resituating them in the domain to practice, he is engaged in theological reflection, critical thinking about the depth dimension of human life. He recognizes that belief is neither the essence of religion nor the primary focus of a flourishing life and that contemporary Western thinking about religion needs to reorient itself in recognition of that.

That reorientation, however, will not be successful if it simply dismisses the role of belief altogether. Although not the essence of religion, belief is far from irrelevant in any dimension of human culture. We do, in fact, believe many things to be true, even if in the movement of contemporary philosophy we find it necessary to rethink what it means to say that something is true. Thus in writing his book *Buddhism Without Beliefs*,[27] Batchelor cannot mean *all* beliefs but rather just those that are no longer believable or those that appear to be dogmatically imposed. As a Buddhist he has very good reasons to reject any dogmatic demand that he believe something that neither inspires nor interests him, nor something that flies in the face of our contemporary standards of logic and evidence. Authentic beliefs are what we honestly think to be true, those that make logical sense to us and that appear to be supported by good evidence. Such beliefs inevitably shape our practice in life. We decide what we decide and do what we do in view of these beliefs and alter our plans of action as these beliefs shift. Belief and practice are mutually correlative.

Understood in this light, "belief" will never be too far from the surface of human life. If the "four truths" become "four tasks," as Batchelor recommends, we must still believe that these are the tasks appropriate to our time and situation and believe that taking them up into our daily practices will eventuate in something worthwhile. The "Buddhism without beliefs" that Batchelor articulates so persuasively is a praxis-based form of Buddhism without *required* beliefs, without the dogmatic imposition of beliefs from previous eras that in our time may have become unbelievable. But that form of Buddhism is nevertheless based on its own alternative set of beliefs—in Batchelor's case, beliefs that have been submitted to several levels of critical questioning. These might include beliefs that life is best practiced in openness, without clinging, and that in our time "awakening" is best characterized as a process of opening up, release, or letting go of patterns of reactivity. Or that questioning is essential to a flourishing life, or that, given the reciprocity of good and evil, learning to "live with the devil" is the most effective way to seek freedom from its grip. Or that the earliest preinstitutional versions of the Buddha dharma may be the most illuminating, or that a fruitful rearticulation of the dharma will require a return to the roots of the Buddhist tradition.

Beliefs such as these and many more currently shape Batchelor's overall life practice and ours. These change over time, of course, but at no point are we without a full repertoire of current beliefs. Batchelor sees clearly how subversive of authentic transformative practice it is when "people transform the dharma into a belief system"[28] or "encase themselves in an armour of fixed opinions,"[29] treating "the dharma as a set of dogmas rather than a liberative practice,"[30] and these insights are important and valid. But this is a matter of how we hold our beliefs, ideas, opinions, thoughts—how we relate to them rather than about whether to have them. Batchelor's writings, like everyone else's, state and recommend hundreds of ideas, thoughts, beliefs, and opinions. Their brilliance is both how well these ideas correlate to real issues in our lives and how skillfully they avoid the overbearing qualities of dogmatic assertion.

Open questioning is the practice that best helps us avoid the ever-present danger of dogmatism. Batchelor's version of this is the recommendation that questioning be the basis of practice. He writes: "If your experience of birth, sickness, aging, and death raises fundamental questions about your existence, then your practice will be driven by the urgent need to come to terms with those questions."[31] Although by one of Batchelor's two definitions of religion what he has said here is the very essence of religious practice, he nevertheless makes a point of referring to this practice of questioning as secular, and this, he says, stands in contrast to what "religious Buddhists" do. Here is how Batchelor puts the contrast: "At the risk of making too broad a generalization, let me suggest that religious Buddhists have tended to base their practice on *beliefs*, whereas secular Buddhists would tend to base their practice on *questions*."[32]

In addition to the breadth of the generalization that Batchelor readily acknowledges, two aspects of this claim seem questionable to me. One is the view of religion as primarily grounded in belief, and the other is the view of secularity as lacking in beliefs. In making a case against this common modern view of religion as belief, we also claimed that belief plays an inevitable role in human life. Those who regard themselves as secular hold as many beliefs as religious people, and in both cases their beliefs have a bearing on practice. Presumably, what you decide to do will be guided by what you believe to be true.

The important role of questioning in these practices is that beliefs and practices are transformed, extended, or reshaped when questions arise and the questioner is "driven by the urgent need to come to terms with those questions."[33] "Such a practice is concerned with finding an authentic and autonomous response to the questions that life poses rather than confirming any doctrinal article of faith."[34] It is important to recognize, however, that when we are driven by a question, what we seek is some kind of answer. Good questions strive toward resolution in satisfactory answers, and good answers—answers that continue over time to function as effective responses to important issues—become beliefs. Questions are not self-sufficient; they aim at and strive toward answers or solutions, even when, or especially when, good answers generate more questions.

Moreover, every question presupposes a set of beliefs that give the question cogency and urgency. The quality of our question "arises dependent" on the character of our current beliefs. This is as true of secular Buddhists as it is of religious Buddhists. Beliefs—what we currently think—set the basis upon which questions can arise at all. If we do not have beliefs, we cannot possibly have questions. So when Batchelor says of religious Buddhists that your "practice will be the logical consequence of your beliefs,"[35] that is equally true of secular Buddhists. On these grounds, we would assume that Batchelor's practice of the four tasks is a logical consequence of his insightful belief that what the tradition has taken to be four noble truths is better conceived ethically as four vital domains of practice.

The stark dichotomy between believing (or thinking) and praxis (or doing) is further undermined when we recognize that one of our most important practices is, in fact, thinking—conceptual practice—even the formation and reformation of coherent, useful beliefs. The practice of thinking is essential to a mature human life and, when fruitful, leads to beliefs that disclose something important about our own here-and-now acts of existence. The tendency in some forms of both traditional Asian Buddhism and contemporary Western Buddhism to valorize "meditation practices" while being disdainful of thinking and conceptual practices weakens the development of Buddhism in the world today and engenders within Buddhism all of the forms of fundamentalism that are so troublesome in other religions.

Two prominent weaknesses are noticeable in this tendency to assert that thinking is inherently problematic. First, it fails to consider how some of the most important forms of Buddhist meditation are conceptual, reflective practices. Many traditional Buddhist meditative practices are exercises in a certain kind of thinking. Batchelor explains one of these in discussing the early Buddhist text *The Grounding of Mindfulness*. "It would be a mistake," he says, "to think that one should meditate on this task [Four Noble Tasks] in the same way as one would pay attention to the breath or the body."[36] Instead, he claims, "the practice of mindfulness includes recollecting the core vision of the dharma,"[37] where "recollecting" means keeping in mind, pondering, thinking. Clarifying this, Batchelor quotes the sutra: "Here a disciple is mindful; he is equipped with the keenest mindfulness and awareness; he recollects well and keeps in mind *what has been said and done in the past*."[38]

Batchelor goes on to explain how "this 'recollective' aspect is obscured as soon as mindfulness is understood as simply being fully attentive in the present moment or remaining in a state of non-judgmental awareness."[39] Instead we are instructed to "keep these ideas in mind and apply them to illuminate whatever is taking place in our experience."[40] Although there are important and effective forms of meditation that do require that we silence our thinking mind, the demand for total silence of the reflective mind is a mistaken and harmful thought.

A second difficulty with the thought that thought must always be eliminated in Buddhist meditation is that it fails to recognize the dangers inherent in unreflective practice. Unreflective praxis—practice that is not continually honed and questioned through critical thinking—is as dangerous as unreflective belief. Both are examples of unwarranted, unjustified blind faith. Practices reify, lose touch with our ideals, and become dogmatic, just like beliefs, but we are less susceptible to that danger when we engage in meditative practices that are structured to encourage openness, questioning, and fearless engagement. Traditional Asian Buddhists might have helped us through this stumbling block more effectively had they stated more clearly and explicitly that the organizational structure for early Buddhism placed philosophical, contemplative practice under the broader rubric of meditative praxis. Philosophy *is* meditation, not its antithesis.

Thinking with clarity and vision is one important form of meditation that requires cultivation just like the others. Thinking that all thinking is harmful renders us both unaware of the role that thinking already plays in our lives and also, because of lack of practice in critical thinking, vulnerable to destructive forms of literalness and fundamentalism. Neither orthodoxy nor orthopraxy—that is, neither dogmatic thought nor dogmatic practice—are healthy developments, but both theory and practice will, in all effective forms of Buddhism, continue to be the central domains of cultivation for our engagement with the "great matter of birth and death." Stephen Batchelor's version of the Buddhist *dharma* articulates this point with impressive clarity.

Secularity and Posttheistic Religion

Secularity—our particular moment in history—is the age of human self-assertion, the epoch of science and technology. To the extent that we consider ourselves secular, we no longer experience ourselves as being observed from above, overseen by powers beyond our own. In this sense, modern subjectivity is secular insofar as we experience our own human agency as supreme and strive toward greater and greater control. Hence Immanuel Kant's answer to the question "What is enlightenment?" is maturity—growing up to capitalize on the rational powers in our own hands so that, standing on our own, we submit the world to deliberation and rational reformation.[41] No one alive today is unaffected by this significant turn of human history into the epoch of humanism.

One danger that we all vaguely sense in this historical development, however, is that our modern drive to control everything is precisely what we can no longer control. Our modern identity may be so thoroughly directed toward the acquisition of human power that our own will to power may already be out of our control. We almost inevitably see the cosmos as being at our disposal, something there for us that we can manipulate toward our own ends and desires. Furthermore, by aligning itself so closely with science, secular thinking tends to identify truth with the empirical, the calculable, the measureable, and thus the spiritual dimension of human life—questions about the very meaning of human life—begin to seem illusory or just vaguely insignificant. Because no other vision of "the Good" has yet arisen to replace "afterlife in heaven" or a "cycle of rebirths/final nirvana," consumerism and other more subtle forms of acquisition have tended to become our default mode of fulfillment, and this is now perhaps the global faith of our secular world.

Nietzsche refers to this development in his famous "death of God" passage in *The Gay Science*.[42] In that potent masterwork, Nietzsche shows how the madman who proclaims the death of God is clearly distraught—he cares deeply about the absence of solid foundations provided by divine oversight and fears the repercussions of this loss. He assumes that, with this loss, the grounds for higher values have been undermined and destroyed. The jeering atheists who just laugh at him are thoughtless, smug, and blindly self-assured in the secular life that they have already adopted. They are perfectly content not to strive for higher values or test their lives in view of stringent ethical ideals. They seem content neither to strive for deeper forms of self-awareness nor to seek new forms of freedom. And in explicitly religious terms, they are quite content not to discipline themselves to ponder the meaning of birth and death. They much prefer their current pursuit of poisonous greed, disdainful aversion, and pleasurable delusion. Although Nietzsche's madman is crazed and disabled by the enormous implications of his cosmic insight, the secular atheists are worse off—they are already dead to any value beyond the most banal forms of self-satisfaction.

In response to the death of God—that is, to our human inability to assert the existence of divine guidance or any other absolute foundation in view of the modern practice of critical thinking—two paths have opened up. The first is reactionary, a form of nostalgia for the premodern past that manifests in fundamentalist, dogmatic attempts to live as though we still reside in some earlier epoch, as though we could still live medieval lives, as though a static conception of human nature can still be taken to sanctify static values. The second path is secularity, which simply accepts the inevitable, rejects the religious past, and tries to make due by focusing elsewhere, like on the "economy" that can only strike us as truly real.

Both reactions cannot help but adopt modern modes of thinking and talking about religion. Both theists and atheists assume that faith is a certain kind of belief—certainty about the truth of otherworldly, supernatural propositions. They both proceed as though the question of the existence of God is ultimately an empirical hypothesis about what really does or doesn't exist "out there," and, like all good modernists, both pursue empirical evidence for their convictions about belief and disbelief. While the hopelessness of the theistic effort may be obvious, we should recognize that contemporary atheism is equally immersed in an untenable, uninspired vision of who we are as human beings. It has nothing to say about the meaning of our lives, nor about the values that we should affirm, since all such talk is thoughtlessly dismissed as "subjective" and "relative."

In the midst of this standoff between theism and atheism, a new and as yet vaguely formed possibility has emerged—the possibility of posttheistic forms of religious life. While atheism is still caught in the grasp of what it must deny—caught in an oppositional relation to theism—posttheism steps onto new ground. Stephen Batchelor's groundbreaking work in *Confession of a Buddhist Atheist* and *After Buddhism* is, from my point of view, really that of a posttheistic Buddhist, where, as he says, Buddhism's "theistic" leap of faith entails afterlives, afterworlds, and other forms of imagined escape from the here and now. Although he does proffer a few arguments against Buddhist afterlife, mostly, like me, he shrugs his shoulders and confesses that he isn't really interested and has more important issues to address. He is "post" wanting to think about it, so that "rebirth" isn't even a serious candidate for belief or disbelief.

Nietzsche's death of God narrative drops the first posttheistic hint that as we come to imagine our real situation on this planet as dependent products of biological and cultural evolution, new forms of enlightened life will emerge. This hint, taken up a half-century later by Heidegger, is that the death of God might allow for a deeper, richer, postmetaphysical sense of spiritual life than any found in traditional religions and that, ironically, this "death" clears the ground for new, revolutionary forms of spirituality that were unimaginable so long as the life-negating, otherworldly structures of theism and the afterlife were the primary religious concerns.

That, it seems to me, is our historical assignment, our calling: to affirm the religious dimension of human life by reenvisioning and reformulating spiritual sensibilities at the cutting edge of contemporary thought, practice, and experience. In contrast to the triumphalism and dogmatism that characterize both theism and atheism, a thoroughly posttheistic religious sensibility would necessarily be experimental, moving forward in humility and openness of thought toward a range of new possibilities for enlightened human life, rather than a search to find the one correct view or practice. It would begin in contemplative practice to build habits of mind and body attuned to openness and inclined to question the instrumental character of current common sense, which imagines ever-new means but never ends, leaving us without ideals and goals suitable to our time.

In this respect a new postsecular orientation would cultivate respect for traditional cultural practices through which things in the world mattered in ways other than our instrumental use of them. In this sense, postsecular, postmetaphysical thinking would be meditative and uniquely attuned to the imaginative dimensions of historical consciousness—contemplating early religious expressions in text and art not as thoughtless believers or critical, disdainful disbelievers but as those in search of our own lineage, asking who we are and who or what we might become, given patterns of dependent arising that have given rise to our identity and situation here and now. In this light, Batchelor's recent interest in the early Buddhist *Nikayas* is one among many promising points of departure for posttheistic forms of spirituality.

Posttheistic religious engagement would recognize that the romantic spirituality that gave rise to our interest in Buddhism in the first place—the quest for authenticity, for wholeness, for self-actualization and self-realization—still harbors the delusory hope of escaping from history and the contingencies of finite beings. Postromantic contemplation would recognize that human beings and human cultures are never complete, that they are not *complete-able* because they are finite, and that there is no final wholeness, since like evolution itself, there is always more to come. It would cultivate the idea that the universe is still experimenting with us and through us and still sharpening its capacity for more comprehensive awareness through our human agency. This kind of meditative historical consciousness will be the best cure both for our lack of religious imagination and for the barren scholasticism that prevents academia from providing leadership on these crucial issues today. The further development of this meditative consciousness would enable us to realize that human beings have already turned out to be far more malleable than our static conceptions of human nature ever allowed and that this opens the future to unimaginable forms of transformation.

I understand that the corrupt and maladaptive character of many modern religions and the antireligious bias of contemporary culture make it tempting to go secular—to refer to the Buddhism of our time as secular Buddhism so that we are not associated with the anachronistic, supernatural thinking that religion often entails. When the religion of one's childhood remains childish, it is natural to think that religion is necessarily or constitutionally childish. But it need not be, and to assume that it is entails a historical mistake based upon an untenable level of essentialism. Religions, including Buddhism, are "empty" of a fixed nature or essence; they are impermanent and come to be what they are dependent on factors that may be or become otherwise.

So, with the Japanese Buddhist leader Shinran, I am inclined to consider secular Buddhism an illusory "easy path" and to encourage all of us to take the more challenging and rewarding route of reenvisioning religion for our time. In other words, we should be willing to continue to call what we are doing and creating just Buddhism—contemporary Buddhism, to be sure, but leaving open all other identities that might inappropriately predetermine what Buddhism will become. It seems to me that the most interesting and revolutionary contribution we can make is to envision and cultivate a contemporary religious sensibility grounded in the long nontheistic tradition of Buddhist thinking and praxis that is fully in accord with the forms of suffering and the possibilities for awakening now becoming available in our time.

PART II

The Moral Dimension of Enlightenment

4

Enlightenment and the Experience of Karma

THE RELATIONSHIP BETWEEN Buddhist enlightenment and the central moral concept of karma is historically complex and invariably important. From the earliest Buddhist writings forward, it is maintained that only those who live lives of a certain karmic quality approach the status of enlightenment. Those whose karma has not been assiduously cultivated are thought to be incapable of even forming an authentic "thought of enlightenment," much less living up to it. On the other hand, it is often the case in Buddhist thought that the concept of karma is set in juxtaposition to the attainment of enlightenment. Those few who attain the highest status of awakening no longer accrue karma, it is claimed; they live in a reality beyond the tragic gravitational pull of karmic action and repercussion.

Reflection on the relation between the moral quality of one's life and its larger repercussions takes place in all cultures. In this domain, the Buddhist concept of karma has the potential to challenge us in significant ways. It may very well be that this Buddhist concept includes some of the most important lessons we can learn from Buddhism. In this chapter we begin to probe some of these issues philosophically rather than historically in hopes of developing our own sense of the relation between what we do and who or what we become.

The early Buddhist sutras set the stage for recognizing the complexities of the concept of karma. There, writers of these early texts produce a recollection of the Buddha's warning about karma: that karmic processes are so complex and mysterious that they are ultimately unfathomable. On these grounds, the Buddha declared it one of the four topics not suited to healthy philosophical meditation, one leading on occasion to "vexation and mad-ness."[1] In spite of this dire warning, however, the Buddha did not heed his own admonition, frequently referring to the workings of karma and thereby encouraging his disciples to do the same. It is important for us to engage in the processes of critical thinking about the concept of karma because Buddhist (and Hindu) teachings on karma and moral life have now entered contemporary currents of Western thought and culture and deserve to be scrutinized for their potential value and weaknesses. The risk in this endeavor *is* serious, of course, because in Asian cultures karma is the primary concept governing the moral sphere of culture. Westerners have faced doubts about critical thinking in this same sphere of culture, when early modern thinkers wondered whether moral conduct would sur-vive critical reflection on the Christian concepts of theistic judgment and heavenly reward. Most have concluded that the benefits of critical think-ing about morality outweigh the risks and that the possibility of further development and refinement in the sphere of human morality warrants energetic effort.

The primary reason that karma is a promising ethical concept for us today is that it appears to propose a natural connection between a human act and its appropriate consequence or, in traditional terms, between sin and suffering, virtue and reward. The connection requires no supernatu-ral intervention: we suffer or succeed because of the natural outcome of our actions themselves, rather than through the subsequent intervention of divine punishment or reward. Moral errors contain their own penal-ties as natural consequences, and every virtue gives rise to its own reward. Although some dimensions of Western culture presuppose such an arrangement today, it is instructive to recall that this kind of understanding was not articulated in the West until Rousseau in the eighteenth century.[2]

Throughout Asia, karma defines the ethical dimension of culture and remains the key to understanding Buddhist morality. Karma is the teach-ing that tells practitioners that it matters what they do throughout their lives and how they do it. It articulates a close relationship between what a person chooses to do and who or what that person becomes over time. The extraordinary sophistication of this early concept should, in fact, be counted as one of the most significant achievements of South Asian cul-ture and an impressive gift to contemporary ethical thinking globally.

A number of scholars[3] have claimed that one of the primary contribu-tions of Buddhism to Indian culture was that it "ethicized" an earlier pre-ethical concept of karma in extending it beyond the sphere of religious ritual by applying it not just to ritual behaviors that pleased the gods but to all good acts.[4] The domain of "all good acts" is, of course, the sphere of ethics as we know it today, and the applicability of the concept of karma to this sphere is the primary question before us now. In this chapter we cultivate what I call a "naturalistic concept of karma." This naturalistic understanding is inherent in the concept of karma as articulated in the many Buddhist versions of it and can and should be developed. This thesis goes further to claim that with further cultivation for the emerging context of contemporary global culture, the concept of karma could constitute a major element in the ethical thinking of the future. Doing that, however, requires critical thinking, and we do that here by raising questions about five dimensions of the concept of karma as it has been understood in the history of Buddhism. Each area of questioning is offered as a way to begin to hone the concept, to separate it from elements of supernatural thinking, and to work toward locating those elements that might be most effective today in the domain of ethics. Following these five exercises in critical thinking, suggestions are offered about the emergence of a naturalized concept of karma.

Karma as the Principle of Ultimate Justice

The first dimension of the Buddhist doctrine of karma that warrants reflective scrutiny is its assertion of ultimate cosmic justice. Most of the world's major religions have longstanding traditions of promise that, at some point, good and evil lives will be rewarded with good and evil consequences, respectively, and that everyone will receive exactly what they deserve. But all of these religions are also forced to admit that this doctrine contradicts what we sometimes experience in our lives. Good people may just as readily be severely injured or die from an accident or die early of disease as anyone else, and people who have lived unjustly and unfairly will not necessarily experience any deprivation in their lives. Some people seem to receive rewards in proportion to the merit of their lives, while others do not. Among those who do not appear to get what they deserve, some seem to receive more than merit would dictate and others less.

That all of these outcomes are common and unsurprising to us should lead us to question the kind of relationship that traditionally has been thought to exist between merit and reward. How should we account for all of the occasions when it appears to be the case that what someone deserves and what he or she in fact gets do not align? One way to face this realization is to conclude, at least provisionally, that the cosmos is largely indifferent to the sphere of human merit as well as to our expectations of justice. If a morally sound person is no more or no less likely to die early of a disease than anyone else, then maturity and honesty of vision on this matter may require that we question traditional assumptions that cosmic justice *must* prevail. Although *we* certainly care about matters of justice, it is not entirely clear that the larger cosmos does as well. It may be that beyond the human sphere we will not be able to find substantial evidence for that kind of concern for justice.

The religious claim that there is a supernatural connection between moral merit and ultimate destiny may derive from our intuitive sense that there *ought* to be such a connection. We all sense that there should be justice, even in settings where it seems to be lacking. That the corporate criminal ought to be punished, that the innocent child ought to have a fair chance to live his or her life rather than suffer from a devastating disease, and that some things ought to be different from what they appear to be are all manifestations of our deep-seated sense of justice. Virtue and reward, vice and punishment, should be systematically related, and where they are not, we all feel a sense of impropriety. But whether that now-intuitive internal sense of justice is sufficient reason to postulate a supernatural scheme of cosmic justice beyond our understanding and experience is an open question that has remained as closed in Buddhism as it has in other religions. The form that this closure takes in Buddhism is the doctrine of rebirth, which plays the same role in Buddhism that heaven does in theistic traditions as the ultimate guarantor of justice. As it is traditionally conceived in Asia, karma requires the metaphysical doctrine of rebirth to support its often counterexperiential claims about the ultimate triumph of cosmic justice for the individual. It is only by means of a literal claim about an afterlife that the inequalities that are so obvious in life can be justified. The question raised here is whether this consolation that we feel through the doctrine of cosmic justice is one that we are justified to maintain. Is there a more honest and truthful response to this very human concern than the one that the Buddhist teachings of rebirth and that the Christian teachings of heaven offer?

Karma, Incentive, and Social Concern

The second justice-related issue regarding karma follows from the first. One criticism that has been leveled against the idea since its introduction in the West is that it may in effect undermine moral concern for others.

This worry is that the idea of karma may be socially and politically dis-empowering in its cultural effect and that, without intending to do this, karma may in fact support social passivity or acquiescence in the face of oppression of various kinds. When we study the history of Buddhism in Asian societies this conclusion is difficult to avoid. This possible negative aspect of the traditional teachings on karma derives again from the link between karma and rebirth formed in order to posit large-scale cosmic justice over long and invisible stretches of time where other more immediate forms of justice appear not to exist.

If one assumes that cosmic justice prevails over numerous lifetimes in order to explain or justify the injustices that we regularly see in life, and if one assumes that therefore the situations of inequality that people find themselves in are essentially of their own making through moral effort or lack of it in previous lives, then it may not seem either necessary or even fair to attempt to equalize opportunities among people or to help those in desperate circumstances. If, for example, we believe that a child being severely abused by his family is now receiving just reward for his past sins, we may find insufficient reason to intervene even when that abuse appears to be destructive to the individual child and to the society. Taken in this vein, the karma/rebirth juxtaposition may sometimes have the effect of undermining our own effort to see that justice is done and to compensate in some way when it is not.

Now, of course, it is an open question—a historical and social-psychological question—whether or to what extent the doctrines of karma and rebirth have ever really had this effect. We know very well that Buddhist concepts of compassion have prominent places in the various traditions, and we can all point to Buddhist examples of compassionate social effort on behalf of the poor and the needy. Nevertheless, we can see where the logic of this belief can and has been taken to lead, in the minds of some people at least, and we can suspect that it may have unjustifiably diminished or undermined concern for the poor and the suffering in all Buddhist cultures. The link between karma and rebirth can quite reasonably be taken to justify nonaction in the socioeconomic and political spheres and may help provide rational support for acquiescence to oppressive neighbors, laws, and regimes. If and when this does occur, then the Buddhist teaching of nonviolence can be distorted into a teaching of nonaction and passivity and be subject to criticism as a failure of courage and justice.

If the truth is that the cosmos is simply indifferent to human questions of merit and justice, that truth makes it all the more important that human beings attend to these matters themselves. If justice is a human concept, invented and evolving in human minds and culture, and nowhere else, then it is up to us alone to see that we follow through on it. If justice is not structured into the universe itself, then it will be a substantial mistake to leave it up to the universe to see that justice is done. Although, given our finitude, human justice will always be imperfect, it may be all the justice we have. Moreover, the fact that religious traditions, including Buddhism, have claimed otherwise may be insufficient reason to accept the assertion of a cosmic justice beyond the human as the basis for our actions in the world. Critical questioning in the West concerning injustices that may be unethically accepted by simply assuming that justice takes place in the afterlife of heaven and hell began to arise in what we now call the modern era of enlightenment. It is therefore only appropriate that those interested in Buddhist enlightenment begin to think carefully and clearly about these issues as well.

The Character of Karmic Outcomes

A third area of inquiry in which to engage the concept of karma concerns the nature of the reward or consequence that might be expected to follow from morally relevant actions. In pursuing this line of questioning, I employ an Aristotelian distinction borrowed from Alasdair MacIntyre that is now common to contemporary ethics between goods that are "externally" or contingently related to a given practice and goods that are "internal" to a practice and that cannot be acquired in any other way.[5] Because the practice under consideration here is any morally relevant action, we want to distinguish between goods or rewards that *may* accompany that moral act but that are only contingently and externally related to it and rewards that are directly linked to the practice, available through no other means and therefore internal to that specific practice.

If we look at a single act, for example an act of extraordinary generosity or kindness, such as when someone goes far out of her way to help someone else through a problem that he has brought upon himself, we can see many possibilities for rewards that might accrue through some contingency entailed in that relation. The person helped may in fact be wealthy and offer a large sum of money in grateful reciprocity. Members of his family may honor the practitioner of kindness, and her reputation in the community for compassion and character might grow. She may become known as a citizen of extraordinary integrity, which could lead to all kinds of indirect rewards. These are all good consequences, and all deserved, but also all contingent outcomes, all goods that are external to the moral act itself. They may or may not be forthcoming. Indeed, on occasion contingent misunderstanding may give rise to exactly the opposite outcome— the same act of generosity may be misunderstood, resented, reviled, or lead to a denigrated reputation that the person never overcomes. Some rewards that derive from an act are, therefore, contingent and will not occur always or necessarily.

The rewards or goods internal to that act of kindness are directly related to the act and are not contingent on anything but the act. When we act generously, we do something incremental to our character—we shape ourselves slightly further into a person who understands how to act generously, is inclined to do so, and does so with increasing ease. We etch that way of behaving just a little more firmly into our character, into who we are. That is true whether the act is positive or negative in character.[6] Whatever we do contributes to the shaping of our character. Generosity, when it becomes an acquired feature of our character, becomes a virtue— in fact one of the central Buddhist virtues, the first of the six perfections, for example. "A virtue is an acquired human quality the possession and exercise of which tends to enable us to achieve those goods which are internal to practices and the lack of which effectively prevents us from achieving any such goods."[7] This is to say that acts of generosity may or may not give rise to external goods like rewards of money or prestige, but they do give rise to a transformation in character that gradually makes us generous, kind, and concerned about the well-being of others. Internal goods derive naturally from the practice as cause.

Our question, then, is what kinds of rewards, or goods, do the Buddhist teachings of karma correlate to virtuous or nonvirtuous acts, and how should we assess that dimension of the doctrine? Familiarity with the tradition prevents us from giving a univocal answer to this question: different texts and different teachers promise many different kinds of rewards for karmically significant acts, depending on who they are and who they happen to be addressing. Both internal and external goods are commonly brought into play. From acts of generosity we get everything from the virtue of generosity as an internal good to great wealth, an external good, with a variety of specific alternatives in between. Teachers often lean heavily one way or the other, from emphasis on external goods such as health and wealth to a strict focus on the internal goods of character, the development of virtues like wisdom and compassion.

Consider the following example from the Dalai Lama, where he is primarily interested in external goods. "As a result of stealing," he writes, "one will lack material wealth."[8] Because we all know that successful thieves and corporate criminals may or may not live their lives lacking in material wealth, we can only agree with this claim insofar as we assume that the author is here referring to an afterlife, some life beyond the end of this one. That is to say that only the metaphysics of rebirth can make this statement plausible. Otherwise, the doctrine of karma cannot truthfully guarantee such an outcome of external rewards.

Had the Dalai Lama been focused on internal goods, he might have said that, as a result of stealing one will have deeply troubled relations with other people, as well as a distorted relation to material goods. As a result of stealing one will find compassion and intimacy more difficult, be further estranged from the society in which one lives, and feel isolated and unable to trust others. As a result of stealing, one will become even more likely to commit other unhealthy acts and may ultimately find oneself in an unfulfilled and diminished existence. These results of the act of stealing have a direct relation to the act; every act pushes one further in some direction of character formation or another and further instantiates one in some particular relationship to the world. External goods, while certainly important, cannot be so easily guaranteed, except insofar as one offers that guarantee metaphysically by referring to lives beyond the current one whether by means of "heaven" or "reincarnation."

Although—promises of personal rebirth aside—there would appear to be no necessary connection between moral achievement and external rewards, there is a sense in which moral achievement does often make external rewards more likely, even if this is never a relation of necessity. This is true because the more human beings enter the equation, the more likely it is that a human sense of justice will intervene, drawing some connection between virtue and reward or sin and suffering. People who characteristically treat others with kindness and just consideration are often treated kindly themselves, although not always. Those who are frequently mean-spirited and selfish are often treated with distain. Honesty in business often pays off in the form of trusting, faithful customers, while the habit of cheating customers will often come back to haunt the merchant. These dimensions of karma and ethical relations are clear to us, and we are thankful that they exist. But it would seem that their existence is human and social, rather than structured into the cosmos. These developments are a result of our own beliefs and desires that justice really ought to prevail.

Therefore all we can say is that things often work this way, not that they always do or that they must. Sometimes unscrupulous businessmen thrive; on occasion, kindness and honesty go completely unrewarded. These occurrences make it impossible for us to claim a *necessary* relation between moral merit and external forms of reward. Although it is clearly true that to some extent virtue is its own reward, what we cannot claim is that other kinds of reward are meted out in the same way. Evidence shows us that they are not, even if the human exercise of justice often directs external rewards toward those who are deserving.

Let us summarize the foregoing by saying that how we comport ourselves ethically has at least three ramifications: (a) it shapes our character and helps determine who or what we become; (b) it helps shape others and the society in which we live, now and into the future; and (c) it encourages others to treat us in ways that correspond to our character—they will often do onto us as we have done onto them, although not always. The first and second outcomes can be counted as goods internal to ethical action; our actions do shape us, and they do have an effect on the world. The third is external, or contingent, in that it may or may not follow from the ethical act. The more human justice there is, the more the distribution of external goods is likely to match the extent of our merit.

Thus, insofar as we can gather evidence on this matter, some dissociation between merit and external goods is important to maintain. Although good acts do lead to the development of good character, being good does not always or necessarily lead to a life of good fortune. Therefore, if there is a contingent relation between human actions and external goods as rewards and merit, it would be wise to articulate a system of ethics and a doctrine of karma that do not rely heavily on this relation in spite of the longstanding Buddhist tradition of doing so for purposes of moral motivation.

Positive and Negative Karma

The fourth question about karma concerns the tendency in Buddhism and other South Asian religions to dwell on karma as a negative and counterenlightening force rather than as an influence that can just as well be positive as negative. The most common way that this issue emerges is when it is claimed that, once enlightened, a person no longer accumulates karma, no matter how long he or she continues to live, and that this end to karma is what enables *parinirvāna,* the highest state in which those who are enlightened exit the cycles of birth and death that ordinary reincarnating or reborn individuals experience in order to dwell "beyond existence and non-existence." The Buddha, for example, was held to have lived in the world for at least four decades without accruing any further residue of karma. Without karma to hold him back, the Buddha entered the ultimate state of *parinirvāna,* thus transcending the human sphere finally and completely.

No doubt this Buddhist teaching was influenced to some extent by earlier Jain and Brahmanical notions of karma. Early Jain teachings on karma are very interesting in this regard since they imagine karma in physical or material terms. Karma is a subtle form of matter that results from all actions that spring from desire, whether good or evil. In this Jain sense, avoiding action through complete withdrawal is the only way to escape the cycles of reincarnation since even a magnanimous act of kindness that derives from the desire that justice or goodness prevail will settle like a kind of material stain on the soul of the actor. Karma is a weight that holds human beings down here in the world so that the transcendence of enlightenment cannot occur. Although these earlier views are distinct from the Buddhist teachings on karma, there are clearly influences and interfusions.

One such influence may be the Buddhist belief that the enlightened are beyond all karma. They live lives and engage in actions that no longer have worldly repercussions or consequences. For a naturalistic conception of karma, however, that idea just does not make sense. In a world of intricate interdependence and movement, nothing stands outside of the web of relations in which we live. Every act and the existence of everything, even the most subtle and seemingly inconsequential, has a bearing on other things. This "bearing" may be so small as to be immeasurable, but we nevertheless cannot imagine a world of causality where anything no longer matters at all. If every act and every movement has an impact, however small, then karma continues to be generated by our lives whether or not we are fully enlightened.

Based on this Buddhist view of intercausality, where every act has a consequence without exceptions, it would be necessary to conceive of karma as taking both positive and negative forms. Acts of enlightenment would have enlightening effects on the world in the same way that acts of un-enlightenment would have destructive effects. Every act has a consequence of a kind that matches the quality and character of the act. This view is ironically found right alongside the opposite view in the history of Buddhist thought. While the Buddha was beyond all karma in the later stages of his enlightened life, he simultaneously had the massive impact on human culture that we continue to feel today. The act of enlightening his disciples brought forth major and obvious cultural consequences, outcomes that were both good for us and good for him. Would not these enormous historical effects be conceived as the outcome of karma? They would not, it seems, only because some of the traditions of early India were focused on enlightenment as the transcendence of the human sphere and the belief that this elevated status required a withdrawal from the activities of human life even while living.

That limitation on the concept of karma is neither persuasive nor helpful for the development of contemporary Buddhism. To see how this might be the case, consider how we now understand these same processes in contemporary neuroscience. Realizations growing out of neuroscience are now eagerly absorbed into the theory and practice of Buddhist meditation. The basic rationale for this collusion is simple. The brain is an organ that alters its structure in conformity to the experience that it undergoes. Whatever regularly comes into one's mind shapes the neural structure of one's brain—temporary mental states are converted into enduring neural structure by growing new neural circuits in the specific area of the brain that is active. Active synapses become more sensitive and more responsive, and they generate the growth of new ones as more blood flow and hence more oxygen are transported to that section of the brain. Inactive connections on the other hand, gradually reduce their capacity and eventually wither away. "Experience-dependent neuroplasticity" demonstrates in a neuroscientific way that no experience is inconsequential.[9] Everything we do, think, feel, or say has a sculpting effect on our brain, and every brain thus shaped engages with the world in some slightly different way.

That, in summary, initiates the development of a naturalized concept of karma, and this way of conceptualizing human experience precludes the traditional Buddhist idea that enlightened beings would engage in actions that in any sense would be "karma-free." Actions, no matter how inconsequential, always have effects, and these effects may be either enslaving or liberating, obscuring or enlightening. Although early South Asian Jains and Buddhists certainly had persuasive reasons to think that all karma is inherently opposed to liberation, once we broaden the concept as we attempt to do here, it is difficult to think that their reasons will be convincing for us. If karma is the enduring repercussions of any act, the

most enlightened of individuals will be generating as much karmic consequence as the most unenlightened, except that the kind or quality of the
karma will determine whether we can count the impact as welcome or
unwelcome. Gandhi and Hitler were contemporaries whose karmic paths
were perhaps equally powerful while being diametrically opposed. The
point here is simply this: forming an adequate contemporary concept of
karma will require universal application—all acts are karmically relevant,
and nothing that occurs in the world is inconsequential.

Understanding Karma Communally

The fifth and final dimension of the concept of karma that we examine is
the extent to which karma can be adequately conceived as a consequence
or destiny that is strictly individual as opposed to one that is social or communal. Although there are a few interesting places in Buddhist philosophy where a collective dimension to karma is broached, in Asanga and
Vasubandhu for example, I think that it is true to say that this concept
has been overwhelmingly understood in individual terms, that is, that
the karma produced by *my* acts is *mine* primarily, rather than ours collectively.[10] For the most part, references to karma in contemporary Buddhist
literature follow the same individualized pattern. From a contemporary
Buddhist point of view, however, there are serious philosophical and ethical difficulties with this way of understanding the impact that human acts
have on our lives. Perhaps most strikingly, the view that my acts and their
repercussions remain enclosed in a personal continuum that never dis-
sipates into the larger society and continues to be forever "mine" rein-
forces a picture of the world as composed of a large number of discreet
and isolated souls, a view that a great deal of Buddhist thought has sought
to undermine. The articulation of this view among the Jains, in Samkhya,
and in other traditions, however, clearly shows the powerful impact of the
concern for ultimate individual destiny in the Indian intellectual/religious
world around the time that Buddhism was developing its vision of the
nature of human life.

Although the primary direction of Buddhist thinking may have been
to undercut the entire question of ultimate individual destiny through the
alternative possibility of *no-self*, the question has continued to surface and
demand an answer. Individuals have continued to focus their concerns
about karma on the impact that it has on them personally and individually. It may very well be, however, that Buddhist attempts to satisfy the

desire behind the question of individual destiny by offering the concept of rebirth to allay fears about the continuation of individual existence has the additional and unwanted effect of blocking further development along the alternative paths clearly laid out in the early teachings. It stands in the way of the achievement of a broader vision of the meanings of no-self, and a more effective and mature understanding of the ways each of us continue to affect the future beyond the time frame of our personal lives. Personal anxieties about death are a powerful force in the mind—so strong that they can prevent other impersonal and transindividual conceptions from rising to the cultural surface. But contemporary Buddhist thought should resist this longstanding human inclination.

The line of thinking that began to develop most explicitly in early Mahayana texts, which imagined complex interrelations among individuals, recognized that the consequences of any act in the world could not be easily localized and isolated. It recognized that effects radiate out from causes in an ultimately uncontainable fashion, rendering lines of partition between selves and between all entities in the world significantly more porous and malleable than we tend to assume. Expanding the image of the bodhisattva, Buddhists began to see how lines of influence and outcome comingle, along family lines and among friends, coworkers, and cocitizens, such that the future for others "arises dependent" in part upon my acts and I "arise dependent" in part upon the shaping powers of the accumulating culture around me. This type of thinking, based heavily on the expanding meaning of "dependent arising," was forcefully present in several dimensions of Buddhist ethics. My suspicion, however, is that we have yet to see the development of this aspect of Buddhism to the extent of its potential and that it has been continually redirected by what must have seemed more pressing questions about individual destiny as "afterlife."

As an example of a possible pattern of "redirection," consider the development of merit transfer, the idea that one might give the rewards from one's own good acts to another person whose karmic status might be in greater jeopardy. Mahayana Buddhists were, of course, particularly attracted to this idea; they sought ways to develop an unselfish concern for the spiritual welfare of all sentient beings and focused intently on methods that enabled them to get out from under the self-centered implications of a personal spiritual quest. The idea that they could pursue the good in their own quest and then, in a compassionate and unselfish meditative gesture, contemplate giving to others whatever good had resulted from that act seemed an excellent middle path between selfish personal quests and compassion for others. But one effect of this teaching was that it still tended to picture the karma or the goodness of an act as a self-enclosed package that was theirs alone and that could be generously given away at some later point if circumstances warranted. As a meditative device used to prevent individuals from coveting and hoarding their own spiritual merit, this may on occasion have been effective. But a problem looms when a skillful meditative device is taken out of that contemplative setting of mental self-cultivation and treated as a picture of what really does happen when we do good things.

It is important to remember that many Buddhist moral teachings are not first of all prescriptions about how to treat others but rather prescriptions for how to treat our own minds in meditation so that we become the kind of moral persons that the tradition envisioned. While it may be very good for us, having done a good deed, to humble ourselves in meditation on it by picturing ourselves giving the merit of that act to others, it is not good for us to misunderstand the moral enterprise by reifying the terms and processes operative within it. What kind of magical or supernatural entity would karma have to be to make such a gift of merit make sense? Focusing so intently on our own moral merit, it is also inevitable that we come to realize that donating our merit to another is itself a really good and generous act, one that cannot help but win us lots of good merit.

What began as a way to drop the meritorious self from consideration ends up slipping it in through the back door in such a way that the entire specter of merit transfer becomes yet another way to picture ourselves as deserving of merit. When seen from the outside, this is doubly problematic, because the one to whom we are supposedly being generous, in fact, gets nothing because, after all, this is mental exercise, while we picture ourselves doubling our own merit, thereby cultivating exactly the pride and self-satisfaction that we wanted to overcome. If the end pursued is understood in terms of humility and unselfishness, entangling ourselves in a mental economy of merit calculation and exchange is not likely to be effective. The practices of merit transfer just fit too smoothly into old habits of self-concern and all too readily block the development of kinds of selflessness envisioned in the bodhisattva ideal. The literal and highly reified conception of karma often presupposed in the practices of merit transfer are philosophically problematic as well as counterproductive to the effort to understand karma as a viable possibility for contemporary ethics.

There are a variety of ways in which an individualized concept of karma continues to perpetuate itself in spite of a wealth of ideas in the Buddhist tradition that would mitigate against it. The basic ideas of impermanence, dependent arising, no-self, and later extensions of these ideas such as "emptiness" are prominent among them. But all of these ideas run aground on the concept of rebirth, and it is there that karma is most problematic. All five critical questions raised so far about karma derive their impact from the association that karma has with rebirth.

The question of rebirth and afterlife is as complicated as it is interesting and therefore not one that I take up in this setting. But let me simply indicate the direction philosophical questioning on this issue might take. First, if this really is an open question about what happens to people after they die, then we would expect that evidence will need to play at least some role, and we would assume that scientific investigation is the best way to gather and assess it. But here we encounter an unsurprising division between pious Hindus and Buddhists who write books gathering what seems to them the incontrovertible evidence for reincarnation and Western scientists who, seeing no evidence whatsoever, do not even raise the question. This is to say that, constrained by a variety of traditional and modern doctrines, this question has not been asked in a serious way, both out of deference to religious belief and because the question itself eludes conclusive response because what it pursues is by definition beyond the world in which we live, that is, fully metaphysical. That leaves most of us in the position of needing to sort out the possibilities ourselves. In the meantime, however, the most honest and therefore spiritually and intellectually compelling response is to admit that we simply do not know what happens to us after we die. Better, it would seem, to allow the mystery and gravity of human mortality to press upon us and to stimulate our asking the kinds of questions that reflect our deepest human concerns than to leap in one direction or the other on the question of afterlife.

The second point, however, is the difficulty that Buddhists have had historically in making a doctrine of rebirth cohere with their other central values. Those who have read through *Abhidharma* literature are familiar with the contortions that Buddhist intellectuals went through in the process of explaining what rebirth might mean in view of the Buddhist claim that there is no permanent or substantial self because all things are both impermanent and dependent on other impermanent conditions. Wherever in Buddhist thought rebirth is given a strong and substantial role, no-self and other dimensions of the teachings are reduced in significance. Wherever the teaching of no-self and related doctrinal elements are given strong and consistent application, very little is left that rebirth could mean.

Philosophers in the future will continue to raise questions about the tension between these two early and important dimensions in Buddhist thought and to examine what possibilities for thought were left unexplored in the Buddhist tradition due to logical difficulties on this one issue. For some, it has already been tempting to suspect that the idea of rebirth in Buddhism is an intellectual relapse, a place within the teachings where practitioners were simply unable or unwilling to consider the radical consequences of their teachings and where they may have fallen prey to the dangers of grasping for the immortal soul or for the kinds of permanence and security that Buddhist psychology warns so perceptively against. These two areas, I suspect, will be the places where the debate about rebirth and its role in the workings of karma will tend to focus. But these are open questions, questions that require cautious, delicate treatment because they are located close to the life force that motivates human beings. Yet that is exactly why they need to be raised as real questions.

In several respects, rebirth stands in the way of our understanding karma in purely ethical terms. Rebirth encourages us to (a) assume a concept of cosmic justice for which we have insufficient evidence; (b) ignore issues of justice in this life on the grounds of speculation about future lives; (c) focus our hopes on external rewards for our actions, like wealth and status in a future life, rather than on the construction of character in this one; (d) conceive of the ultimate goal as a form of quiescence that accrues no karma at all; and (e) conceive of our lives in strictly individual terms, as a personal continuum through many lives, rather than collectively, where individuals share in a communal destiny, contributing their lives and efforts to that collective destiny. Although at the time when Buddhism first emerged, karma and rebirth continued to be linked together in order to make the newly emerging domain of ethics viable, today, ironically, given the cultural evolution of ethical understanding, karma may need to be disconnected from the metaphysics of rebirth in order to continue the development of Buddhist ethics.[11] If the early Buddhists did ethicize the concept of karma by lifting it out of the sphere of religious ritual by applying it to all of our morally relevant actions, then carrying through on that ethicization will require that the link between karma and rebirth be questioned, perhaps altered. Among Buddhists today, educated in a world of science and favorably disposed to contemporary standards for the articulation of truth, a naturalized concept of karma without supernatural preconditions will more likely be both persuasive and motivationally functional.[12]

Toward a Contemporary Understanding of Karma

How would we develop such a concept? Here are just a few suggestions. A naturalistic theory of karma would treat choice and character as mutually determining, each arising dependent on the other. It would show how the choices we make, one by one, shape our character, and how the character that we have constructed, choice by choice, sets limits on the range of possibilities that we will be able to consider in each future decision. Karma implies that once we have made a choice and acted on it, it will always be with us, and we will always be the one who at that moment and under those conditions embraced that path of action. The past, on this view, is never something that once happened to us and is now over; instead, it is the network of causes and conditions that has already shaped us and that is right now setting conditions for every choice and move we make. From the very moment of an act on, we *are* that choice, which has been appropriated into our character along with countless others. In this light human freedom becomes highly visible, and awesome in its gravity, but is noticeable only to one who has realized the far-reaching and irreversible impact on oneself and others of choices made, of karma.

The concept of karma brings this pattern of freedom in self-cultivation clearly to the fore and does so with great insight and natural subtlety. It highlights a structure of personal accountability in which every act contains its own internal, natural rewards or consequences, even if Buddhists sometimes succumbed to the temptation to offer a variety of external rewards as well. Although money does talk, promising it when it may or may not be forthcoming is a questionable strategy of motivation. Better to teach, as Buddhists have, that the best things in life are free and that the very best of these is the freedom to cultivate oneself into someone who is wise, insightful, compassionate, and magnanimous.[13] This freedom, however, operates under strict and always fluctuating conditions. A mature concept of karma would encourage people to recognize the finitude of freedom and choice and all of the ways we are shaped by forces far beyond our control. Although always attempting to extend our ethical imaginations, and

therefore our freedom, failure simultaneously to recognize the encompassing forces of nature, society, and history places us in a precarious position
and renders our choices naive. Our choices and our lives arise dependent
on these larger forces, and, in view of them, mindfulness and reverence are
appropriate responses.

If the solitary ethical decisions we have been focusing on so far have the
power to move us in the direction of greater forms of human excellence,
or the opposite, then how much more so the unconscious "non-choices"
that we make every day in the form of habits and customs that deepen
over time and engrave their mark into our character. Some accounts of
karma are exceptionally insightful in that their understanding of character
development takes full account of the enormous importance of ordinary
daily practice or customs of behavior, what we habitually do during the day
often without reflection or choice—the ways we do our work and manage
our time, the ways we daydream, or cultivate resentment, or lose ourselves
in distractions, down to the very way we eat and breathe.

This is clearly a strong point in Buddhist ethics. On this understanding of karma, which was closely related to the development of meditation,
ethics is largely a matter of daily practice, understood as the self-conscious
cultivation of ordinary life and mentality toward the approximation of
an ideal defined by images of human excellence, the awakened arhats
and bodhisattvas.[14] To an extent not found in other religious and philosophical traditions, Buddhists saw that ethics is only rarely about difficult
and monumental decisions and that, in preparing ourselves for life, it is
much more important to focus on what we do with ourselves moment
by moment than it is to attempt to imagine how we will solve the major
moral crises when they arrive. They seem to have realized that it is only
through disciplined practices of daily self-cultivation that we would be in
a mental position to handle the big issues when they do come up. They
also claimed, insightfully, that the self is malleable and open to this kind
of ethical transformation, and here we see the impact of the concept of no-
self as it was developed in various dimensions of the tradition.

Moreover, the Buddhist doctrine of no-self is one of the best among
several places in the teachings where we can begin to see beyond the individual interpretation of karma that has dominated the tradition so far.
If karma is to be a truly comprehensive teaching about human actions
and their effects, extensive development of all of the ways in which the
effects of our acts radiate into other selves and into social structures
will need to be grafted onto the doctrine of karma as it currently stands.

This extension of the doctrine has already begun, however, and will not be difficult to pursue because it can be grounded on the extraordinary Mahayana teaching of emptiness, the Buddhist vision of the interpenetration of all beings. Following this vision, we can imagine a collective understanding of karma that overcomes limitations deriving from the concept's original foundation in the individualized spirituality of early Buddhist monasticism.

A naturalized philosophical account of the Buddhist idea of karma might insightfully reflect these and other dimensions of our human situation. Separated from elements of supernatural thinking that have been associated with karma since its inception, its basic tenets of freedom, decision, and accountability are impressive and clearly show us something important about the human situation, including the project of self-construction, both individually and collectively conceived. I conclude, therefore, imagining elements in the concept of karma having the potential to be truly effective in the effort to design strategies of ethical education that are both honest to the requirements of thinking in our time and profoundly enabling in the quest for human enlightenment.

5

Enlightenment and the Moral Dimension of Zen Training

IN 2003 PRACTITIONERS and admirers of the Zen tradition were shocked by the criticism leveled by Brian Victoria upon the amoral or immoral way that Zen masters in Japan had responded to the government's summons to take an active role in the recruitment and training of young men to serve Japanese expansionism, imperialism, and military aggression against neighboring countries. Victoria's critique raised serious questions for the Zen tradition both in Japan and beyond. How, he asks, could Zen "enlightenment" manifest itself in actions that seemed consistently amoral and thoughtless? How could Zen enlightenment give rise to anything less than morally admirable actions? How could enlightened Zen masters participate as advocates in the brutal military conquest of Buddhist peoples and nations throughout Asia, without ever questioning the moral quality of that aggressive enterprise?

Although himself a fully ordained Zen priest in the Japanese tradition, Victoria's publications have shaken the world of Zen in Japan and in the West. His books document how Zen masters became advocates of Japanese military values, co-opted by the Japanese government into rationalizing the militarization of Japanese society in the 1930s and 1940s by proclaiming the "unity of Zen and war."[1] Beyond this willingness to construct ideological links between military aggression and the teachings of Zen, Victoria describes how certain acclaimed Zen masters showed "complete and utter indifference to the pain and suffering of the victims of Japanese aggression."[2] He asks how it was possible that acknowledged Zen masters had witnessed "what were so clearly war atrocities committed against Chinese civilians, young and old, without having confronted the moral implications of . . . this mindless brutality."[3]

This chapter seeks an adequate response to these questions by assessing the role that morality has played in the Japanese Zen tradition and in the end by considering how the Zen tradition might extend itself in response to the moral crisis that Victoria's questions have brought to light.

Locating Morality in Zen

Startled by the impact of these revelations, some Buddhists have responded to Victoria's devastating criticism by claiming that those who demonstrated such "moral blindness" were obviously not enlightened—they were not *true* Zen masters.[4] Given the sheer numbers of authenticated Zen masters whose actions in the war fit this pattern, however, and the scarcity of those who comported themselves otherwise, this response is inadequate. In my judgment, a more honest and intellectually disciplined conclusion would be that these Zen masters were indeed enlightened according to the tradition's own criteria but that, by these internal, defining criteria, Zen enlightenment lacks a substantial moral dimension.[5]

This understanding will of course be counterintuitive for many of us because by "enlightenment" we want to mean an attainment of human excellence that is comprehensive and complete. By "enlightenment" we want to mean an opening of the human mind to the way things really are, an end to the human perversions of greed, hatred, and delusion—a comprehensive form of human excellence. When projected onto historical examples of enlightenment from the past, however, this desire undermines our ability to understand differences between instances of enlightenment, that is, to understand them historically as they actually were and are. Historically considered, every attainment of enlightenment, like everything else human, has a particular character, one that takes different forms in different settings, cultures, and epochs. And in the Zen tradition, enlightenment has been conceived and experienced in a way that does not include morality as a substantial or central element. This is not something that has always been hidden or denied in Zen. Indeed, there were times when the transmoral character of enlightenment was flaunted, times when true enlightenment required a corresponding claim to have gone beyond the distinction between good and evil. Morality has rarely been a matter of primary interest in Zen history.

This is not to say, of course, that traditional Zen masters were necessarily immoral or even amoral. No doubt more than a few masters in Zen history have been moral exemplars in their communities. But I conclude, following Tom Kasulis, Chris Ives, and others, that this is not directly attributable to their Zen training so much as it is to their participation in the traditions of East Asian Confucian morality, as well as to the moral teachings of the broader Chinese Buddhist tradition. In other words, Zen masters, like everyone else in East Asia, lived moral lives and expressed themselves morally *to the extent of* their absorption of the Confucian and Buddhist culture in which they lived. Wherever moral stature is a component of the character of a Zen master, that stature would be the result of something other than Zen training. This conclusion seems justified because if we search for evidence of substantive interest in morality in the two dimensions of the Zen tradition where we would most expect to find it—in the vast canon of Zen sacred literature and in the full repertoire of Zen practices—we discover that it is largely absent.

Reading widely in the enormous Zen canon that chronicles many centuries of Zen history, we find no mention of what happened when Zen masters faced moral dilemmas like the ones that Brian Victoria described in modern Japan, or any other for that matter. What happened, for example, when a Zen master had to decide between speaking on behalf of peasant farmers who were impoverished and starving in a time of famine and supporting the wealthy ruling powers of the region? How did Zen masters respond when a local regime governed through intimidation and cruelty or when corruption was blatant, widespread, and devastating to the society? What happened when a donor to a Zen monastery asked in return for substantial favors that seriously compromised the values of the Buddhist tradition? How were moral issues like these decided, and how did such decisions draw upon the awakened minds of Zen masters?

The answer is that, for the most part, we do not know, because the authors of Zen texts did not consider incidences like these to be worthy examples of the "function" or "skill" of great Zen minds. In fact, they don't even mention occasions of moral significance when describing the great masters of Zen. In composing the tradition's great texts, authors directed their descriptions and praise instead toward what they took to be situations in life that, to their minds, most fully disclosed the character of awakened Zen life. Even though the vast *Transmission of the Lamp* literature describes thousands of occasions in which a master's Zen mind came to fruition in some specific worldly context, virtually none of these call upon the *moral* capacities of their exemplars.[6] This is significant, and from it we ought to conclude that, not just in twentieth-century Japan but throughout the East Asian Zen tradition as well, morality was neither an explicit concern of practice or praise nor a dimension of human life upon which anyone expected Zen enlightenment to have a significant bearing.

Moreover, morality appears to have been largely absent from the overall education that Zen monasteries have traditionally offered.[7] Zen practice, for reasons associated with its particular conception of enlightenment, directed the minds of practitioners elsewhere. In the extensive repertoire of Zen practices, none appear to be intentionally and directly focused on the powers of moral reflection; none appear to aim explicitly at the cultivation of generosity, kindness, forgiveness, empathy, regard for the suffering of others, justice, or compassion. And if we inquire about social/ethical outcome, asking whether mastery of Zen practice has tended to lead to the explicit morality of social engagement, whether *satori* culminates in greater constructive involvement in society, greater compassion for the suffering of ordinary people, or more concern for the sociopolitical whole, the answer is "generally not." At no point in the history of East Asian Zen was skillful engagement in social/moral issues considered to be one of the primary consequences of Zen enlightenment.

Why not? Why would Zen *satori* not naturally encompass a kind of moral wisdom and become manifest in activities of compassion and concern for others? Buddhist philosophy provides the best theoretical background and overall answer to that question. It claims, by way of the concept of "dependent arising," that whatever comes into being is irrevocably shaped by the conditions that give rise to it. Thus we become what we do insofar as our practices are the primary factors that shape the character of our participation in the world. As the East Asian Confucian tradition had long maintained, moral sensitivity is a function of conditioning through practice and learning, rather than primarily a matter of sudden insight or a fully ingrained natural birthright. Although morality was thought to be within human beings as an innate potential, unless it has been cultivated there through appropriately moral practices, it will not come to fruition or be actualized.[8] This is true of virtually everything. If you don't practice meditation, or architecture, or cooking, or tennis, you won't be good at it. If you do not practice moral reflection, you will similarly not be good at it, because such reflection is essential to morally mature human life. Without the development of a basis for morality through explicit reflective practice, mature moral intuitions will have no grounds from which to arise.

As we know, Zen training focuses elsewhere. It is a highly specialized form of training that emphasizes a number of features: submission to the guidance of skilled teachers, rigorous physical discipline, exacting mastery of ritual procedure, calming or *samatha* types of meditation that clear the mind of thinking processes, focused meditations on nonanalytical topics like *kōans* and capping phrases, a variety of practices of silence, the cultivation of direct perception without conceptual mediation, and a quest for intuitive understanding. Enlightenment in Zen arises dependent upon the particular character and texture of these modes of training. It will therefore inevitably feature dimensions of human excellence that align with these determining conditions.

The enlightened Zen master will tend to be characterized by mindfulness, self-discipline, endurance, stability, self-control, courage, confidence, loyalty, powers of mental concentration, immediacy, mental presence and, focus, including the ability to set aside the peripheral in order to stay focused on what is essential. Given that orientation, little or no attention will have been given in this training to other dimensions of human life, including those that pertain to morality. If these other dimensions of character are never or rarely mentioned in Zen canonical literature, and if the primary monastic practices do not intentionally target the cultivation of these sensibilities, then it would be unreasonable to expect them to be necessary components of the outcome of Zen monastic culture.

A morally exemplary person by contrast is someone who has undergone a different kind of training. The aim of moral training is to instill the desire for justice, a desire, against the pull of most instinct, to treat others as we would hope they might treat us. Such training must address conflict of motive or interest and must include reflection on human relations, including difficult and ambiguous situations. Moral training does not dwell on a metaphysical concept of nondualism; instead it focuses on nondualism with respect to the relative interests and needs of oneself and others. Expertise in matters of moral significance requires considerable experience in the complexity of human relations and extensive practice in moral thinking. What earlier Mahayana Buddhists called "skill-in-means" is essential to human moral excellence because effective consideration of how to act must take into account particular features of the life and character of each person implicated in the situation.

But moral excellence is not just a matter of "means." It is a further dimension of moral excellence to determine appropriate "ends" with skill and integrity. The fact that even thieves can practice skill-in-means and mindful concentration shows us the necessity of deep reflection on authentic moral ends. Lacking sufficient concern for appropriate goals in the moral sphere, nothing provides guidance for choices that have moral bearing. Since so much of Zen training focused on a state of "no-mind," a state of mind prior to conscious thinking of any kind, little room remained for the development of the reflective dimension of human character. Without it, however, the expectation of morally admirable lives has little basis.

Following the war, D.T. Suzuki acknowledged this weakness in the Zen tradition in Japan. He wrote: "Present-day Zen priests have no knowledge or learning and therefore are unable to think about things independently or formulate their own independent opinions. This is a great failing of Zen priests."[9] Suzuki harbored no assumption that Zen *satori* would enable moral excellence. "With satori alone," he wrote, "it is impossible [for Zen priests] to shoulder their responsibilities as leaders of society ... by itself satori is unable to judge the right and wrong of war. With regard to disputes in the ordinary world, it is necessary to employ intellectual discrimination."[10] Going further, he opened the possibility that a more comprehensive *satori* might encompass intellectual powers: "I wish to foster in Zen priests the power to increasingly think about things independently. A satori which lacks this element should be taken to the middle of the Pacific Ocean and sent straight to the bottom!"[11] What Suzuki's claim calls for is a thorough reconsideration of the character of Zen enlightenment on the grounds that *satori* as it now stands is inapplicable to important moral matters, matters about which a Zen master cannot afford to be naïve.

Zen Enlightenment in Life

To what is Zen *satori*, as traditionally defined, thought to be applicable? In what spheres of life will a spontaneous, unreflective mode of comportment be likely to yield actions that we would find admirable? Two domains seem most receptive to this Zen state of mind: first, any aspect of life that is not structurally complex and, second, any sphere of life that has been fully mastered and is, as a result, well known. The first domain encompasses relatively simple activities, activities for which little or no thought is required, where few subtle choices need to be made and practitioners can see immediately how to respond. Such situations in life are increasingly rare, however, and even when we do encounter them, much of our fluency in them is attributable to our past mastery of these situations rather than to their simplicity.

The second domain is therefore more revealing. We can be spontaneous and engage fluently "without thinking" in any activity whose contours and demands are already well known to us. In these areas of life, the grounds for unmediated intuition are already solidly in place. Here we can imagine the craftsman who knows his work and materials so well that for most dimensions of the craft no thought is required. Indeed, in some of these circumstances, thought simply gets in the way. The potter who knows in the muscles of her hands how to shape the clay will proceed brilliantly on some tasks without thinking. The rules and principles of her craft need not be conscious; indeed, they may never have been known in an explicit conceptual form. On these same grounds of practice and experience, the skilled athlete can make moves without consulting the principles of the game; indeed, if she does consult them, her moves will be too slow, too self-conscious to succeed.

Some great athletes and potters are, when asked, unable to articulate the principles of their discipline because, embedded in their practice, they have never stood back to consider how they do what they do. Their moves have always proceeded without thoughtful consideration of this theoretical kind. But it is a mistake to conclude from this, as some Zen practitioners have, that knowing the principles of a craft is somehow detrimental to its practice or that it is irrelevant to practice. Indeed, there are limitations to what someone can accomplish without thinking even in relatively simple disciplines. The potter or athlete who has studied the theory of his or her craft or sport will have enormous advantages at just those junctures where reflection provides opportunities for flexibility, imagination, and insight. Having never reflected on the principles that govern what they do, nor on the full spectrum of possible moves, their options are significantly limited in comparison to the practitioner who stands back to get reflective distance on his or her activity. An irony of Zen history is that many of the great masters of Zen attained their elevated status in part because of their non-Zen skills, their skills of persuasion, or analysis, or social understanding, for example. Thus even in areas where spontaneity is valuable, thinking is sometimes its basis and always its resource.

Now, refining the issue further, we can ask: In matters of moral significance, how does spontaneous action "prior to reflection" fare? Here we can distinguish between two types of spontaneity in two different types of people—one whose acts proceed spontaneously on the basis of unreflective participation in prevailing moral custom and another whose acts proceed spontaneously on the basis of a cultivated sensitivity through previous moral reflection. The first of these types has not grappled with questions of moral significance. Typically, such a person does not see the need for moral thought and responds to moral situations in a spontaneous and straightforward way by following established patterns of behavior that were taught and learned in childhood. As long as the situations that this person encounters are simple or straightforward in terms of the moral customs already in his or her mind, customarily acceptable actions are likely to result. But as soon as a situation arises that does not conform to custom, this person will have no resources to call upon in making a decision.

Moreover, such a person will never be in a position to judge the adequacy of the moral customs currently in effect. Both of these conditions pertain to the Zen masters Victoria and Suzuki describe: they were unable to recognize that their current situations could not be adequately handled through past custom and were ill equipped to think for themselves about how to solve these new problems. Their training had not prepared them to see how the moral customs of loyalty and patriotism that they practiced might themselves generate immoral instincts and outcomes. The groundwork for an admirable moral response to the crisis of their time had not been laid.

The second kind of spontaneous practitioner acts out of a deep reservoir of moral reflection. This person can act in most cases without thinking because he or she has examined cases like these before, perhaps both in theory and in the conscious practice of mindfulness. Such a person can often proceed without thinking because this sustaining background of reflection is more than adequate to encompass situations that arise. Whenever it is not adequate, such a person is practiced in matters of moral deliberation. He or she can step back out of immediate action and into further reflection in order to consider what options for action are most viable. Simple moral situations can be handled without thinking, flowing smoothly and effortlessly from a deeply cultivated moral wisdom. Complex or previously unknown situations are, by contrast, recognized as such and immediately give rise to thinking rather than to spontaneous, habitual action. Past experience in explicit moral deliberation provides the resources that enable one to respond thoughtfully to unfamiliar or unexpected situations. It also gives one the capacity to challenge traditional moral practices and customs in facing an unfamiliar situation that does not fit into previous models of behavior. In this sense, it is thinking—conscious reflection—there in the background that enables the moral improvisation that would befit the image of a Zen master's flexibility and spontaneity.

No-Thought and Thinking in Zen

From this perspective, one of the greatest dangers to the Zen tradition is its ever-present temptation to be disdainful of conceptual thinking. In the moral sphere, this is especially dangerous because responding to complex moral issues with sound judgment requires clarity of thought. Wherever Zen interprets its no-mind doctrine literally, moral difficulties like the ones that Victoria documents in Japan will eventually surface. Similarly troublesome is the claim that "Zen mind" is "beyond good and evil," precisely because it is regularly proclaimed without inviting or allowing open reflection on what that might mean. In what sense is the Zen master beyond good and evil? The inability to answer that question with intellectual and moral clarity opens the gates of Zen to the possibility of moral travesty.

That these extreme interpretations of Zen can be found in Yasutani Hakuun Roshi, one of the best-known Zen masters of twentieth-century Japan and, for Western practitioners, one of the most influential Zen masters, is a clear warning sign. Teaching, without significant qualification, that "Buddhism has clearly demonstrated that discriminative thinking lies at the root of delusion"[12] and that "thought is the sickness of the human mind"[13] does more to undermine the possibility of "wisdom and compassion" than it does to enable it. If we have not developed the arts of reflection and imagination in the domain of morality, our actions will be vulnerable to a whole host of dangers, even to those that the early Buddhists had diagnosed so clearly—greed, hatred, and delusion. As early Buddhist thought shows, morality is a fundamental dimension of life, one that requires both reflection and the training of one's vision through daily practice.

The conception or "thought of enlightenment" that guides Buddhist practice also shapes its outcome. The thought of enlightenment in Zen, inscribed into the design of its practices and imagined in literary accounts of Zen masters, covers a very specific range of human ideals. Morality, as we have seen, plays no substantial role in that image of an ideal human life. This is the point or thesis of the Neo-Confucian critique of the Zen tradition in China, Korea, and Japan—that the form of enlightenment to which Zen practice gives rise is insufficiently comprehensive. Although these Neo-Confucian sages were inspired and deeply influenced by the Zen tradition, they concluded that the image and conception of enlightenment in Zen was far too limited.

Specifically, they thought that Zen lacked a substantial moral dimension, that it did not encourage inspired social/political participation, and that its contribution to the culture as a whole was seriously lacking. They also thought that quite often the anti-rational pronouncements of Zen masters were counterproductive—did they not realize that the coherence and viability of the culture as a whole depended upon leaders who had the knowledge, deliberative capacity, and moral sensitivity to work for the betterment of the whole society? Although Neo-Confucian critiques of Zen were often tempted into hyperbolic excess, they had realized something important about the way Zen Buddhism had come to develop throughout East Asia. Some of their points are still germane, and for the most part the Zen tradition has not gone very far in responding to them.[14]

This is clearly Suzuki's point in his postwar remark that "the opportunity was lost to develop a world vision within Japanese spirituality that was sufficiently extensive and comprehensive."[15] The spirit of Zen was limited, he concedes, and therefore in need of extension and further cultivation. Like all religious traditions, Zen has gone through historical periods when practitioners assume its current form of practice and attainment to be unsurpassable and other periods when it has been able to grow and extend itself.

There are two important images in the Zen tradition that encourage each of these two tendencies, one toward conservation of the past and one toward innovation and change. The first is based on the historic claim that every instance of Zen enlightenment is identical to all others insofar as the "stamp" of the master has been placed upon the mind of the disciple in a "mind-to-mind transmission" of enlightenment from the Buddha down through all the patriarchs of Zen. This image is inherently conservative. It is based on the desire to preserve the tradition "as it has always been," on the thought that any change in the meaning and experience of enlightenment would be a "fall" from the fully enlightened status of the Buddha himself.

The second image derives from the Chinese Zen claim that every authentic enlightenment "goes beyond" the teacher and the tradition as it was inherited. This account is based on the realization that the most exciting Zen masters were creative, that their actions extended the tradition in unforeseen directions. It seems to recognize that the success of the tradition's efforts to preserve the vitality of Zen is located in its ability to criticize itself and to develop in new directions in response to the new possibilities and situations that emerge.

These two images are clearly in tension; their messages feature the contrasting poles of stability and change, permanence and impermanence. The first image has a tendency to reify the Zen thought of enlightenment. It assumes that enlightenment has a fixed essence, that, unlike everything else from a Buddhist point of view, it is neither impermanent nor dependent upon conditions. A practitioner under the influence of this image assumes the unsurpassability of the tradition that is being handed down, and has therefore been provided no reason to question it or to pursue anything beyond its current state. Historically, this is probably the position that has most often been promulgated in Zen. There have been times in the history of Zen, however, when this reification was not the dominant path and when important and historic advances in the East Asian Buddhist thought of enlightenment were achieved. In such times or among representatives of the tradition such as these, there is the excitement of open questions and a fearless diversification among practitioners who refuse the objectification of the goal of Zen.

In my judgment, the question on which the Zen tradition faces its most important challenge today is the meaning of Zen "no-mind" and its relation to the full scope of enlightened life. If the state of enlightenment that is sought in Zen is literally "without thinking," then the dominance of that one guiding thought will render further self-conscious movement in the tradition impossible. It seems to me that the Zen tradition needs to re-engage the question of the relation between thinking and the form of awakening that is "without thinking." The reasons for this need are amply demonstrated in the Zen masters chronicled by Victoria who were largely unprepared to face the moral challenges of their time.

Lacking the resources of clear reflection that can only be generated through practice, Zen masters would be unable to assess their own goal. Without thinking, they will not have been able to consider how a spontaneous state of "no-thought" stands in the overall scope of human life. Cultivating an understanding of one's own goal is essential because only through such an account can one grasp or explain how its benefits should be balanced against other values that are also important in admirable human lives. Deliberation about ends—about ideals like enlightenment— are reflective enterprises. To the extent that Zen practitioners are "without thinking," they will have no choice but to take it on faith that their inherited goals are adequate because they will not have developed the skills that would allow them to think clearly about or enter into conversation and debate about the kind of life that they seek, live, and teach to others.

It is certainly not the case that deliberation has been missing altogether in the history of Zen. But it is true, I believe, that its practice has been undermined by a tendency to take the "no-thought" doctrine literally. As a result, what reflection there is has become constricted and, at times, convoluted. Thinking and openly discussing the "thought of enlightenment" is not encouraged in Zen monastic settings as they sometimes are in some other forms of Buddhism. As a result, ideas are not honed and developed in such a way that they can be elevated through practice. Given the kinds of practices that are dominant, the stamp of enlightenment that monks receive in Zen does not include the skills of reflection, conversation, reasoning, debating, organizing, or planning. All of these capacities, it seems to me, are essential to ideal forms of human life, components of a truly comprehensive concept and practice of enlightenment. The extent to which Zen practice has no bearing on these basic human capacities is the extent to which Zen enlightenment must be considered a partial and limited achievement, something subordinate to a more comprehensive understanding of enlightenment that would need to be sought beyond the Zen tradition.

Zen training also inculcates a certain relation to authority and hierarchy that undermines the opportunity for monks to develop these skills. It would be unreasonable to expect that, after practicing decades of unquestioning subservience to monastic authorities, this habit of subordination would simply go away once a monk became a leader in the Zen tradition. When called upon by Japanese officials, some Zen masters appear to have simply placed themselves in the service of the government's imperialistic goals without facing the incongruence between those goals and their own principles. Loyalty and patriotism were simply extolled by Zen masters as enlightened virtues.[16]

Had the tradition developed its practitioners' skill in considering the scope of these virtues, Zen leaders might have been able to see how limited and potentially problematic loyalty and patriotism are as virtues. Only in thought can one begin to see that patriotism is among nations what self-centeredness is among persons. If Zen practitioners had been encouraged to engage in debate on the meaning of nondualism, they might have more easily recognized the dangers of the dualism between "us" and "them" that advocates of the "unity of Zen and war" could not see. That advanced

Zen practitioners so easily adopted this form of dualism is one sign that the thought of enlightenment in Zen has been insufficiently comprehensive. Had Zen masters continued to practice Zen's own grounding in the tradition of Buddhist philosophy, they might have been in a much better position to face this crisis.

If, as Zen leaders claimed in the midst of the war effort, "It is not the responsibility of Zen priests to comment about what is going on in the world," then we must ask: What, then, is their responsibility?[17] And why is Zen enlightenment *not* able to shed light on what is going on in the world? Given these serious limitations on the scope of Zen, imposed by the tradition's own self-definition, how then should we formulate a thought of enlightenment that *is* comprehensive enough to provide us with vision about what is going on in the world? Thus the question is inevitable: Does Zen enlightenment bring the whole person to a higher, more mature, more comprehensive level of human vision and action, or is it limited to very specific segments of life? Can Zen discipline benefit everyone, including those who engage in reflective disciplines, or is Zen necessarily limited to having an effect on unreflective life?

If the tradition insists on these significant limitations, then that would amount to an admission that Zen practice cannot be good training for people who occupy prominent and important positions in a society—that Zen practice is not appropriate training for prime ministers, urban planners, directors of human resources, engineers, ambassadors, physicians, judges, lawyers, business leaders, scientists, teachers, parents, and many more. A contemporary society that does not place these kinds of people in positions of significance is currently unimaginable; these are the people who will lead us into the future. If Zen is not applicable to these essentially reflective disciplines and to the people who inhabit them, then its usefulness to our future will be highly circumscribed.

So to what in human life *does* Zen apply? Does it enhance and provide depth of perspective *only* to those activities that can be done without thinking? I do not think so, and the implicit claim in the Zen tradition that this is so unnecessarily sells the tradition short. It seems to me that a more comprehensive way to understand the meditative cultivation of mind is that it deepens our contact with the world in every sphere of our activity—it puts us into contact with the depth dimension of *any* sphere of human life, whether more or less reflective. If that is so, then beyond the forms of cultural life that have traditionally been affected by Zen—swordsmanship, calligraphy, the tea ceremony, and so on—people in widely diverse forms of life could benefit from the deepening of sensitivities that Zen practice makes possible. But this broadening of the scope of Zen would only be possible insofar as the Zen tradition expands and develops its "thought of enlightenment"—the understanding a practitioner has of the point and the consequence of Zen training. And this can only be accomplished by practicing the arts of thinking that have for so long been banished in Zen. The tradition needs to ask once again: What is enlightenment? In doing so, it needs to be prepared to learn from other non-Zen sources so that its concept of enlightenment is comprehensive enough to give rise to human lives that we really do admire.

Should the tradition be flexible and responsive enough to do that, it will recover one of its own traditional formulas, most notably its own critique of the concept of enlightenment in East Asia that forced the tradition to "go beyond" itself. Among its *kōans* will need to be included a question that is applicable to the life of every one of us: Who or what should I or could I become; what kind of person should I be? This question is essential to any effort to re-engage the creative cultural work of the Zen tradition. Like every tradition of any sort, Zen will need continually to reimagine and rethink itself in order to avoid stagnation and irrelevance. It will need to "go beyond itself," not just once but perpetually. If Zen purports to bring about some form of self-transcendence—an emptying or deepening of the self—a sophisticated understanding of that transformation must be cultivated in at least some segments of the tradition. The Zen tradition will need to respond to the claim, made by Brian Victoria, D.T. Suzuki, and others that, whatever its other impressive strengths, Zen training in its current form leaves even the most awakened practitioners in a state of moral immaturity and vulnerability. It will need to respond by rethinking and expanding Zen training, extending Zen meditation to include practices that are relevant to the cultivation of moral excellence, as well as to other reflective powers that are essential to admirable forms of human life.

Enlightenment and the Persistence of Human Fallibility

THE IMAGES OF enlightened human lives that have been passed down to us may be Zen Buddhism's greatest contribution to human culture. These images are extraordinary in the history of Buddhism for their human specificity. Each Zen master is depicted in the vast Zen literary corpus with a unique persona, with personality traits that individuate each of them in a way that highlights their humanity. By the time the Zen "recorded sayings" literature was being composed in the tenth and eleventh centuries, this focus on the uniquely human quality of enlightened lives had only rarely made its appearance in Mahayana Buddhist literature. In Mahayana sutras, for example, bodhisattvas are characteristically imagined to have transcended the human realm altogether. They are pictured with unlimited knowledge and power. Given their lack of limitations, we read about them staging extraordinary miracles as their ordinary mode of daily life. Bodhisattvas were described as traveling to or dwelling in far-off universes and living "infinite" lives. The level of transcendence imagined beyond the human sphere was so great that the *Daśabhūmika sūtra*, a text that purports to articulate ten stages through which bodhisattvas would develop, begins the very first stage at a level already far beyond human limitations as we know them. No one reading such a text would have ever known or heard about any living being who was even remotely like these bodhisattvas. As a consequence of that feature, these texts could not be useful as models for the lives of their readers; they had other religious functions beyond describing the human dimension of bodhisattva practice.

The Zen "discourse records" (*yu-lu*), by contrast, describe what appear to be actual human lives, even if extraordinary ones. Arranged genealogically in the *Transmission of the Lamp* literature in order to stress lineages of particular styles of enlightenment, this literature provided what purported to be biographical sketches of each Zen master. Some of them were so famous that their biographical accounts warranted lengthy entries, while others, less well known, might receive a paragraph of the most basic information. The longer, more important segments gathered stories that developed the distinct personality traits of a Zen master and were relatively consistent from story to story. These Zen masters became famous for their particular "style," the unique way that they expressed their enlightenment in daily life and, most especially, their individual style of teaching and awakening their disciples. Reading these stories, we imagine real teachers working in the garden, lecturing in the dharma hall, meeting disciples in the hallway—or, as the Zen saying has it, "chopping wood and carrying water."

What we do not see in these "golden age" Zen masters, however, are difficulties, problems, weaknesses, and other characteristics that would make them more like us, that is, "human, all too human." Naturally so. These were reports from disciples that served to distinguish and elevate their particular lineage of Zen. As these were edited over centuries of Zen history, we see a tendency toward the miraculous, an elevation just slightly up beyond the human. That tendency toward transcendence begins to undermine the use these stories had as guides for the human quest that Buddhists today must undertake, even if these incredible Zen masters still display unique personalities.

What is interesting about the modern "historical consciousness" that most people in the world now share is that even in the depiction of our heroes we demand the truth and will not be satisfied with implausible inflations or miracle stores that cannot be factually verified. Historical accuracy is one of the distinguishing features of modern human culture, and it is clear that when we provide accounts of the greatest among us for posterity, all of the relevant facts available to us, including or especially weaknesses and failures, will be included. The question that we pose in this chapter concerns what that will mean for the image and standing of Zen masters. If the description of Zen lives cannot simply eliminate stories that seem to show unenlightened human frailty, how are we to imagine the contemporary meaning of "enlightenment"? Can "imperfection" and "enlightenment" go together? In exploring this question, we highlight the remarkable career of one twentieth-century Zen teacher, Hakuyu Maezumi, whose human fallibility is woven together with an enlightened presence that was persuasive to many who knew him.

Hakuyū Taizan Maezumi Rōshi (1931–1995) was the founder of the Zen Center of Los Angeles (ZCLA) and one of the seminal figures in the history of American Zen Buddhism. His charismatic image as a Zen master helped define Zen for American culture, and by giving authorization to twelve dharma heirs, his legacy continues to shape the further development of Zen practice in the West. Although an impressive and groundbreaking Zen master by any standard, the story of Maezumi Roshi's life is not without ambiguity and controversy. Indeed, it is difficult not to sense some degree of tragedy in this story. This double-edged complexity in the life of the Zen master is the primary element that differentiates the account of Maezumi's life from the idealized narratives of classical Zen masters and, for that reason, one significant factor that defines both his personal image and the overall image of contemporary American Zen.

The first part of this chapter is a biographical account of the life of Maezumi that serves to contextualize the development and character of his Zen enlightenment. This account follows the chronological format of traditional Zen histories by describing his early life and training in Japanese Zen all the way through to his death in 1995. In this case, however, our narrative includes the difficulties that have partially undermined Maezumi's status as an enlightened Zen master. The second part stands back from his life story to examine the image of Maezumi Roshi as a Zen master. It asks what this image is, how it has been formed, and to what extent Maezumi's Zen image aligns with the paradigmatic lives of the classical Zen tradition. What did enlightenment look like in the life of this one Japanese American Zen master, and how does that image alter the ongoing tradition?

Maezumi's Early Life and Zen Training

Hakuyu Maezumi was born directly into the cultural world of Japanese Zen Buddhism on February 24, 1931, in Otawara City, Tochigi Prefecture. His father, Hakujun Kuroda Roshi, was an important priest in the Sōtō lineage of Zen Buddhism, serving in a variety of important administrative positions including head of the Sōtō sect's Supreme Court.[1] Partly as a consequence of his significant position within the Zen sect, all six of his surviving sons would later become Zen priests. Although Maezumi was one of six brothers in the Kuroda family, rather than adopt his father's surname, as would have been customary, he was given his mother's family name—Maezumi—in order to perpetuate that family name, since his mother had no brothers to extend their lineage.[2]

Shortly after the Japanese attack on Pearl Harbor and the beginning of the Pacific segment of the Second World War, Maezumi at age eleven was ordained a Sōtō Zen monk on March 25, 1942.[3] Given the ordination name Taizan (Great Mountain), he began the discipline of Zen training at his father's temple, Koshin-ji.[4] Although simultaneously attending the local school, the young novice was focused on Zen training, which he already knew would be his lifelong vocation. Maezumi began to learn English in his teens through contact with American soldiers who were stationed in his home area after the war. During one period of time American occupation soldiers employed his father's temple as their base, giving the young monk direct contact with American-English language and culture, a factor that would later effect his entire life and career.[5]

At the age of sixteen, while continuing his training to become a Sōtō priest, Maezumi left home to go to Tokyo to begin study under Koryu Osaka Roshi, a lay Rinzai Zen master and friend of Maezumi's father.[6] Koryu Roshi focused on Zen training for the laity, an emphasis that would years later be of great significance to Maezumi. It is also important to note that his work with Koryu Roshi initiated the unusual circumstances of Maezumi's hybrid Zen education that blurred the traditional boundaries of separation between the two most prominent Zen institutions in Japan. Four years later he began his university studies at Komazawa University, the primary center of Sōtō Zen education, graduating with degrees in East Asian philosophy and literature in 1954.[7] A year later at age twenty-four, Maezumi was given dharma transmission (*shihō*) by his father[8] and completed his training at the two principle Sōtō monasteries, Eiheiji and Sōjiji, where he performed the "honorary abbot" or *zuise* ceremony that same year.

Then, probably because of his English-language skills, Maezumi was given assignment by the Sōtō School of Zen to relocate to the United States to serve Japanese immigrants as a priest in California. Traveling by way of an inexpensive one-way ticket on a freighter ship, Maezumi took up residence in Los Angeles in 1956 at the age of twenty-five.[9] His assignment was to perform priestly duties at Zenshuji Temple, the Sōtō headquarters in the United States, at that time under the leadership of Togan Sumi.[10] Although this work was often conducted in Japanese, there were numerous English-language dimensions to the task, including ministering to the second and third generations of Japanese immigrants for whom English was becoming the dominant language. Maezumi's responsibilities as a Sōtō Zen priest stationed in California included weekly services, funerals, memorials, weddings, and other ceremonies required by the immigrant population of California. These were difficult times economically, in Japan and in the United States, and Maezumi held a series of part-time jobs to make ends meet, working whenever he could as a gardener and a transla-tor for Japanese businesses in Los Angeles.

In spite of the widespread lack of interest in rigorous Zen training in his new environment, Maezumi continued his own advancement in the study of Zen after arrival in the new world, engaging in meditation, *kōan* study, and textual study whenever he had the opportunity. He read Dōgen's *Shōbōgenzō* with Reirin Yamada Roshi, the bishop of the American Sōtō mission, and engaged in serious *kōan* study with Nyogen Senzaki, a Rinzai Zen teacher who was at that time teaching in Los Angeles. Senzaki was the first Zen teacher to reside in the United States and had already accepted several European American students interested in Zen, among them Robert Aitken.[11] His influence on Maezumi includes the previously unimaginable idea that Zen practices might be of interest to people whose heritage was not originally Buddhist.

Indeed, by the late 1950s that interest was already developing in San Francisco among a handful of beat poets and writers. What was particu-larly attractive about Zen, however, was not the rigorous *zazen* and *kōan* study that Maezumi and others would be teaching a decade later but rather the unusual discourse and eccentric behaviors of the masters of the "golden age" of Chinese Chan described in the classic literature of Zen that at that time was being translated and narrated by D.T. Suzuki. Given the disciplinary character of postwar American culture, the "discipline" of Zen was not initially what would attract attention to this spiritual tradition. In spite of lack of interest among his own parishioners at Zenshuji in Los Angeles, Maezumi held weekly *zazen* meditation sessions at the temple. It would not be long, however, before interest in Zen meditation would spread through the youth movement in American culture.

Perhaps most significant for the formation of his identity as a teacher of Zen, Maezumi met Hakuun Yasutani Roshi, becoming a disciple in the early 1960s and pushing his interest in *kōan* studies to fruition in the late 1960s, just as he was forming ZCLA.[12] Yasutani and his teacher, Daiun Harada, were instrumental in the revitalization of Zen in Japan that was beginning to take place after the war. These teachers combined Rinzai and Sōtō styles of teaching in a way that ignored the traditional bifurcation between these two schools of Zen. They revised Rinzai *kōan* practice in the setting of Sōtō emphasis on *shikantaza* (just sitting). Yasutani stressed rigorous discipline in Zen training and focused on the prospects of "sudden awakening" as the goal of Zen. Eventually this would be the formula for Zen that would attract non-Asian interest, and the success of a book by one of Yasutani's students—Phillip Kapleau—would lay the foundations for American Zen by describing rigorous Zen practice in a way that would attract a widespread following. Yasutani was the Zen master featured in *The Three Pillars of Zen*,[13] and as a result his fame spread quickly in the United States and Japan. When Yasutani visited the United States for lectures and *sesshin* trainings, Maezumi served as translator and interpreter.[14] Their relationship was fundamental to the Zen identity that Maezumi was fashioning during that period of time.

In 1969 Maezumi returned to Japan to complete his *kōan* training under Yasutani Roshi, placing the newly formed ZCLA under the leadership of his foremost student and eventual heir, Bernie Glassman. Fourteen months later, in December 1970, Maezumi Roshi received *inka* approval from Yasutani Roshi.[15] In 1970 Koryu Osaka Roshi, the friend of Maezumi's father and the Rinzai Zen teacher with whom Maezumi had studied in the 1950s while at Komazawa University, came to ZCLA, there renewing the teacher–student relationship that they had cultivated years earlier. Over the next several years, Maezumi completed his *kōan* training with Koryu Roshi and in 1973 received *inka* authorization in his lineage as well.[16] This series of relationships put Maezumi in the unusual position of having received Zen authorization from three different Zen masters in three distinct lineages, Sōtō, Rinzai, and the Harada-Yasutani line.

Maezumi Roshi at the Zen Center of Los Angeles

Due primarily to the widely read literature of the beat poets and the books of D. T. Suzuki, serious interest in Zen among European Americans began to develop in the mid-1960s. Several non-Japanese Americans began to attend Maezumi's weekly *zazen* gatherings at Zenshuji in Los Angeles to experiment with these novel practices. Purportedly because some parishioners and the other priests were skeptical or critical of this outreach to those outside of the Japanese community, Maezumi soon moved his meditation group out of the temple, first into an apartment on Serrano Street in the Wilshire district and then, in 1967, into a house in the Korea-town section of central Los Angeles.[17] The house was named the Los Angeles

Zendo and was incorporated under that name in 1968.[18] Soon thereafter the name was changed to the Zen Center of Los Angeles. Maezumi's father, Baian Hakujun Kuroda, was named the honorary founder of the institution, which was registered as a Sōtō temple and given the name Busshinji (Buddha Truth Temple).[19] There was a profound sense that something important was about to happen to the dharma in the United States. Maezumi attended the opening ceremony for the Tassajara Zen Mountain Center in July of 1967 joining Suzuki Roshi, Katagiri Roshi, and other important Zen teachers at this historic event. No doubt Suzuki's remarkable success in San Francisco impressed Maezumi deeply.[20] Yasutani Roshi began a series of visits to ZCLA in the late 1960s both to work with Maezumi on his *kōan* practice and on occasion to conduct some of the earliest and most influential *sesshins* (meditation retreats) in American Zen history. At that point in time Maezumi was just completing his own studies with Yasutani, becoming a *rōshi* of full standing in the Japanese Zen tradition. Receiving *inka* approval from Yasutani Roshi solidified Maezumi's authority as a Zen master in America just at the moment when attention to Zen in the West was about to boom.

And boom it did. The Zen Center of Los Angeles grew exponentially in the early 1970s and by the end of that decade it was clearly one of the most vibrant and significant religious institutions in the city. Interest in Zen had continued to develop among non-Asian Americans, and Maezumi Roshi's persona captured the attention of hundreds of new converts to *zazen* meditation. Urban properties adjacent to the original Zendo in Los Angeles were purchased for residential and religious purposes. At its height in the early 1980s, ZCLA occupied almost all of one full city block, including several multistoried apartment buildings. Among the youth of America, Zen symbolized what was new and exciting about the globalization that was transforming American culture, and the rapid growth of ZCLA embodied that symbolism brilliantly.

The regimen of practice at ZCLA was rigorous and for the most part orthodox. Traditional Sōtō ceremonial procedures were painstakingly learned, practiced, and maintained. Trainees and visitors spent long hours in *zazen,* including weeklong *sesshins* at regular intervals. Woven into this meditation schedule was a traditional *kōan* curriculum. Maezumi and other senior teachers assigned *kōans* taking the mental and spiritual disposition of each student into account. The psychological pressure behind *kōan* study was accentuated through the requirement of periodic *dokusan* practice—one-on-one private interviews between master and disciple with the intention of pushing the *kōan* through to its conclusion. Visiting teachers from elsewhere in the United States and Japan were regular guests at ZCLA, often giving *teishō* lectures and performing the traditional ceremonies of Zen. Although Maezumi would encourage his American dharma heirs to innovate and to build a truly American Zen tradition, at his own center he maintained strict adherence to orthodox Sōtō practices, thereby offering a meticulous transmission of the dharma in a new setting.

In 1975 Maezumi married Martha Ekyo Maezumi with whom he had three children, Kirsten Mitsuyo, Yuri Jundo, and Shira Yoshimi, who were raised at ZCLA and later in Idyllwild.[21] Their lives unfolded at the very center of this extraordinary development in American religion and added an element of domesticity to Maezumi's image that departed to some extent from the monastic environment that the Zen master was intent on cultivating. Although Maezumi was by all accounts a loving father, his attention was clearly focused on the historic Zen enterprise that he had founded.

Under the lens of this focus, the Zen Center prospered as no one could have imagined. Membership lists grew weekly. Dozens of new and curious visitors arrived at the center every weekend to be introduced to Zen practice. Hundreds of lay practitioners became regular members who would frequent the center for meditation and instruction. And through the early 1980s over a hundred full-time practitioners resided at ZCLA doing *zazen* morning and night every day and engaging in regular weeklong *sesshins*. Publications such as an early book titled *The Way of Everyday Life* and a Zen periodical called *The Ten Directions* began to be disseminated and were read all over the English-speaking world, focusing more and more attention on Maezumi and ZCLA. New affiliate centers began to be formed. Maezumi and his principle students envisioned a network of interrelated Zen centers throughout the United States, North America, and Europe and began to implement a plan. Land in the San Jacinto mountains near Idyllwild California was purchased, and a Zen Mountain Center for *sesshins* and intensive training was launched. In 1976 Maezumi founded the Kuroda Institute for the Study of Buddhism and Human Values as an educational arm of ZCLA to encourage scholarly attention to the Zen tradition.[22] The Institute organized and funded conferences, colloquia, and publications.

Although initially a counterculture movement, as the Zen movement morphed into a mainstream cultural institution, Zen practice in Los Angeles became increasingly established across the full socioeconomic spectrum. Practitioners included physicians, attorneys, psychiatrists, and professors, along with carpenters, electricians, and professionals from all occupational fields. Maezumi Roshi gave the Buddhist precepts to more than five hundred people, ordained sixty-eight priests, and gave dharma transmission to twelve of his close students.[23] At its height in the early 1980s, ZCLA was one of the most vibrant and exciting religious institutions in the country, and Maezumi Roshi was the most widely known and admired Zen master in the West. For many people, his image symbolized the spiritual brilliance of Zen.

Zen Crisis and the End of Life

In 1983, at the height of Maezumi's influence and the success of his innovative Zen organization, two crises brought an end to the upward surge of his Zen movement and began to undermine the Zen master's image. One of these was the disclosure that Maezumi had had sexual relationships with several of his female students, including one of the recipients of his dharma transmission. This disclosure immediately split the community, throwing it into turmoil and controversy. While the "free-love" atmosphere of the 1970s certainly prevailed at the Zen Center as a widespread assumption, it nevertheless shocked practitioners that the Zen master had compromised his position of authority as a spiritual leader and had violated his marriage in this way. Simultaneous to that troublesome disclosure, a second revelation further damaged Maezumi's image as an authentic Zen master. Although his alcohol consumption practices were relatively well known at ZCLA and up to this point generally accepted, at this time both Maezumi and the community realized that his drinking was out of control.[24] Under enormous pressure and in emotional turmoil, Maezumi openly discussed the difficulties his drinking had caused and voluntarily checked himself into an alcohol rehabilitation center.

Meanwhile, in his absence, Zen Center practitioners attempted to reconcile themselves to these now widely perceived shortcomings in the Zen master whom they had previously considered invulnerable to worldly problems. Many practitioners left ZCLA in anger, disappointment, or disillusionment. One dharma heir, Charlotte Joko Beck, having already departed Los Angeles to form a new center in San Diego, renounced affiliation with ZCLA and Maezumi.[25] Although Maezumi returned to the Zen Center in less than a month, now seemingly in control of his drinking, other problems related to these crises continued to compound. Membership roles at ZCLA shrunk quickly and dramatically within months after these disclosures, and the once thriving organization struggled to maintain itself. As monthly bills began to accrue debt, properties adjacent to the Zendo were sold, and over the next several years ZCLA scaled down to a considerably diminished level of operation. By the time Maezumi had worked through his remorse and gathered himself to the point that he could respond constructively to the situation, the damage had already been done. ZCLA was a shadow of its former prominence. Maezumi's wife and children had left their home at the Zen Center and moved to the mountain community of Idyllwild near the Zen Mountain Center, and only a handful of faithful practitioners remained in residence at ZCLA.[26]

Deeply apologetic and remorseful about the damage he had caused, Maezumi struggled to regain himself spiritually. Close associates recall that it was many years before Maezumi returned to anything like his former exuberance and confidence, the spirit of Zen that had so animated his teachings. Even then the damage to the reputation and standing of ZCLA would not abate, and although the Center continued uninterrupted through Maezumi's life, it did not recover the powerful spiritual image that it once radiated. Maezumi continued his practice of teaching for over a decade beyond the crisis, gradually winning back former and new members, but the memories and effects of failure were never entirely thrown off. One effect of the crisis, however, was that leading disciples of Maezumi took the occasion to disperse around North America, founding Zen centers in Maezumi's lineage elsewhere while beginning the long process of experimenting with innovative formulas for a truly American Zen. Although Maezumi was himself tarnished by the diminishment of ZCLA and its reputation, his heirs extended the tradition through the formation of Zen centers all over the continent.

Very late at night on May 15, 1995, Maezumi Roshi died suddenly and unexpectedly at the age of sixty-four while visiting his family and Sōtō Zen leaders in Japan. Controversy surrounds Maezumi's death as it had the later part of his life. Receiving the news of Maezumi's death by telephone and in a state of shock, ZCLA leaders flew to Tokyo to attend the Japanese funeral services and cremation. They were told by family members in Japan that their teacher had died of a heart attack in bed. This understanding of Maezumi's death still held sway three months later when an elaborate memorial event was held at ZCLA on August 27, 1995. Over the next few months, however, it was learned that in fact Maezumi had drowned in the bathtub of his brother's house under the influence of alcohol. This fact had been concealed by Maezumi's Japanese family in order to maintain

the dignity of his substantial legacy. Even Maezumi's wife and central cir-
cle of students had been unaware of the actual cause of his death.[27]

The truth about Maezumi's death came to light when Wendy Egyoku
Nakao, Maezumi's eventual successor at ZCLA, obtained a copy of the
death certificate from Japan so that the Zen master's family could qualify
to benefit from the life insurance policy that had been taken out in his
name. The death certificate specified the cause of death as drowning and
noted the presence of alcohol in his blood.[28] When confronted with this
discrepancy, Maezumi's brothers disclosed the full story. Maezumi had
been at the family home and temple, dining and drinking with his brothers, but had planned to travel back to Tokyo that night to be with another
of his brothers and to stay there. Although clearly exhausted and advised
against this journey, Maezumi set out for Tokyo by train. Apparently
asleep, he missed the appropriate train station, thus extending his journey
even further. When he finally arrived at his brother's home late at night,
Maezumi announced that he would bathe and then go to bed. The next
morning, Maezumi's brother found him drowned in the bathtub.

Concerned that the alcohol-related circumstances of Maezumi's death
would undermine the Zen master's international reputation, his brothers decided to withhold the truth. When asked for an English translation
of the death certificate for insurance use in the United States, they did
not comply. But when the Japanese-language certificate arrived in Los
Angeles, it was translated, thus initiating what would still be a slow process of full disclosure.[29] It was decided at ZCLA not to make a general
announcement of these death details, since what they had thought to be
the cause of death had already been announced publically. Gradually, however, the truth leaked and began to circulate as a rumor among ZCLA
leaders until finally in 1997 the ZCLA Sangha was given a full and formal
account of the Zen master's death.[30] From that point forward, Maezumi's
death would be yet another element of controversy shaping the image of
this important Zen master.

The Zen Image of Maezumi Roshi

How do the sources of our knowledge of the life of Maezumi Roshi differ from those through which we have come to understand the classical
masters of Zen? How do we know about the Zen masters of antiquity? The
evidence available to us from East Asian antiquity is limited and very specific in orientation. Images of classical Zen masters come to us through

literature written by later participants within each master's Zen lineage and were composed with the intention of cultivating the mythos of these masters and the lineage as a whole. Narratives giving account of the lives and personas of Zen masters in earlier epochs of Zen history bear remarkable resemblance, especially those written to narrate the early centuries of Zen's legendary history. These narratives follow a unified model and were edited over time to fit uniformly into the comprehensive documents that transmit the tradition as a whole—the *Transmission of the Lamp* literature.

One byproduct of this uniformity in the narrative accounts is a corresponding similarity in the lives and personas of the Zen masters they depict. Classical Zen masters are identifiable as Zen masters precisely because they say and do Zen-like things and lead lives that are recognizably "Zen" in identity. All of these stories begin, proceed, and end in much the same way. For example, accounts of the deaths of Zen masters bear remarkable similarity—Zen masters are presented in such a way that they die at a time and in a manner of their own choosing; the power of their Zen-disciplined wills dominates from the moment of their awakening all the way through death. Some are imagined to die seated in the lotus posture engaged in deep meditative concentration having just composed a traditional death poem. Their Zen practice and Zen minds are understood to be flawless from beginning to end.

Tracing these narratives back to their probable compositions, historians have found over and over that these stories are much more the products of evolving traditions than they are of firsthand report. The lives of the most famous Zen masters are saturated with legend, and their historical foundations are often unrecoverable. Much of this literature was composed many decades or even centuries after the lives of the masters they depicted. We point this out because these traditional methods of historical representation will not be duplicated in the cases of contemporary Zen masters like Taizan Maezumi. Firsthand accounts by followers and detractors are now deposited in our archives not as a well-edited, unified story about a contemporary master but as scattered representations from a variety of points of view. It is hard to imagine that these sources will ever disappear, contained as they are now in digital format and available to anyone anywhere. So although the importance of a Zen master will grow and evolve depending upon the later success of his or her legacy, as was true in earlier epochs, it is unlikely ever to be the case that the firsthand accounts of their lives will be drastically altered, deleted, or lost. This appears to be the case with Maezumi Roshi. Unlike earlier Zen masters, what we have available to document the life of Maezumi are a wide variety of historical materials composed both by Maezumi and hundreds of individuals who knew him personally. Although some of these reports are permeated with admiration, they are quite unlike the legend-based accounts of classical Zen masters.

How does our image of Maezumi as a Zen master come to be constructed? If we are thorough and take the time to work through the evidence at our disposal, the sources are amazingly voluminous. We have recorded talks by Maezumi, essays and books written by him, books and essays written about Maezumi by those who knew him best, film footage of Maezumi both in formal dharma talks and informal circumstances. The list of resources goes further: we have films about Maezumi, photographs by the hundreds—probably thousands—newspaper articles, journal articles, and magazine articles that have discussed Maezumi's life at one stage or another. And it is still possible to gather verbal accounts from the hundreds of people who knew him in one context or another, along with verbal accounts from his families in both Japan and the United States. The volume of evidence from which to construct a thorough account of the life of this Zen master is enormous. This chapter simply adds a further layer to this evolving tradition, based as it is on the archive of print, electronic, and verbal resources and written by one who also had occasional contact with Maezumi during his life.

For classical Zen masters we have one or sometimes several well-edited, tradition-sanctioned accounts typically written decades or centuries after the Zen master's life. For Maezumi we have a vast archive of firsthand images, most of which are "edited" only by the varying perspectives of those who have provided us with their story. In the former case, we gain an image of the Zen master conceived as an ideal. In the latter, we obtain judgments of every conceivable kind. The accuracy, realism, and perspectival variation of the latter curtail the extent to which an ideal can be imposed on the historical narratives by a subsequent idealizing tradition. From this point on in the history of Zen, we have the opportunity to see not just what a Zen master is supposed to be like but also the extent to which particular masters actually lived up to that image.

The Character of Maezumi's Enlightenment

We learn about the enlightened character of famous Zen masters from antiquity by reading texts that describe their "sayings and doings." These "discourse record" texts purport to be firsthand accounts of the many ways that the great masters of the past expressed their enlightenment in everyday situations. Stories giving expression to Maezumi Roshi's character—the way his enlightenment was manifest in actual life situations—are voluminous. We find them scattered throughout the literature of disciples discussing the life of the teacher, many of these now enshrined in text and on film. As it often occurred in classical Zen, however, these scattered stories eventually come together into larger, more comprehensive accounts that hope to express a full and complete image of the master's enlightenment. Surprisingly, this coalescence of stories has already begun to occur for Taizan Maezumi.

In 1986 award-winning novelist, disciple, and dharma heir Peter Matthiessen published his journals from the years 1969 to 1982 under the title *Nine-Headed Dragon River*.[31] These journal entries tell numerous stories that express the character of Maezumi, incidents in their student–teacher relationship from which we gain an internal glimpse of the Zen master's mind and persona. Then, in 1999, poet, writer, and filmmaker Philomene Long published a book titled *American Zen Bones*.[32] Inspired by her long-time discipleship and friendship with Maezumi, Long gathered stories from the students of Maezumi and put them together into a text that is explicitly modeled on the classical Zen discourse record literature. Following this classical model, there is no chronology and no order of topics. As readers move from page to page, they get glimpses of Maezumi saying and doing unusual and interesting things. In this text, Maezumi's "discourse record" would fit seamlessly into the classic *Transmission of the Lamp*.

Several years later, Sean Murphy published a book taking something close to this same discourse record format. In *One Bird, One Stone: 108 American Zen Stories*[33] we read a series of stories about Maezumi but in this case juxtaposed to and joined together with stories from the lives of other famous American Zen masters. This is extraordinary literature in that it adopts a genre from classical Zen history and weaves into it a very new segment of Zen history. For our purposes, these stories, along with many others, give a clear account of ways in which the character of Maezumi's Zen emerged in everyday life.

One feature of the persona of Maezumi that appears in many accounts of him is the way his physical presence made an impression on people. We have already seen how Maezumi's teachings highlighted the physicality of *zazen*, and he frequently taught students to sense their *hara* (center) and to gather themselves into that central domain of poise. Followers of Maezumi describe him as maintaining that center at all times. As a result, Maezumi is often described as "charismatic in a calm way." Calmness and charisma are often considered opposing traits, but Maezumi's "calm charisma" was something for which he was widely admired and often warrants mention in the literature describing him. Student descriptions of Maezumi refer to his dharma name, Taizen (Great Mountain), as if that metaphor perfectly captured the solidity of his physical presence. He is described as a "small man with a huge presence" and as projecting a "confident beauty."[34] Peter Matthiessen wrote that "he moved beautifully, leaving no trace, like a bird across the sky."[35] He loved gardening and took great pleasure in the rigors of physical labor. One student described him as having "black fire in his eyes," saying that Maezumi lived a kind of freedom that made him unpredictable and uncategorizable.[36]

Maezumi's quick wit and sense of humor are frequently mentioned by those who spent time with him and are clearly demonstrated in many of the stories about him. His charisma included the capacity to see clearly into the situations directly in front of him and to respond with insight. Consider, for example, the following story.

Maezumi Roshi was sitting on the front porch of the Zen Center one evening with one of his students when a disheveled, inebriated, and extremely depressed-looking man staggered up to them.

"Whaarsh it like," the man slurred, ". . . to be enlightened?'
Maezumi looked at the man quietly.
"Very depressing," he answered.[37]

Related to the physicality and strength of his presence is the temper that Maezumi was well known to exhibit on occasion. All close disciples tell and write stories about it. When he got angry Maezumi would rage with passion and energy until the matter was settled. He would not hold back, one disciple explained, because he was very "comfortable with his anger."[38] "Being comfortable with anger" meant being able to trust that what was done in anger would not turn out later to be a source of deep regret. Although anger is often a state out of which monumental mistakes are made, wherever that is not the case anger is less to be feared because it is more an expression of honest vision than an immature, self-centered loss of perspective. In all of these accounts the assumption is that Maezumi's Zen anger operated under the framework of his Zen vision, that in some sense it was intended as one form that his teaching practice would take. Peter Matthiessen wrote that his teacher would "push all of my buttons, keeping me off balance."[39] And by all accounts when the occasion for anger had passed, so had the anger. It "left no residue," one student claimed.[40] When it was over, there was nothing left to infect the next encounter with the person who had just incited his anger. In that sense, Maezumi's anger was something far more or far less than anger.

Juxtaposed to this side of Maezumi is another dimension of his character in which his Zen persona took a soft and sensitive form. One of his dharma heirs describes Maezumi as "grandmotherly" in relating to students.[41] Although some students needed vibrant energy or stern discipline, others needed sensitivity and care. One story in *American Zen Bones* is titled "Just Cry":

> Luli Jiren Madero had a daughter who was born a dwarf. Her family was very loving and close, but still the condition caused a great deal of hardship and pain for the child had to undergo multiple surgeries for her condition. One day, Jiren went to a private interview with Maezumi to find comfort. After telling Roshi her story, he reached into the sleeve of his robe and produced two clean handkerchiefs. He handed one to her, kept the other for himself, and they both cried.[42]

Maezumi was one of the first Zen masters to ordain women, including women with children. His personal character included the innovative sense and courage to break new ground in Buddhism. There was something inherently experimental about the cultural atmosphere in the United States when Maezumi taught Zen. The diversity of backgrounds and sense of freedom were extraordinary, and Maezumi reveled in this sense of the times. Pat O'Hara wrote that "Maezumi Roshi came to this country as a young man and just fell in love with the freedom and real thirst for the dharma here. He seemed very open to new traditions, and part of it was that he empowered a lot of women."[43]

Another dimension to Maezumi's character and persona was his dedication to the task of teaching. Everyone who knew Maezumi and worked closely with him called him a "workaholic"; some teased him about this obsession with the dharma.[44] He made himself available for teaching purposes every day of the week and around the clock. As Daido Loori claimed, "His life belonged to his students."[45] This dedication to others did not appear to prevent Maezumi from being a deeply introspective and self-aware Zen master. Although frequently in public visibility, he also maintained a strict meditation practice and valued opportunities for introspection and thoughtful reflection. As we know, however, different dimensions of our characters emerge in different sets of circumstance, and in Maezumi's case this is certainly true of his persona after the scandals that damaged his Zen Center in the mid-1980s. And it is to that transformation that we now turn.

Scandalous Images

As we have seen, in 1983 the vulnerability and humanity of Maezumi Roshi were brought to light in two interconnected instances of criticism. First, several sexual affairs with female students were disclosed, causing serious interpersonal turmoil at the Zen Center. As students began to see how these affairs represented mistakes in moral judgment, Maezumi's alcohol consumption practices quickly came to be seen as one source of the problem, now appearing in new light as alcoholism rather than as an innocent, playful, and unproblematic love of liquor. For some students these revelations proved to be the end of their Zen careers. They were massively disillusioned, and when the illusions were gone there was nothing left to bolster their interest in Zen. For other students, these shortcomings were gradually reconciled with the belief that Maezumi was an awakened Zen master. Although they too were disillusioned, these were illusions that they would gladly shed, illusions that had previously encouraged them to think that being a Zen master meant being invulnerable to all human frailty. Once the aura of magic was lifted from their understanding of Zen, what it meant to practice Zen and to seek awakening underwent a transformation.[46]

Maezumi's love of drinking was longstanding and never hidden. When he was in San Francisco visiting Shunryo Suzuki, Maezumi would sometimes take Suzuki's wife out drinking, since Suzuki himself took very little interest in these activities.[47] Maezumi often joined his students and colleagues on social occasions, both at ZCLA and out on the road. And students at ZCLA knew that one way to get Maezumi into a good conversation was to arrive with liquor as an offering. They often assumed, though, that these social practices constituted a "time-out" from their practice of Zen and from Maezumi's teaching. But there are no time-outs in life. Peter Matthiessen writes that when he attributed his own sluggishness in *zazen* one day to the *sake* that they had consumed the night before, Maezumi snapped back that *"sake* is one thing, and *zazen* is another. They have nothing to do with each other!"[48]

As a skillful, therapeutic response to a student's petty excuse for weak practice, Maezumi's strongly worded barb was no doubt effective. But in retrospect, it may be possible to see in that response a significant lacunae developing in Maezumi's own rationalizations about alcohol consumption. After all, Buddhist philosophy argues against thinking of any two activities as starkly separated. It dwells insightfully on the deep interconnection between all things. Nothing stands on its own; nothing is really separate from anything else. Liquor consumption and the practice of *zazen* are not unrelated. In fact, they are intimately bound up with each other; they both have a significant bearing on one's state of mind. Failure to admit that alcohol affects mental discipline, mindfulness, and many other aspects of life prevents one from looking directly at this important relationship and recognizing that serious problems may be concealed there.

It may be that over time liquor came to play a particular role in Maezumi's Zen personality. He was known to have a highly attuned sense of humor while drinking. Students recall quick-minded jokes and puns, even occasions when Maezumi would break into hilarious skits such as geisha impersonations.[49] It is not easy to be funny in a second language, and Maezumi may have been aided by the dampening of inhibition that alcohol provides. More to the point, though, there could have been a significant relationship developing over time between alcohol consumption and the spontaneous and unique verbal behaviors expected of an authentic Zen master. Improvised, unusual behavior is more easily initiated under the influence of alcohol, and accounts of Maezumi saying strongly worded and unusual things while drinking are clearly present in stories about him.

So one may wonder to what extent the expectations of spontaneous Zen behaviors might have contributed to the desire for alcohol to help give rise to uninhibited, non-self-conscious actions and expressions. Suzuki Roshi is an interesting contrast on this point. He reportedly did not drink much and did not like the feelings of intoxication.[50] He was also not known for shocking, eccentric Zen-like actions or words. Suzuki's power as a Zen master derived from a subdued wisdom, a quiet reserve that seemed to exude compassion and insight. Although in some moods Maezumi displayed a similar power of reserve, in other moods or on other occasions there was an eccentric energy to his persona, and it may have been that during the late 1970s and early 1980s this dimension of the Zen master was frequently initiated by the influences of alcohol.

Several weeks spent at Scripps Alcohol Rehabilitation Center were enough to educate Maezumi on the dangers of alcoholism. He admitted that he had never given it much thought before. This casual attitude toward alcohol is widespread in Japan where a "disease" called "alcoholism" is simply not recognized, at least not in that era. Having received that education, Maezumi saw what he could not see before; he understood how his actions and relations to other people were affected by his desire for and consumption of liquor. Both he and his students began to see how one problem—drinking—may have set the stage for the other problematic action that marred Maezumi's Zen image.

The historical records seem to show that there were no sex scandals in medieval Zen monasteries. There were also no women. ZCLA was born at the height of a global revolution in sexuality made possible by advancements in birth control. Social changes, especially the women's movement, made the isolation of genders seem archaic and pointless. ZCLA, without being aware of this, would have been a laboratory of social experiment in gender relations. It was not clear that the opening up of sexual relations that came to be assumed at that time would exclude one participant—the Zen master—but that turned out to be precisely the requirement. As one practitioner claimed in the Zen Center film, "I had no idea that in 1984 in Los Angeles matters of sexual conduct between consenting adults would be so uproarious."[51] Essentially, nothing in this experiment was clear, or it wasn't until Maezumi's sexual relations struck many practitioners as deeply inappropriate and scandalous.

Once out of rehabilitation and educated on issues related to alcohol, Maezumi himself considered it "scandalous." "It's true," he said on film, "being alcoholic you become loose about morals. I agree that this negative part should be closely observed to become aware of it. Being an alcoholic, I didn't see the immoral things I did. It's really outrageous."[52] Students say that Maezumi never made excuses and that he took full responsibility for his own failures. Never defending himself, he was the most severe critic of his behavior. Indeed, it was Maezumi himself who argued against those at the Zen Center who were more inclined to hide these problems from the public. Maezumi insisted that the chaotic situation that he had caused at ZCLA should be openly and honestly discussed in a documentary film about the Center that had been scheduled to be shot even though the film crew arrived right at the height of the turmoil and exodus from the Zen Center.[53]

Wendy Egyoku Nakao has said that Maezumi "spent the rest of his life trying to make up for his errors."[54] As his attendant during the early 1990s, she claims that Maezumi faced serious levels of depression upon recognizing what his unmindful behaviors had wrought. Due to the exodus from ZCLA after the scandals, the busyness that had consumed Maezumi before 1983 receded to some extent. Now, just when he might have least wanted it, he had free time for introspection and reflection. Those close to Maezumi after 1983 report that there was a significant change in the Roshi's personality. Facing an empty *zendō* on the occasion of a dharma talk was something Maezumi had not seen for years, and he understood very clearly what had caused the decline. Looking directly at that effect of his own actions was devastating, and Maezumi took it upon himself to shoulder that blame with unrelenting ferocity. His self-criticism did not abate, even when followers suggested to him in all candor that self-condemnation was no longer necessary.[55]

Other contemporary Zen masters have faced scandals in their careers. These other cases show us that the presence of some form of ethical failure may or may not come to invalidate or alter perceptions of the authenticity of a Zen master's enlightenment. Sometimes it does, and in these cases others conclude that ethical errors of judgment show that a Zen master had not attained what before he had appeared to have attained. In Maezumi's case, those who knew him throughout his life— both students and non-students—claim that the depth of Maezumi's enlightenment is indisputable given the evidence that his life presented. Overwhelmingly, those who had spent substantial time with him remained convinced that the depth of Maezumi's enlightenment was authentic and beyond serious doubt. No one, they claim, could have demonstrated this level of personal presence and depth of character and not have ascended to remarkable levels of Zen insight; no one could have faked the level of clarity and compassion that Maezumi's life so clearly demonstrated.

Depictions of Death

It is a tragedy of some significance that alcohol consumption figured into the death of Maezumi Roshi. It is tragic because Maezumi appeared to have overcome his desire and need for alcohol. He had lived for twelve years without drinking; liquor played no discernable role in his life during that period of time, except as a constant reminder of the mistakes that had partly undermined his lifelong ambition to serve the dharma.

Apparently Maezumi considered himself to have achieved sufficient control over alcohol that he could indulge while in Japan where the social expectation of drinking was virtually unquestionable and then simply stop when he returned to the United States. He had accomplished that before with success and no doubt assumed he would this time as well. It would be hard to overestimate the strength and stamina of character that Maezumi would have achieved in his later life. For the last twelve years of his life, the moral and spiritual struggle within him was intense. He battled with levels of guilt and a profundity of disappointment that are difficult to imagine, and he did so while continuing his practice of teaching Zen. He knew how devastating his errors had been to ZCLA and to the dharma in America more broadly conceived. He had disappointed everyone and let the momentum of the dharma slip out of his hands. The tragic sensibility in this judgment did not escape Maezumi for a moment during that period of time. Although profoundly ashamed of his mistakes, he knew that he had to gather himself and his energies into a new effort of enormous proportions just at the moment in life when most of us begin to relax a little, to coast on the momentum of earlier achievements. This he did admirably, although always apologetically. No doubt the disciplinarian character of his lifelong Zen training served him well in this. It taught him how to let go of the past just enough to keep focused on the present moment of challenge. And although that present would always be shadowed by the weight of his past, Maezumi did manage to regroup his energies and purposes to the point that he rebuilt the Zen Center that he had mistakenly undermined.

At first glance, the circumstances of Maezumi's death would seem worlds apart from the idealized deaths of the great masters of the golden age of Zen. Images of their deaths are marked by perfect control of circumstances and timing. There are no tragedies in the narratives of classical Zen. These images, of course, come to us not from firsthand reports so much as through the editing powers of the evolving tradition. If we have a choice when writing the history of great founders of our group, how would we have them die—in ignominious circumstances or in mastery and triumph? In Maezumi's contemporary case, there appear to be few choices. The facts of the matter just are what they are, in spite of the initial efforts on the part of the Zen master's brothers to edit out the potentially demeaning details of drowning in a bathtub under the influence of alcohol.

Taking a second look at the timing and circumstances of Maezumi Roshi's death, however, something more comes into view. First is the issue of timing. While the classical masters of Zen appear to choose the time of their own death, Maezumi's death was obviously unchosen. Ironically, however, and in retrospect, it would be hard to imagine better timing. Maezumi had just spent a dozen years working through the damage to his Zen Center that his own actions and choices had wrought and all this with considerable success. There really was not much more to be done; the rest would be up to his successors, the dozen dharma heirs who were already well on their way to distinguishing themselves for the quality and innovation of their Zen teachings.

Several students note that Maezumi had come to feel that rather than furthering the mission of Zen in America, he was now "standing in its way."[56] By this he meant that the new era of Zen in the West that he had helped to initiate would not really get underway until the older generation of immigrant Zen masters from Asia were replaced by Americans, Europeans, Latin Americans, and so on throughout the world. Maezumi referred to himself as a "stepping stone."[57] He knew very clearly that the traditions from Japan that he had taught would be gradually altered and improved under indigenous circumstances and that, as the Buddha had said, this impermanence was the true condition of the world. Although he certainly did not look forward to his retirement and death, he understood that these events would open up the dharma in the West to transformations that even he could not anticipate. Maezumi had lived sixty-four years, all in good health, and had maintained his strength, humility, and sense of humor throughout. Those who remember him at the end of his life recall a wizened, compassionate, and humble Zen master still fully within the power of his Zen mind. Leaving that image under those circumstances would be far from tragic.

Indeed, the unchosen but impeccable timing of Maezumi's death was even more interesting. He had just made his final trip to his homeland. He had gone there in part to participate in the memorial service for his mother, whom he loved and respected with great sincerity. Perhaps most important, he had traveled to Japan to finalize his dharma transmission to Bernard Glassman, his first and foremost disciple. In Zen tradition this is the final and official act of turning a legacy over to a successor, and in classical Zen it often happened in the final days of a master's life. That the poem Maezumi inscribed on the official *inka* certificate would also be his Zen death poem is perhaps as beautifully choreographed a departure as anyone could imagine. Maezumi had paid his last respects to his mother, his brothers, and his homeland; had visited the leaders of the Sōtō sect with whom he had worked all of his life; and had undergone formal ceremonies of transmission to his successor. If that wasn't a magnificently timed death, it would only be on behalf of the three children that he was leaving behind in America.

The other factor mentioned—the circumstances of his death—provides another way to make sense of Maezumi's legacy. His death under the influence of alcohol was tragic in the same way that his earlier alcoholism and sexual misjudgments had been. In them we see a Zen master of obvious greatness brought down to humbling proportions. However much Maezumi Roshi may have dreaded this outcome, it could very well be that among his greatest contributions to the global Zen movement now in formation is that the story of his life has helped to humanize our concept and image of Zen masters. We can now see a great Zen master as human in all the ways we are. Maezumi was by all accounts an impressive Zen master—someone who it was impossible not to love and respect—but with weaknesses and vulnerabilities that derive from the simple fact that he was also finite and human. While living a truly profound and visionary Zen life, Maezumi Roshi was at the same time vulnerable to the tragedies of life and mortality.

By humanizing our understanding of what it means to be a Zen master, Maezumi shows us that mastery in Zen is not mastery in everything in life. There are other dimensions to life that are not automatically cultivated or enlightened once a certain depth of Zen mind has been attained. These other dimensions—many of them, including the moral dimensions having to do with sexual relations and substance use—have to be cultivated on their own, even though Zen mindfulness may be the overarching skill that most effectively allows one to enlarge oneself in these other spheres. Reflecting on Maezumi's life and legacy helps us get beyond a "magical" understanding of Zen enlightenment wherein everything in life is perfected at the moment when the results of Zen practice come to fruition. It helps bring contemporary Zen to a maturity that we typically evade when we look at classical images of Zen masters, a maturity that need not consider Zen masters as enlightened gods in order to hold them in admiration and deep respect. If this is part of Taizan Maezumi's legacy to the global Zen tradition, that could very well prove to be a monumental contribution.

7

The Thought of Enlightenment and the Dilemma of Human Achievement

WE BEGIN THIS chapter with the Buddhist concept of *bodhicitta,* or the "thought of or aspiration for enlightenment." The thought of enlightenment is a concept of an ideal form of life, one that, as it begins to take shape in the mind, gives rise to a distinction between our current way of living and another way of life to which this "thought" calls us. As it matures in the mind, a thought of enlightenment becomes an aspiration, a motivational force that may enable some degree of transformative movement in the direction of the ideal. Buddhists recognized relatively early in the tradition the importance of this thought. Without some conception of a better and more satisfying possibility for life, motivation for self-transformation would be altogether missing. Recognizing the central role played by *bodhicitta,* Buddhist texts began to extol the thought of enlightenment and to focus significant attention on this initial point of departure in the quest for enlightenment.

This Buddhist conception of admirable goals or ends is analogous in important ways to the Platonic/Aristotelian "idea of the good." Both of these fundamental concepts—the thought of enlightenment and the idea of the good—stake out for participants in their cultures how it is that human lives may be integrated around a quest for the highest goal of human excellence. In what follows, we work back and forth between Buddhist and Western sources (both Greek and Christian) in order to reflect on the relation between a concept of ideal ends and the possibility of human achievement.

Barriers to Human Achievement

It may be that the reason early Buddhists singled out "desire" as the most pervasive root of unenlightened life is that in following the path of our first-order, instinctual appetites we lose the opportunity to prioritize and to develop our desires around a well-conceived thought of enlightenment. Those who spend their lives pursuing whatever they happen to need, want, and crave have not had, or taken, the opportunity to shape their pursuits around a carefully honed image of what kind of life it might be best to lead. They lack a thought of enlightenment that can effectively stimulate and guide movement toward a better form of life. Following immediate and unevaluated desires as ends, human beings forgo the possibility of integrating a life around a higher order ideal. Such a life may still be largely in conformity with the standards of conventional morality, since such conformity will often prudently be seen to enable successful pursuit of even more desires. That is, we understand that getting what we want will require basic abilities to get along with other human beings. But this consideration of means still leaves the ends that they serve unevaluated, and without that more important level of reflection, the integrity of life cannot be developed and the steady dissipation of one's energies and overall life is virtually assured.

Failure to place a thought of enlightenment out ahead of our activities as their criterion and end is not the only way to fail in the quest to integrate our lives around an identity that we have ourselves chosen. In fact, a somewhat less egregious mode of failure is even more painful. Consider the situation of those who have deliberated and to some extent adopted a thought of enlightenment and who, moreover, do evaluate their desires in light of this image of the good. However, when this evaluation is not motivationally strong enough to influence actual choices, these people find themselves divided and judged by the standard that they themselves have adopted rather than effectively motivated by it. In this situation, the self-image that is meant to guide one's life is insufficiently developed and too weak to motivate or to direct daily practice. By living one's life in this way, the desires that do successfully move someone to act are not the ones that have been chosen, and this bifurcation is experienced as a painful form of disintegration.

All of us, I assume, feel the pinch of this description to some extent, and Saint Paul's articulation of the dilemma in the book of Romans is the paradigmatic expression of it. Famously describing the human condition, he writes: "For I do not do the good that I will, but the evil that I do not will, that I do."[1] The reason Paul's description of this moral bind is more useful than a description of the person who wantonly pursues first-order desires is that, at this point in the development of human culture, most people find themselves confronted by a more or less internalized standard by which their choices and actions are assessed. Perhaps not everyone suffers the pangs of conscience and self-awareness, but today I think it is fair to say that most do, at least to some degree.

Akrasia, or weakness of the will, is one form of division within the self, a division in which two distinct aspects of the self move in different directions. Paul's version of this division is conceptualized as the battle between "flesh" and "spirit" with the "will" caught between them.[2] But if we open the Pauline question somewhat to ask "Why is it that we seem *always* unable to achieve the highest good that we know to be our most exalted end and fulfillment?" we find several answers—in addition to the early Christian understanding of original sin—that are worth consideration.

Why Are Ultimate Ideals Unattainable?

The first of several reasons for our inability to achieve the most exalted level of our aspirations entails inquiry into the character of ideals. The divinely ordained "law" that Paul sought to enact in his own life is one form of the idea of the good, an *ideal* that has been placed out before human beings as an image of the "best way to live" or as the most exalted life achievement to which they could possibly aspire. Ideals are projections of the very best that can be thought to pertain to us; they are those aspirations "than which no greater can right now be thought,"[3] at least not at this point in time.

Although ideals are imagined in the mind, these acts of imagination are not simply fantasy. What we imagine in true ideals are images of the good that realistically belong to us, those in pursuit of which we foster the highest forms of excellence of which we are in fact capable. An act of imagination in which we fantasize an identity for ourselves that we could not possibly achieve is far from ideal. But certain ideals really do align with our background, character, and potential in this particular time and place. However, whenever it occurs that through practice, energetic effort, or some other mechanism of change we alter ourselves by moving toward such an actual and plausible ideal, something extraordinary occurs. In acts of practice, the foundations are established for the projection of a new and somewhat transformed version of that ideal. Any movement toward an ideal establishes the conditions under which our perspective is elevated, thus affording at least a slight revision of the ideal itself, one that in effect alters the goal by enriching its conception.

This is true even of the notoriously "set-in-stone" Ten Commandments. Ongoing debate throughout the history of Jewish and Christian thought enabled richer conceptions of what living up to each commandment would actually entail. Jesus' famous line in reference to the law, "You have heard it said of old . . . but I say onto you . . ."[4] is just one of many such elevations of the meaning of the good. Although the particular commandment appears to remain the same through history, what the commandment means and what it requires of practitioners undergoes such far-reaching change that in fact something else is being "commanded." Similarly, Buddhist history can be read insightfully as the unfolding of the thought of enlightenment and the experience of enlightenment over time. As historical conditions and the practices aimed at enlightenment change, so does enlightenment, both the conception that people have of it and their experience of it. This change in ideals occurs at different levels, within one individual life of seeking and in whole traditions through history.

Understanding ideals in this vein, as historically moving projections, provides one way for us to understand why we always look *up* to ideals, never fully achieving the level of excellence they demand. By their nature, ideals always stand out ahead of us as images of our own potential perfection, projections of ideal ends that we know to be our own but which we nevertheless cannot right now fully actualize. As the point of departure from which those ideals are articulated shifts, so do the ideals. A couple of examples of this pattern are when enlightenment was opened to the laity as a real possibility and when the development of the "bodhisattva vow" made compassionate engagement on behalf of others a primary and indispensable element of the meaning of enlightenment.[5]

Structured into the ongoing elevation of ideals, therefore, is some degree of frustration, an inevitable inability to complete the task based on our capacity always to envision more and more. But this is the same frustration that is built into our efforts to improve in any serious domain of practice, from cooking to math, from the violin to golf. What we actually manage to do and what we feel we ought to be able to do are, at every point along the way, at variance. No matter how much we improve, we can always catch glimpses of greater levels of excellence beyond where we are right now. Thus maturation occurs not just in our capacity to practice an ideal but also in our ability to envision and conceptualize the ideal.

A second and obverse reason for our incapacity to occupy the level of our ideals is the ongoing development and deepening of introspection. Nietzsche's genealogical insight that the advent of Christianity served to develop new forms of human self-consciousness was just the suggestion we needed to begin to see the role that prayerful introspection and the mental image of God's omniscience have played in the development of conscience in the West. If in religious practice we seriously believe that God always knows the quality of our inner thoughts, motives, and desires—not just our outer acts—we will also have strong incentive to practice awareness of our own inner life, the workings of which are otherwise unknown to us. Our understanding of God's vision of our inner life becomes in effect our own vision. When individual theism as opposed to the collective religions of earlier culture came into being, so did psychological introspection—self-knowledge and self-assessment emerged as whole new domains of human awareness. Although for the most part lacking the strong theistic focus of Western religions, an analogous development of the skills of introspection occurred in the context of Buddhist meditation. The deeper a meditator looked for "poisonous" traces of "greed, hatred, and delusion," or subtle signs of the "five hindrances," the more likely it became that previously unknown forms of them would come to light.

This is to say that the more and the harder we look within to judge whether in fact we have lived in accord with a particular idea of the good or thought of enlightenment, the better we will become at identifying ways in which we have not in fact lived that way. Introspective self-evaluation, like any other skill, can be fine-tuned and enhanced to establish nuanced standards that were literally inconceivable before. No matter how good a nun or opera singer or anything else one might become, one's skills of critical assessment and self-judgment will always mature along with those skills to outstrip one's accomplishments. As is the case with ideals, insufficiencies constitute a moving target. As we work toward eliminating weaknesses, deeper and more intractable versions of them will appear through the ongoing development of our skills of introspective self-assessment. As the Buddhist thought of enlightenment developed, so did sensitivity to deeply seeded tendencies to unenlightened thoughts, feelings, and behaviors. Thus if we are on the move at all in life, both our capacity to imagine worthy ideals *and* our capacity to criticize ourselves for not living up to these ideals grows and develops.

A third reason why we cannot completely fulfill the divine law or live up to our highest thought of enlightenment—a reason even more basic than the previous two—is our fundamental human finitude. Frequently, the choices that we face in life are not between the opposing forces of good and evil but rather between conflicting goods or between two equally troublesome or harmful choices. We regularly choose what to do among a complex set of possibilities, many of which are well worth our consideration but all of which cannot possibly be actualized. I cannot be the scholar, *and* the father, *and* the athlete, *and* the citizen of my community that my ideal tells me I ought to be because, as we always say, there simply isn't enough time. This dilemma is structured into the shape of our finitude—the limitations of our achievements will always be greater than the limitations on our ability to conceive the content of the good. Our sense of "ought" is broadly expandable but *not* our capacity to live in satisfied accord with that sense. In Buddhism the simultaneous juxtaposition of the demands of meditative isolation and the demands of compassion motivated "social engagement," along with many other demands beyond these, actually serve to prevent the full actualization of any of them, and this finitude is structured into the human situation no matter how single-mindedly we attempt to focus on fulfilling the demands of these ideals.

Given these realizations, it is essential to deal wisely with the unachievability of our ideals without undermining confidence and the determination of our efforts. Rather than avoid this paradox, Zen Buddhists meditate precisely on this impossibility in their vows to rededicate and energize their practice:

> *Sentient beings are numberless, I vow to enlighten them.*
> *Cravings and attachments are inexhaustible, I vow to put an end to them.*
> *Reality is boundless, I vow to comprehend it.*
> *The Buddhist path is uncompleteable, I vow to attain it.*

Saint Paul's frustration over his imperfectability led him to ecstatic abandon in relation to the ethical tasks of self-completion and thus to the experience of grace, a freedom from the "law" that in fact helped empower its partial fulfillment. This theological outcome appeared in Buddhism too, although there as a relatively late and somewhat rare exception rather than as a longstanding pattern.[6] One reason, I think, that a Pauline-style conclusion would not be normative in that tradition, besides the primarily nontheistic orientation of Buddhism, is that Buddhist meditative practices were aimed at a kind of wisdom or insight (*prajna*) that was defined precisely in terms of a life-changing recognition and acceptance of the finitude of all dependent things. All things become what they are dependent on, an extensive set of finite conditions, they claimed.

The Spiritual Ramifications of Dependence

Everything depends. What we can accomplish just depends. While it does depend on the quality of our choices, the energy of our motivations, the skill of our acts, and other internal factors that we may partially control, it also depends on countless factors and constraints beyond our control—the economy, political battles, the particulars of any moment in history. Understanding these structures and the particularities of our own situation imparts wisdom with respect to who we have become, along with the encouragement and lure of who we may yet become. From this point of view, self-flagellation over human limitations, of which both Buddhists and Christians have occasionally been guilty, seem both unproductive and unwise. The relevant challenge is to accomplish what we can, not what we can't, and the place to focus most deliberately is present possibility rather than past failure.

This form of wisdom is the point of the Serenity Prayer recited in Alcoholics Anonymous and attributed to the Christian theologian Reinhold Niebuhr: "Lord, Grant me the serenity to accept the things I cannot change, the courage to change the things I can, and the wisdom to know the difference." There are Buddhist versions of this formula. To paraphrase translations of Shantideva in the eighth century: "If there is a solution to the problem you face, then why are you sitting there wallowing in dejection? And what exactly is the point of wallowing in dejection if there is no solution to your problem?"[7]

The goal in this respect would be a mature recognition of human finitude that would make possible both motivational encouragement toward optimum action and an appropriate form of humility. Although humility is typically understood in terms of a lack of self-awareness—an unselfconsciousness with respect to our own merit—it might be better to consider how a deeper form of humility entails an enhanced clarity of mind with respect to who we are and what we have done rather than an absence of such clarity. Self-effacement is certainly an appropriate gesture or sign of humility, but it will ring true only when it issues from a lucid grasp of who we are in relation to others and to the actual conditions in which we live. Like its opposite—various forms of self-aggrandizement—self-abasement is often the result of a false sense of self, one way among many that we can get trapped within ourselves and misjudge the reality of our situation. When humility is authentic, it is generated by insight into the relation between who or what we really are and the larger context in which we live. No matter how refined or how powerful we are, that refinement and that power are miniscule in proportion to the larger world from which we have received virtually everything. When this recognition dawns on us, humility is often manifest in the form of gratitude. Indeed, most fundamentally, humility is a thoroughgoing recognition of the extent to which not just our accomplishments but also our very being have come to us as gifts in whose creation we played little or no role.

What is the relationship between this kind of humility and our concerted self-effort, between our striving for ideals and the recognition of our complete dependence on forces far beyond our own? How does the individual Buddhist effort to conceive and pursue a thought of enlightenment cohere with a profound recognition that, without the support of powers beyond our own, there would be neither striving nor striver? All religions with a long enough history seem at some point to find themselves confronted with this question. The Pauline-Augustinian-Lutheran encounter with the transcendence of God and the necessity of grace is given cogent modern articulation in Friedrich Schleiermacher's sense that religion itself arises out of a distinctively human feeling of "absolute dependence."[8]

The central Buddhist concept of "dependent arising" captures something like this same sense but in a different key. Although human beings are understood to be absolutely dependent, what our lives and our enlightenments depend upon is dispersed throughout the cosmos of causes. What we are dependent on, the "whence" of our dependence, as Schleiermacher translations call it, is everywhere around us. And even though the power behind or within all particular causes can be conceived in unified terms, as the image of "Buddha-nature" or as "emptiness" itself, Buddhists have frequently maintained that mindful, constant focus on the actual appearance of their dispersion throughout the world of particular factors is a spiritually healthy way to foster acknowledgement of dependence and to express appropriate gratitude. If we are always looking for the one ultimate source—the Buddha or the *Dharmakaya*—we will often fail to recognize the presence of that reality everywhere around us in the complex world of other people and other factors all right here in the present moment.

Buddhists have also been well aware of the opposite weakness—the tendencies to get lost in the dispersion of particular factors to the point that a deeper sense of integrity or overarching unity is either lost or never developed. This spiritual weakness is manifest in a habitual failure to sense the numinous quality within the entities around us. The world flattens out into innumerable meaningless things.

Karma, Spiritual Discipline, and Transcendence

The question of our dependence upon factors beyond us has a bearing on how we might best understand the Buddhist teachings on karma. The issue of individual merit—karmic merit—is, in my judgment, one upon which many Buddhist treatises fail to follow through on their own principles. It is one theoretical matter upon which to test the sophistication of particular Buddhist concepts of "no-self." Wherever karmic merit is conceived individually, such that my acts accrue merit or demerit for me alone, then we can easily see that the no-self teaching has been undermined or reduced in significance, because thinking of karma in these strictly individual terms assumes a clear and substantial separation of "my self" or "my karma" from other individuals and from larger contexts of community.

How can karmic merit be understood otherwise? On the spirit of Buddhist principles, we are encouraged to realize how everything has its existence within larger contexts of conditions and dependencies. Recognizing that our very selves are utterly dependent upon factors out beyond us, we can see the limits of the idea of meritorious achievement conceived in strictly individual terms. Whatever we have accomplished would never have occurred if it were not for the cooperation of countless of others—those who have farmed for us, those who have built houses for us, those who have educated us, and so on. Our accomplishments are hardly "ours" once we begin to factor in all of the conditions that had to be supplied to us in order to make our work possible at all.

That our achievements are in all these ways utterly dependent need not eliminate all sense of accomplishment. It does redefine and qualify it, however, by distributing the merit behind accomplishment in just proportion to the real sources of empowerment. Moreover, a humility appropriate to that recognition understands that gifts received always, by necessity, outstrip gifts given and that the dividing line between the two is always porous and open to erasure. The traditional Buddhist way of saying this is that our merit and our receipt of gifts are *non-dual*; they cannot be ultimately separated. Thus the merit that I deserve is thoroughly comingled with all those people and things upon which I have been utterly dependent for the event of my life and its achievements. Once the merit of achievement has been decentered from the self, "enlightenment" can no longer be conceived in simplistic terms as an individual accomplishment. The appearance of a truly magnanimous, truly extraordinary individual can only be the achievement of a whole culture—indeed, of the cosmos itself—of everything that has conspired knowingly and unknowingly to produce anything of greatness. Understanding this, an appropriate Buddhist response to spiritual achievement would be a posture of humility and gratitude that is measured by the extent of that recognition.

In this context of thought, we can appreciate Paul Ricoeur's articulation of what he called the "dialectic of ownership and dispossession ... of self-affirmation and self-effacement."[9] As finite beings we cannot simultaneously engage the imperative of self-mastery that energetic striving demands and the ecstasy of humble self-abandonment, but we can nonetheless experience both of them in turn and in relation to each other. Each pole in the dialectic both limits and enables the other. Nevertheless, I wonder whether there is a sense in which this dialectic might receive at least some degree of its urgency from a presupposed separation between self and other than self that is more extensive than the Buddhist no-self and dependent arising concepts would suggest. If so, realizations that diminish the dichotomy of self and other would also diminish the play of the dialectic thus described. If the self's sense of ownership is diminished to some extent due to increased awareness of interdependence, so would its corresponding experience of affirmation or dispossession. But that difference is simply one of degree, since it is inevitable that at times one pole or another would dominate our experience. At times we affirm ourselves in the discipline of our work, both spiritual and otherwise. At other times we sense the extent to which all of this is a gift and that we are never the ultimate source of anything. When heightened, both of these experiences impart powerful spiritual affects.

Although the Paul-Augustine-Lutheran line of tradition would seem to have reduced the significance of the law in Christian thought, I do not think that this has diminished the role implicitly played in subsequent theologies by the "idea of the good" as an ethical ideal. Looking at it from this Buddhist-inspired point of view, we might say that the law has simply been replaced by a much more sophisticated thought of enlightenment, one in which human character, dependence, and a more nuanced understanding of transcendence have been taken into account. The idea of the good in these theologies has been refined, in other words, such that it corresponds to the historical transformation humanity has undergone.

Incorporating forgiveness and an understanding of the multilateral structures of transcendence into an idea of the good functions both to mitigate the condemnation that arises from the judgment of the law and to provide empowering images of grace that impel further movement and refinement in life. From this angle of vision then, the reason that the law is no longer binding in the way that it was before for Paul is that it has been replaced by a significantly more comprehensive thought of enlightenment. Where early Jews and Christians were once trapped between their own inclinations and the inclinations demanded of them by the divinely given law, post-Pauline theologies increasingly focus on the transformation and elevation of inclinations through the grace of ongoing enlightenment.

There is a line of tradition in Buddhism that says, much to the appreciation of Western romantic Buddhists, that the way to find the appropriate image of enlightenment is to gaze deeply within, that in meditative interiority you will see what it is that you should be. We should qualify that account however by adding that the ideals you will discover within are possibilities for enlightenment placed there by your culture through language and education. For the most part, ideals are adopted from traditions and then adapted to particular life situations far more than they are discovered or invented by individuals. Having learned this from philosophers like Hegel and Gadamer, we now understand more of what it means to belong to a tradition, a belonging that entails the enormous benefit of inheriting finely articulated, long-tested possibilities for life that have widespread credence in our communities as images of human excellence.

Having accepted our inheritance, our freedom consists in choosing among these images, combining them with others, and transforming or adapting them to fit our particular circumstances in such a way that our own uniqueness is manifest. Traditional possibilities are the inherited forms from which our own thought of enlightenment will be sculpted. In this sense, rather than being constraints on freedom, traditions are the condition of its possibility, the ground from which our own unique constructions will grow. Our task is to decide what that cultivation of inheritance will entail in our own individual cases, shaped as we are by our particular circumstances and character, and then to put those decisions to the test in practice.

On these grounds, one important point upon which many of us might demur from many traditional versions of the idea of the good or the thought of enlightenment concerns the singularity or plurality of its content. Most Buddhists have assumed that to will enlightenment is to will one thing—exactly what the Buddha achieved. From their ahistorical point of view, any deviation from that form of enlightenment could only be understood as a diminishment. Given, however, the range of images available to us now through global history and literature, we cannot avoid a considerably more open and pluralistic conception of good lives, one that is reticent to impose a set of requirements that all strivers must meet. Cultures and individual lives are now so unavoidably diverse that ideals of personal excellence will also admit of a wide range of characteristics. No singular form of the good and no particular thought of enlightenment will be comprehensive enough to encompass all possibilities for excellence that will arise even in one culture at one time, much less in the course of human history.

This is the justification, I assume, for Alastair MacIntyre's famously circular definition of "the good life" in *After Virtue* where he claimed that "The good life for man is the life spent pursuing the good life for man."[10] This sentence provides a formal definition of "the good life" without specifying in advance or permanently the particular content of the good, which is historically variable. MacIntyre's definition claims, with subtle insight, that the most important thing to realize about the pursuit of enlightenment is that we should honestly spend our lives pursuing it, wherever that will lead us beyond the current capacity of our imaginations. Zen master Dōgen's Buddhist way of putting this is "the path is realization"—being on the path of self-transformation is the goal itself. What the shape of that honestly pursued enlightenment will be must vary in accordance with circumstances and points of departure. The long histories of Christian and Buddhist hagiography are excellent places to witness this diversity, as is the historically honed truth of the formal structure that MacIntyre brings to our attention.

At least one qualification on the relativity or relativism that we sense in that definition is important: That the particular content of the good is relative to the situation and character of the seeker, as well as to his or her historical location, should not in any way diminish the absolute character of the ethical demand placed upon the one in pursuit. Indeed, we will, at the end of our lives, take responsibility for nothing more seriously than the character of the ideals or the thought of enlightenment in terms of which we have shaped our lives. What is good for me to pursue in my life is a matter about which I stand to be right or wrong—either successful in sculpting a life befitting my circumstances or seriously mistaken as evidenced in an unethical and failed life, or any of the innumerable possibilities between these poles. And although we will not be able to conceive of that quest as an effort to hold a teaching or standard that is timeless and cannot be transcended, we will nevertheless experience a demand for truth in this venture as binding as any we can imagine.

Although this demand will still be felt as the need to "get it right," to live the best possible kind of life on grounds that we ourselves have chosen and justified in the context of our own language and tradition, the most important dimension of this quest is the ongoing, lifelong effort to deepen the ideals that guide and shape that sense of "right." "Depth" here entails the comprehensiveness and the integration of ideals, a gathering of all relevant dimensions of the good that takes the form of human integrity. As a guiding norm and rule for thought, the "integrity of life"[11] encourages us to engage in thoughtful integration, the act of bringing all the particular goods we encounter into more comprehensive relationships aimed finally at the integrity of the good itself—that is, enlightenment. When effective, such an orientation for ethical thinking also becomes a form of mindfulness in practical engagement, an attentiveness that guards and enriches whatever it is that we can authentically judge to be good, true, and beautiful.

PART III

Language and the Experience of Enlightenment

8

Language in Zen Enlightenment

THIS CHAPTER ASPIRES to articulate an alternative to what has been a fundamental component of Western-language interpretations of Zen experience—the idea that Zen enlightenment is an undistorted, "pure experience" of "things as they are" beyond the shaping power of language. This alternative consists of an interpretation of Zen practice and enlightenment that acknowledges numerous ways in which language and linguistically articulated social practice have shaped and made possible distinctively "Zen" modes of experience. Our critical focus is restricted to the normative status of "our" (Western-language) claim that Zen experience transcends language, a position either developed or assumed in virtually all English-language works on Zen that attempt to articulate what "enlightenment" is. The primary concern here is not, therefore, grounded in a text-based descriptive claim about what East Asians have thought or said about the relation between language and Zen experience. Instead it asserts that regardless of how East Asians have understood the role of language in Zen experience, as contemporary interpreters of Zen, we are no longer justified in thinking that this kind of religious experience (or any other) stands altogether beyond the shaping power of language and culture.

We begin with an account of modern Western interpretations of the role of language in Zen, a critical exploration of presuppositions and cultural origins in the West. Although the assertion that Zen enlightenment transcends language is ubiquitous to English-language works on Zen Buddhism, I characterize the position and outline my argument against it by focusing on two influential versions of that position, Erich Fromm's seminal essay "Psychoanalysis and Zen Buddhism" and T.P. Kasulis' important book, *Zen Action: Zen Person,* which constitute the first two stages in the development of our understanding of the role of language in Zen experience. This section is followed by a four-part articulation of ways in which language can be thought to have a more substantial role in the Zen experience of "awakening."

Enlightenment as the Transcendence of Language

Erich Fromm's widely influential essay "Psychoanalysis and Zen Buddhism," presented at a conference in 1957 and then published in 1960,[1] is interesting for our purposes because, in formulating his interpretation of enlightenment in both the Zen and psychoanalytic traditions, it takes up the question of language. Moreover, while acknowledging at the outset that his understanding of Zen has developed primarily through the English language works of D.T. Suzuki, Fromm goes on to present a considerably more thorough and systematic position on the issue of language than Suzuki ever did. This surplus of articulation beyond his source inspires us to ask: What are the origins and genealogy of this influential understanding of the relation between language and experience that Fromm so naturally attributes to Zen? More important, though, this section seeks to outline Fromm's position as the mainstream position for English-language works on Zen and to put it into critical perspective.

The focal point of Fromm's position is a sharp contrast between the mediating, conditioning effects of language and enlightenment, understood as an "immediate, intuitive grasp of reality."[2] Although he discusses at some length the role that language plays in "conditioning" the mind, Fromm's emphasis is on the extent to which this influence is a negative one. Because the conditioning power of language "prevents awareness of reality,"[3] the goal of both humanistic psychology and Zen Buddhism is a liberation from linguistic and cultural conditioning.

A whole series of connected metaphors shape this understanding. Language is figured as a "filter," a "veil," a "screen," an "obstruction," a "distortion," a form of "alienation," a system of "fictional" "categories," and "clothing" placed upon naked reality. On these terms, language is taken as an interpolation between the knowing subject and objective reality that inevitably causes distortion. The implication here is that although linguistic mediation is very common, it can and ought to be avoided because language falsifies reality. In the rare and liberating cases where language is circumvented, as in Zen, there is an "immediate, undistorted grasp of reality." We "see reality as it is."[4] Having adopted this point of departure, Fromm holds that the goal of Zen must be to "rid myself of this social filter of language"[5] and to overcome the "false consciousness"[6] that it generates.

Presupposed in this account, and therefore neither articulated nor argued for, is the belief that language is an avoidable and optional element in human experience. Language is taken to be independent of and separable from both subject and object in the same way that a tool or instrument is separate from the worker and what is worked upon. Here Fromm draws upon metaphors of utility and the "instrumental" theory of language, the dominant understanding of language in modern Western thought. Because of the extent of its dominance, this theory's applicability to Zen seemed "natural" to Fromm and others.[7] My argument, however, is that this way of locating language in relation to human experience is misleading and that the kind of prelinguistic experience based upon it and valorized by Fromm is neither possible nor desirable.

A second presupposition that supports Fromm's position on language is the modern dichotomy between thought and feeling or between "cerebration" and "affection." Although the precise terms of the relation are not worked out, language is exclusively associated with the domain of "thought" and not with "feelings." Enlightenment, however, "the intuitive grasp of reality,"[8] is a felt experience that cannot be thought. Although the concepts embedded within language may be useful tools, more often than not they are misused in a way that hides reality behind a conceptual "screen," beyond the reach of unmediated feelings.

Fromm's imagery in the development of this dualism between directly felt reality and linguistically "filtered" thinking is drawn from a particular reading of Plato:

> The cerebrating person is the alienated person, the person in the cave who, as in Plato's allegory, sees only shadows and mistakes them for immediate reality. ... The full experience [of reality] actually exists only up to the moment when it is expressed in language ... words more and more take the place of experience.[9]

Enlightenment is therefore "not an intellectual act, but an affective experience,"[10] a difference that "constitutes one of the basic difficulties the Western student has in trying to understand Zen. The West, for two thousand years ... has believed that a final answer to the problem of existence can be given in thought."[11]

What Fromm has left out of this account of "Western thought," how-ever, is precisely the tradition in which he stands, the tradition from which most of his ideas about language and experience, feeling and thought, have been drawn. Attributing his reflections to Zen, he neglects to locate their diverse origins in eighteenth-century pietism, in the nineteenth-century relegation of "religion" to the domain of "feeling," in romanticism, and in the existentialist appropriation of romanticism not only current but domi-nant when Fromm's essay was written.

Regardless of its origins, however, several contemporary realizations throw Fromm's independent domain of feeling into question. First, lan-guage extends far beyond the domain of thought. Feelings, like thoughts, are shaped and molded by the language that we have (instrumentally) taken merely to express them. Feelings and the language of feelings always interfuse. To know one is to have some kind of acquaintance with the other. If we did have feelings to which no complex of words could ever apply in any sense, we would know neither what those feelings were nor that we had them. Second, "cerebration" and "affection" are not inde-pendent domains that can be so easily separated. Feelings are inevitably associated with thoughts and thoughts with feelings. Language, concepts, and feelings interpenetrate each other such that none is independent of the others, each incorporating the effects of the others within its very "essence."

As the essay continues, however, Fromm backs off from the position he has been developing. Changing metaphors, he says that enlighten-ment involves the "whole person," which presumably would include other dimensions of human experience, together with feelings, in a more com-plex relationship than previously assumed. If this kind of interrelationship prevails, then no domain could be entirely innocent of language and the shaping effects of culture and history.

Finally, it seems that Fromm's views on language are linked to his views on the relation between the self and society. On this view, enlightenment requires that the individual transcend society because "most of what is in our consciousness is 'false consciousness' and it is essentially society that fills us with these fictitious and unreal notions. But the effect of society is not only to funnel fictions into our consciousness, [it is] also to prevent awareness of reality."[12] If this is true, then the goal of practitioners in both Zen and psychoanalysis must be to "transcend the limits of ... society and ... become a citizen of the world, a cosmopolitan."[13] Both traditions of practice, Fromm asserts, would seek to produce "the whole man-minus that part of man which corresponds to his society."[14]

The viability of Fromm's understanding of Zen enlightenment, and of the relation between language and human life generally, turns on the possibility of making the act of subtraction just mentioned. If "the social" is already there in the always evolving nature of the human, then the subtraction of one from the other would not be possible without destroying what is basic to human experience.

Fromm's hierarchical dichotomy between the universal and the particular sets the stage for his placement of language in Zen. Enlightenment is identification with the universal in human nature, the attainment of which requires that the particular must be transcended. And since languages are unique or particular to each society, the differences they structure into particular cultures must be renounced in order to attain the depth of universality. The character of Zen *satori*, therefore, would not be related in any significant way to the histories, cultures, and languages of East Asian societies. This point is so central to Fromm's enterprise that his final sentence confirms it in the form of a rhetorical question:

> How could such [Western] understanding [of Zen] be possible, were it not for the fact that the "Buddha Nature is in all of us," that man and existence are universal categories, and that the immediate grasp of reality, waking up, and enlightenment, are universal experiences?[15]

Without devaluing many of the important humanistic consequences of this universalist thought, it would be difficult today not to be aware of its shortcomings. Most decisively, it eliminates what is valuable and interesting in cultural studies—the particular institutions, beliefs, and practices of a culture. In refusing to acknowledge experiential difference between cultures, it fails to understand Zen enlightenment as a unique and impressive cultural achievement particular to East Asian societies. In effect, this prevents Fromm from learning anything new from Zen because his claim entails that he already understands the universal experience to which it aspires. The guiding thought of this chapter is that the attainment of what Alasdair Macintyre has called "tradition-free individuals"[16] is an unworthy goal—East or West—and that for us to improve upon it would require greater attentiveness to the role that language plays in the pursuit of excellence in any culture.

Transcending Language Relatively

Sensitivity to Zen language and to the particularity of Japanese culture is precisely what T.P. Kasulis brings to his important book *Zen Action: Zen Person*.[17] The text opens with a discussion of the unique character of Japanese language, moves into a philosophical discussion of Buddhist theories of language, and demonstrates a well-cultivated appreciation of Japanese poetic language all the way through. Just two decades later, Kasulis had an access to Zen that Fromm did not.

Kasulis' version of the relation between language and Zen experience is more complex, partly because he is working out of original Buddhist sources, partly because his account has attained a greater philosophical rigor, and partly—perhaps most importantly—because he is working back and forth between two quite different views of language. One view follows the basic structure of Fromm's understanding: the Zen master is free of the screening effects of language so that his experience is direct and unmediated. The second view, inspired by a different set of sources, argues convincingly that being human means being fully situated within a particular cultural milieu and that full transcendence is not possible. Working between these two positions both deepens Kasulis' account of language in Zen and, in the end, undermines it.

Under the constraints of Kasulis' first position, most of Fromm's metaphors reappear. Language is a "filter," a "screen," a "tool," an "overlay," a "covering," a "distortion," an "obstruction," and extra "baggage." As for Fromm, these metaphors carry with them traditional associations with some form of dualism. In Kasulis' case, the essential dichotomy, which sometimes carries temporal connotations, is between an initial moment of unmediated contact and subsequent "filtering" through linguistic categories. The specific terms of the dichotomy are "raw data" versus "meaning," "pure experience" versus "conceptual overlay," "original image" versus "blurring through conceptual filters," "prereflective awareness" versus "reflective categories," "primordial given" versus "linguistic construct," and so on. Given this dichotomy as background, how does enlightenment come to be construed in Kasulis' account? If language and concepts "cover over" the "raw data" of "pure experience," enlightenment would require that "one must overcome the tendency to filter experience through previously learned categories."[18] In the moment of awakening we "return to the state before we put on the first filters."[19] Having made this return, "the master does not immediately filter his direct experience."[20]

For him, things "manifest themselves just as they are,"[21] without labels, distinctions, judgments, or meaning.

The alternative account offered in this chapter is based upon the thought that this foundational dichotomy between the "primordial given" and a subsequent attribution of meaning is untenable. In support of this claim I argue that human perception is always—even for the Zen master— already linguistically shaped and that there is no human access to a pre-linguistic, objective "given." Kasulis' claim here is based on a temporal distinction: "the Zen master does not immediately filter his direct experience."[22] He does that later, if and when the situation requires it. First, there is "immediate, non-verbal intuition of *Prajñā*. Then, if one finds it necessary to describe or analyze phenomena, one will be cognizant of which aspects of the primordial experience are being highlighted and which hidden by distinctions."[23]

The irony of this account is that it attributes nondualistic, undichotomized experience to the unenlightened and a cumbersome bifurcation to the Zen master. Whereas those who are unenlightened experience meaning right in the things themselves, the Zen master experiences in succession both the "things in themselves" and their socially ascribed meaning and is, therefore, charged with the constant task of comparing them. The point here, however, is that this division within the Zen master cannot hold.

One way to locate the problem is to notice in the previous quote that the movement from primordial experience to linguistic articulation cannot occur without presupposing distinctions, judgments, and meanings already present within the primordial. One would only "find it necessary to describe or analyze phenomena"[24] if there were some distinction—some criterion of necessity—already present in the primordial. Necessary with respect to what? In contrast to what? In terms of what context of meaning? The impetus to make the move from nonconceptual to conceptual shows the prior presence of the conceptual in the supposed preconceptual. The claim that the enlightened "will be cognizant of which aspects of the primordial experience are being highlighted and which hidden by distinctions"[25] already implicitly recognizes the presence within the primordial of both cognition and differentiated aspects. Furthermore, the portrait of the Zen master as needing to hold one access to the world up against another for comparison[26] must render problematic any claim to immediacy and spontaneity.

But what is really rendered problematic throughout is the adequacy of modern epistemology as the background in terms of which Zen experience can be understood. This background is what modern Western interpretations of Buddhism have consistently assumed. Kasulis' understanding of Nagarjuna, drawn from the best interpretations available, shows this most clearly. Here the issues of representation and subject–object relations, the central issues in modern philosophy, are introduced. Nagarjuna is taken to demonstrate that "there is an unbridgeable gap between the concepts and their supposed referents."[27] Concepts or "language structures do overlap with structures found in our experience of concrete phenomena, but the overlap is fortuitous, not necessary."[28]

Although, as Kasulis puts it, "the gap between such concepts and their referents is not so great that language is to be avoided entirely,"[29] the enlightened know that it is "not to be totally trusted."[30] Trusted for what? Trusted for accurate representation, the representation of the primordially given within the domain of the conceptually constructed. But if, as many contemporary thinkers now conclude,[31] language and concepts are already there deeply involved in the very presentation of "things as they are," then accuracy of representation and related problems in epistemology are not the primary issues at stake.

It may also be the case that this epistemological framework is problematic for understanding Buddhist thought generally. When we assume this framework, we imply that Buddhists arrived at the same intellectual crossroads as their Western counterparts but, at that point, came to a different conclusion. Western thinkers responded to the problem of the "gap" by seeking well-grounded bridges between subjective concepts and objective referents, whereas Buddhists rejected that line of thought, deciding, for example, that the gap is unbridgeable and therefore requires the abandonment of the project of accurate representation. Although our purpose here is not to assert it, it is entirely conceivable that Buddhists did not in fact arrive at this same intellectual impasse, and that, beyond coming to a different answer to the same basic question, they were not even asking that question. To treat Buddhists as skeptics is to make their texts respond to problems that they may never have had.

At the beginning of this section we found that Kasulis' text is complicated by the fact that he is working between two different and contrasting views of the relation between language and experience. While the first view aligns with Fromm's, the second position goes in a different direction, not only qualifying and adding depth to the first but undercutting and subverting it. The second dimension of Kasulis' text points toward the understanding of Zen language that this chapter offers as an alternative to the theory that has dominated modern interpretation. At the time of writing, it would appear that Kasulis stood between two different paradigms of thought on this issue—one fully structuralist and another poststructuralist[32]—and his text tries to reconcile them by bringing the insights of the second within the framework provided by the first. Although that reconciliation is not, in my opinion, successful, Kasulis' attempt to work with an alternative view of language may in the end be the decisive significance of his text.

The focal point of Kasulis' second, qualifying account is the finitude and historicity of all human life, including enlightened life. Unlike Fromm's universal person, "who must transcend the limits of his society,"[33] Kasulis' account of enlightenment proceeds under the realization that human beings are always situated in particular time, space, and culture. Whereas Fromm takes a transcendental state as the goal, Kasulis concludes that "we cannot find our full sense of personhood by totally rejecting our historical conditions and seeking an ahistorical original face."[34] Kasulis' Zen master "does not transcend the world—he is firmly implanted in it." He "does not undo his conditionality; rather, he understands its nature and its limits."[35]

This realization, inspired, according to the text, by Heidegger, Wittgenstein, and Dōgen, ultimately undermines Kasulis' overall account of the place of language in Zen experience. This can be seen not just in the tensions that it introduces into his text but also in another look at his sources. Setting Dōgen aside, since his Zen view is at issue in our interpretations, we notice that, in articulating their positions, both Heidegger and Wittgenstein were working out an explicit rejection of the overarching epistemological framework to which Kasulis' text still appeals. What Heidegger and Wittgenstein have to say about language either argues against this modern (Cartesian) paradigm or assumes its demise. At present, it is hard to see how the two points of departure for reflection on language could be reconciled and united.

Because of the incongruity of these two frameworks, Kasulis' excellent chapter, "The Person as Act," ends up arguing in two directions. The first sets out the transcendental goal: the Zen master is "without presuppositions."[36] Undetermined by the past, he encounters everything as if for the "first time."[37] The second line argues convincingly that this ahistorical, uncontextualized ideal is neither possible nor in keeping with the world ensconced character of the Zen master. Aware of the tension between them,

Kasulis negotiates a compromise that acknowledges human finitude while maintaining the transcendental framework: enlightenment means being relatively less determined by language and cultural inheritance.

Resources for an Alternative Theory

In what follows we attempt to work out, in four steps, an alternative account of the relation between language and Zen experience. Like others, this account stands within a tradition of thought and, from that perspective, seeks to be influenced and informed by the best contemporary thinking on the matter. It is well known that the issue of language was central to late-twentieth-century thought. Picking up on the insights of Heidegger and Wittgenstein, poststructuralist theories of language have been at the forefront of discussions in academic fields that have been influenced by similar developments from Kuhnian philosophy of science to deconstruction, feminism, and postcolonial theory.

Drawing upon this discussion, this chapter asks: What would it mean for our understanding of Zen to have undergone the transformation in perspective afforded by the "linguistic turn" in contemporary Western thought? The foregoing discussion of the dominant (modern Western) model of the role of language in Zen has staked out how the critique of that model would proceed and how an alternative to it would be initiated. The force of both critique and alternative is the realization that language is embedded in all human experience, even at the primitive level of perception.

Language in Perception and Understanding

As we have seen, our understanding of Zen experience has presupposed a structural dichotomy between the immediately given data of experience and a subsequent interpretation that we (knowingly or unknowingly) place upon that data. Contemporary thinkers, however, deny this dichotomy by exposing the "myth of the given."[38] They claim that even the most immediate perception is already structured by some linguistically constituted cognitive context and that there is no human access to a world prior to interpretation.[39]

The first to make this assertion was Heidegger in section 32 of *Being and Time*.[40] There the claim is made that whenever we encounter something, we encounter it "as" something in particular. We see this as a book, that as a door, and so on. Anything not experienced as something in particular (or in general) is simply not experienced. Because this hermeneutical "as" is linguistically shaped, language is always implicated in our experience. Language, and its entire history of involvement in thought and practice, functions to set up a context of significance within which perception occurs. By means of language, the world (the given) is focused and organized in advance of every encounter with entities, persons, or situations. Thus when we see something, we have already interpreted it—immediately—as whatever it is. Assigning it an interpretation is not something we do after seeing it. It is the very shape that seeing has already taken. On Heidegger's terms then, interpretation is not an additional procedure that we conduct upon the given. Instead, it constitutes the basic structure of our "being in the world."

Two qualifications are important here. First, this is not to say, as some have, that everything is reducible to linguistic projection. It is rather to claim that we experience everything through the medium of language. Although what a particular word or sentence refers to is often extralinguistic, it appears to us as the reality it is through language. Second, this is not to say that there is no such thing as nontheoretical experience. The simple, perceptual seeing something as what it is in the midst of our activity in the world does not require our thinking about it. No reflective mediation is required. The point, however, is that the results of past reflection—the formation of concepts—is passed along to all participants in a culture through its language. We do not have to reflect on the concept of a door, or define it, in order to experience that shape as a door and to use it in accordance with its appropriate "sense." Language, therefore, is not to be located only at the level of concept and predication. It is also present at the level of perception in such a way that perception, language, and thinking are all interdependent.

Without this linguistically shaped sense that informs our direct awareness of things, the daily life of a Zen master would be problematic at best. One must be able to perceive those lines on the wall as a door in order to know how to exit the meditation hall. Inability to understand these sounds as a question, that sound as a meditation bell, and so on would render even the most basic functions of the Zen master impossible. Inability to experience a monastery fire immediately as a fire, as a threat, as a demand for action, as requiring the evacuation of others, as extinguishable by water, and so on would render the Zen master helpless and incapable of spontaneous, Zen-like response. No Zen text disputes this; in fact, they all assume it. They assume the everyday function of distinctions and understanding by means of which things are experienced as what they are, fully laden with meaning and significance. It is on the basis of this background that distinctively Zen actions and discourse are performed.

The instrumental theory of language is not wrong in asserting that language functions as an instrument or tool that we use for our own purposes. We do, in fact, use language. But this theory is insufficient insofar as it sees this as the only location of language and insofar as it understands human beings to have an independent and controlling relation to language. Every act of use or control, whether discursive or not, is already structured for us by the linguistically shaped contours of our cultural inheritance. Moreover, transcending these contours, getting back behind them, is no more desirable than it is possible. Not only are we mistaken when we understand the Zen master to have achieved this state, but we also render him incapable of the worldly "function" for which he is famous.

One implication of this theory for our understanding of the self is that individuality comes to be situated upon the foundations of community, culture, history, and language. The individual self develops upon this foundation as an inheritor of the cultural achievements that have come to fruition in that tradition. Thus situated, the individual develops a capacity for involvement within the socially structured world. Language and culture function to make human experience what it is by structuring, in advance, a perceptual field of relevant features, self-evident relations, possible responses, and so on.

On this foundation, the Zen master thinks and acts "naturally," without abstract reflection, in response to the immediate situation. But, in contrast to Kasulis' image of the Zen master as relatively less "determined," let us entertain the opposite possibility. Because he is an advanced instantiation of the cultural ideal, the Zen master can be understood to be "relatively more" determined and shaped by the Zen community's linguistically articulated image of excellence. The behavior, perception, and understanding of any Zen practitioner is, in this way, internally structured by the language and culture of Zen. Since this is true of all participants in a culture, it is a further, derivative task to decide how the "excellence" of the Zen master is to be distinguished from the competence level of the ordinary practitioner. Both, however, share this (ultimately ungrounded) foundation in cultural history. If this is true, then understanding the awakened Zen master will require as much sensitivity as possible to the Zen community within which he stands and the role that language plays in the constitution of that community.

Language in Zen Community

Because language is a communal or social practice, one consequence of a reassessment of the role of language in Zen is that community is granted a greater significance than it has in modern interpretations. Rather than grounding meaning and experience in the private sphere of the individual subject (personal intuitions, intentions, desires, and so forth), we stress the fundamental importance of the shared language of the Zen Buddhist monastic world. More basic than individual subjectivity is communal intersubjectivity, in this case the linguistically shaped sense of Zen that held monks together as a community in pursuit of common goals. On this interpretation, therefore, language is taken to be the power to form that commonality and to shape and sustain the monks' shared concern for the possibility of "awakening."

This way of proceeding—understanding Zen personal experience by way of the linguistically shaped world of the monastery—stands in sharp contrast to early interpretations of Zen like Fromm's. Recall that for Fromm, authentic Zen experience entailed the transcendence of one's society. Consequently, Fromm shows no interest in Zen monastic life or in the discursive practices that organize it. These would be figured as elements needing to be transcended rather than as the undergirding context that has made some form of enlightened transcendence possible.[41] Early interpretations of Zen, guided as they were by the modern valorization of individualism in its many forms, could not appreciate the significance of this sociolinguistic background. Indeed, American "beat Zen" was commonly understood as a radical rejection of communal participation in stark contrast to the collective character of the Zen literature that served as its inspiration. More recently, interest in Zen's communal background has taken hold, among both Western practitioners of Zen and academic analysts.

The two Western thinkers that Kasulis draws upon, Heidegger and Wittgenstein, are precisely the ones who initiated this interest in the communal background of thought. Heidegger's critique of modern individualism focused on language.[42] Communication, he claimed, is not the transmission of individual thoughts and desires from the interior of one autonomous person to another. It is rather a reciprocally influential interaction within shared contexts of significance established and maintained in language. Similarly, Wittgenstein understood discourse as participation in diverse "language games."[43] On this model Zen monks would be pictured as participating in the shared concerns of the monastic community that were constituted and presented in the language they spoke and in the linguistically shaped practices and activities that held them together in their "game"—the pursuit of awakening. Their language provided a medium within which this common enterprise could take shape and directed each of them toward the always evolving image of excellence that it projected.

We saw earlier how Fromm's modern understanding of the self led him to assume that Zen must be another form of individualism that rejects social influence. For him, the true self eschews what others think and say, taking upon himself what Harold Bloom has aptly called the romantic "anxiety of influence."[44] Although no adequate interpretation could deny the critical, subversive dimension of Zen, this account stresses the extent to which that dimension rests upon a much more basic submission to the tradition of Zen. The accomplished monk is a repository of the community's purposes, values, practices, and beliefs and only secondarily, upon that basis, an individual agent who takes the tradition up into critical scrutiny. The capacity for critical distance, however, is based upon and derived from a prior mastery of the monastic language game. Through the process of Zen training, the language and practice of the institution become the very ground of the mind upon which the monk as individual agent can function fluently and meaningfully. Understood in this way, language is far more than a tool for use in expression and communication. The language that the Zen master "uses" to teach his students would also be what he is teaching. Learning Zen would depend upon learning Zen language and the appropriate distinctions built into it. Some degree of fluency in this language would be prerequisite to experiencing what Zen is about.

If this is true, then Zen experience would be dependent upon prior education or socialization in the skills, customs, and beliefs valued by the Zen monastic community. The novice monk who enters this context of training is gradually formed into the kind of self for whom Zen experience is a possibility.[45] Our modern inclination has been to understand the Zen monastery as a voluntary community of individuals who come to that institution in personal pursuit of a goal that they already essentially understand. What further study of Zen history has shown, however, is that we have overlooked the extent to which monasteries served as educational and vocational institutions for boys.

Upon entrance to the monastery, postulates might neither understand nor value the pursuit of awakening. That understanding and that valuing were precisely what they were there to acquire. Acquiring them entailed a gradual restructuring of the monk's desires, behaviors, and beliefs. Zen concerns and Zen practices would slowly take shape in the novice's mind, replacing or reshaping whatever concerns and practices were there before. The process of acquisition, furthermore, was a lengthy and in-depth education in the language and practice of Zen that placed great priority on the imitation of role models. Because the abbot and senior monks embodied the purpose of the institution, the pedagogical method of imitating their gestures, speech, and concerns could hardly be improved upon.

From the point of view of Fromm's work, it would be unimaginable that the pursuit of Zen "freedom" would result from the acquisition of socially accepted, institutionally mandated conventions and practices. Yet so it now seems. Understanding—even Zen understanding—is a social and linguistic practice into which participants must be initiated. This is true even of Zen's most radical conventions—the critique and disruption of conventions, a skill acquired only at the most advanced stages of Zen training.

A new set of metaphors is involved in our thinking that language might have such a role in Zen experience. H.G. Gadamer's hermeneutical inquiries are a rich source for many of these.[46] In his terms, language is not a barrier, obstructing access; it is a "reservoir" of possibilities that it holds open to those who participate in it. Language is not a "clothing" that hides the truth; it is a "medium" through which truth becomes manifest. Language is not a "veil" preventing vision; it is a "window" that opens vision. Following the suggestions evoked by these metaphors, James Boyd White outlines the domain of language as follows:

> Language, after all, is the repository of the kinds of meaning and relation that make a culture what it is. In it ... one can find the terms by which the natural world is classified and represented, those by which the social universe is constituted, and those terms of motive and value by which action is directed and judged. In a sense we literally are the language that we speak, for the particular culture that makes us a "we"—that defines and connects us, that differentiates us from others—is enacted and embedded in our language.[47]

Language in Zen Rhetoric

Within the foundational context of the Zen monastic world, laid out in broad but specific terms by the language of that time and place, a very unusual, precise, and exclusive language game was played. This discursive game was so exclusive and so difficult to play that only advanced members of the Zen monastic world could participate. This extraordinary rhetoric was clearly separate from other ways of speaking common to the everyday life of the monastery, such as the "normal" language of daily monastic operations, the socioeconomic language that enabled the monastery to remain in functional relation to the nonmonastic world, and even the mythical-narrative language that had given rise to Zen and that had been appropriated into ritual practices. Beyond all these modes of communication, there was a kind of Zen rhetoric that was incorporated into explicit Zen practice. This unique rhetoric was closely linked to the experience of enlightenment, not just as its presupposed background but as its initiating source and consequential outcome.

The essential feature of this rhetoric is its strictly emancipatory intention. By means of its "otherness" to ordinary discourse, and therefore to ordinary "mind," Zen rhetoric sought to free its speakers and hearers, writers and readers, from the constraints of conventional modes of human comportment. The otherness of Zen rhetoric was typically twofold, juxtaposing itself both to the classical language of established Buddhist institutions and to the conventional language of everyday East Asian life. Identifiably Zen rhetoric was marked by a persistent refusal to talk about ordinary matters in ordinary ways. Indeed, the discursive practice of "talking about"—that is, propositional, representational discourse—was resolutely avoided. This reversal of priorities can be seen historically in the gradual movement away from both mythical/confessional and theoretical/philosophical discussions of enlightenment. The earliest Zen texts still attempt to propose true statements about enlightenment. Later texts abandoned this effort. In later classical texts, if enlightenment figured into the text at all, it did so obliquely and often with irony. While enlightenment could be rhetorically evoked, it could not be discussed. Increasingly, the language of Zen masters embodied the "un-graspability" of the matters about which they spoke.

This close relation between Zen rhetoric and the experience of "sudden awakening" is evident virtually everywhere in classical Zen texts, perhaps most prominently in the *Transmission of the Lamp* texts, which narrate accounts of the experience of awakening.[48] The phrase "at these words, so and so was awakened" is one of the most common in those texts. Awakening occurs not in the absence of language but fully in its presence as the focal point of its evocation and emergence. In the famous example of Linji's enlightenment account, the narrative reports: "At these words,

Linji attained great enlightenment."[49] Now awakened, Linji is anything but silent. Words give rise to the experience and then issue from it immediately and spontaneously. Linji's "discourse of awakening" is so powerful, in fact, that his teacher, Huangbo, predicts that he will "sit upon the tongue of every person on earth."[50] Linji's practice is heavily focused on language, a linguistic practice that, in both spoken and textual form, served to disseminate a particular kind of religious rhetoric throughout the East Asian Buddhist world.

One of the most common contexts for the experience of awakening given in these texts is that of narrative accounts of "encounter dialogue" between practitioners of Zen. These linguistic events, transmitted to all subsequent practitioners through classic texts, supplied the basic models for Zen rhetoric. Expertise or fluency in dialogical encounter was taken to be demonstrative of depth in Zen experience. One had to be so agile—so prereflectively quick in response—that the dialogue could continue of its own accord without "faltering." "Argument" in this context was clearly subordinate to the act of demonstration. One sought to have the language of the event show or demonstrate the point rather than to argue for it syllogistically. Presupposed here is a view that language works on the mind, brings about effects, and transforms experience. The crucial or focal word in a dialogue came to be called a "turning word,"[51] the word upon which the point of the encounter "turns" and the word carrying the power to turn the mind of participants, audience, or reader. The *Record of Linji* calls this "speaking a word apropos of the moment,"[52] a word perfectly suited to exposing the depth of the present moment and situation.

Some Zen texts describe the dialogical encounter between two Zen masters, or between student and master, as coming to conclusion in a nonverbal act—a gesture, a shout, or a kick. Having come to the limits of language, the final stroke of the dialogue is pure act, a "direct pointing" to the point of Zen. This dimension of Zen practice was retroactively traced back to Bodhidharma, the legendary founder of Zen, who, having dispensed with linguistic signs, taught directly through act and silence. But from the perspective of this interpretation, direct pointing still falls within the domain of language. Acts of pointing are potentially readable signs; they point beyond themselves to something present but hidden from ordinary view. Pointing is not direct contact. It makes direct contact possible and therefore always entails whatever indirection or mediation the pointer itself introduces. Nevertheless, the practical emphasis of nonverbal signs in Zen enhances the effective otherness and strangeness of Zen rhetoric.

Released from the conventions of "using" language for the purposes of literal representation, a Zen way with language is necessarily unusual. Zen texts and the masters who are credited with having spoken them are famous for their improvisation along unconventional lines. Instead of following conventional discursive patterns, they wander off in inventive and creative ways. These ways are meant to be disruptive for the reader or hearer. Their meaning is hard to locate, and it is precisely in the search for it that the commonly held sense of things is dislodged. Zen discourse of this sort fulfills its function precisely as a transgression on everyday language and common sense. In the disorientation that results from it, the interlocutors or readers are themselves thrown into question, sometimes by upsetting their normal position as those who understand and act on the world as subjects.

The otherness of Zen language is most powerful in the pressure that it places upon subjectivity. It introduces radical discontinuities into the subject's world and seeks some kind of significant disclosure as a result. This discontinuity can be overstressed, however. Zen rhetoric was, indeed, a radical departure from the East Asian Buddhist scholastic tradition, but that departure was as much a connection to the tradition as a disconnection. Radical Zen discourse extends and maintains the tradition by drawing upon its previously latent resources. Only romantically, following Fromm, can we conceive of a transformation in a tradition as so radical a break that all connections are severed to the previous history of that culture. The invention of new ways of speaking and new ways of understanding speaking can only occur within the parameters of the existing vocabulary any language has at its disposal. Romantic doctrines of creativity *ex nihilo*, when applied to Zen, will inevitably fail to account for the extent to which "training" is the essence of Zen.

Figuring Zen as a liberating rejection of tradition, we fail to appreciate the extent to which the enlightening effects of Zen are themselves the result of an in-depth submission to this tradition. Entering the monastery was itself an act of submitting the mind to a lifetime of reshaping that occurs through the language and social practices of Zen. Having trained in this way, true creativity is possible, but not before. One can speak the language of Zen freely only after having learned it and having taken into oneself its purposes and intentions. Training in this rhetorical practice provides the background out of which the Zen master's freedom can be performed. This suggests a restatement of the point of this section—that if Zen rhetoric both evokes awakening and is, in turn, evoked by it, then there is an important and interesting correspondence between this discursive practice and the goal of Zen. Understanding this correspondence, however, requires a departure from the romantic and transcendental grounds that have guided our reading of Zen texts thus far.

Language in Meditation and Silence

If there is one place in Zen where we would most expect to find that language has indeed been circumvented, it is within the central practices of meditation and contemplative silence. Western interpretations of Zen have typically taken this nondiscursive dimension of Zen practice as the basis for a claim that enlightenment transcends language and avoids its mediating function. A strong textual basis for this understanding of the matter can be easily located throughout Zen literature from the Chinese classics through contemporary Zen manuals. Many of the founding narratives of Zen and many of the tradition's primary symbols juxtapose the immediacy of meditative silence with the mediating functions of discourse and concept. The Zen tradition traces its sacred lineage to the Buddha's silent transmission of the dharma to Mahākāśyapa, through Vimalakīrti's "thunderous silence" to Bodhidharma's nine years of silent, "wall-gazing" meditation. The founding formula of classical Zen, describing Bodhidharma's "wordless dharma," valorizes "direct experience" as a remedy for the Buddhist tradition's dependence on language and text. In its terms Zen is: "A special transmission outside the sutras, not dependent on language and texts, direct pointing to mind, one sees the true nature of things and becomes the Buddha."[53]

From the perspective of this understanding of language in Zen, what evokes particular interest are the rhetorical practices entailed in making this claim to linguistic transcendence, especially the irony generated when one speaks against speaking or when one writes an antitextual text. On rare occasions, in fact, this irony emerges into the text's reflexive awareness as, for example, when a Zen text is able to see that "saying that there is no dharma that can be spoken is called speaking the dharma."[54] But whatever connections East Asians have or have not been able to make between language and silence, our Western interpretations have been naive in taking their antilanguage rhetoric literally and have failed to appreciate the ironic fact that this was their most powerful religious language. Becoming more attentive to this dimension of Zen, we would learn to look behind what is said (the antilanguage doctrine) to the discursive practice of saying it.

Reading in that way we would notice that every effort to relegate language to a subordinate position is itself linguistically produced, thereby continually placing language in a more fundamental position than its particular message.

But aside from the critique of language and the conceptual dichotomy between language and silence, we are still tempted to claim that the practice of nondiscursive meditation, at its deepest levels, is independent of language and that the experience of the accomplished meditator is thoroughly nonlinguistic. Yet this is not so for the same kinds of reasons that have been presented for the presence of language in perception and for the role that communal intersubjectivity plays in the constitution of individual subjectivity. In fact, it might be possible to make the opposite case, that, given the range and subtlety of their vocabulary of meditative silence, the experience of silence in Zen is the most highly nuanced, linguistically articulate—that is, "significant"—such experience in the world.

What does a "vocabulary of silence" have to do with its experience, besides supplying the terms for its communication? Initially, it makes silence noticeable. Although silence was available for experience long before Zen, only when the teaching of silence was generated and regenerated did it really become interesting. Before its articulation in language, silence was not much of anything; no one attended to it (at least not in view of Zen interests).

Moreover, whatever linguisticality there is to the various doctrines of silent immediacy is also present in the contours of the experience of immediacy. The voluminous presence within the Zen tradition of symbols and myths of silence, of instructions and manuals on meditation, and of continuous discussion of these sacred artifacts "frames" the experience of silence in Zen as the particular kind of experience that it is. Silence in Zen is not just the absence of sound. It is "symbolic of awakening," "highly profound," "the foundation of any authentic practice," "the atmosphere most treasured and cultivated in monastic life," "unnerving," "capable of evoking insight," and so on. All of these elements of understanding and many more set the stage for the experience of silence in Zen; they make it what it is. Change them and we change the experience. All of this is to say, once again, that a reciprocal, interdependent relationship exists between direct experience (perception), language, and concepts. The actual contour of the experience of silence is dependent in part on the vocabularies and theories that relate to it and vice versa.

Although modern interpretations have generally taken traditional Zen meditative claims as a rejection of language, one dimension of our hypothesis here is that these claims are not directed at language so much as they are at discursive textual practices and reflective thinking. The traditional assertion that Zen experience is "direct" appears to be bound up with the Zen critique of other, more scholarly branches of Buddhism. That the early foundational rhetoric of Zen was thoroughly connected to the ongoing political competition between Buddhist sects for prestige and patronage has been documented for some time now.[55] Early Zen literature intends to stake out a convincing alternative to prominent competitors and takes as its critical target their grounding in intellectual, textual practices. Juxtaposed with these literary, philosophical practices, then, are the Zen practices of silence and prereflective spontaneity. Serious practitioners defined themselves in terms of a concern for the cultivation of prereflective experience, an experience and responsiveness that did not require explicit cognitive mediation.

On the terms of this chapter, the claim to have transcended language is distinct from the claim to a kind of experience that is prior to conceptual reflection. Understood in this way, the experience of sudden awakening in Zen is immediate but only in the sense that it is not mediated by self-conscious reflection on the part of the experiencer. It is, however, thoroughly interpenetrated by the forces of linguistic shaping that are communicated through the institutions, practices, and beliefs of the community and its underlying tradition. While a great deal of experience is, in fact, prior to conceptual reflection, none is prior to the norms, values, and language of the culture within which the experiencer has been raised.

It is entirely possible that Zen writers have not denied the role that linguistic, conceptual categories play in the formation of prereflective experience because, given what other intellectual issues they seem to have faced, the question would simply not have come up. If this is true, then the premodern Zen tradition should not be thought to have made either assertion or denial on this issue.[56] The focus of this chapter, however, is on the modern Western understanding of Zen experience, for which that question not only came up but has received a unanimous and consistent answer. In this case both question and answer have much more to do with what has been going on in Western culture than they do with Zen.

To understand the status of the modern claim that Zen meditative experience is beyond the shaping power of language and culture, we must consider the language of this claim in relation to its content.

Although this language would typically go unnoticed, when examined, it dismantles its own basis. If Zen experience is "signless," then no sign of any sort derives from it, not even "the signless." If, in the experience, something is experienced as absent, such as signs, then a distinction is in fact present, as are the signs that enable its emergence. On the other hand, if nothing is experienced as either present or absent, then no experience has taken place and no assertions of any kind would be made. Because an experience of the "uninterpreted" must be interpreted in order to be experienced as such, a claim about it deserves no special status. It would be judged on terms similar to other assertions, on grounds of who said it, how, with what support, and so on. Partly because of its firm background in Buddhist thought, the Zen tradition seems always to have had a well-developed understanding of the fact that whatever is said about the experience of awakening, whether descriptive, doctrinal, or practical, has no greater status than any other assertion and is no less subject to critical scrutiny. Indeed, criteria in this area may have been more rigorous.

It is also worth noticing that claims about otherworldly kinds of experience seem to have been relatively unimportant in Zen, including claims, for example, about "ultimate unity," "pure consciousness," "contentlessness," "transcendence," and so on. The focus in Zen is more often on worldliness—on action, function, and immediate response. As Kasulis makes very clear, the Zen master is "firmly implanted in the world."[57] This kind of experience obviously presupposes a solid world of clear distinctions within which spontaneous action can be confidently performed. Moving freely, without reflection, requires that one be fully familiar with the world and thoroughly at home in it.

The fact that this particular familiarity, a Zen orientation within the world, results from a radical process of disorientation also shows us something important about the relation between language and silence in Zen. Silence served in Zen as the "other" of discourse. It functioned to bring its opposite—language—into view by providing a perspective on language that is as distanced as it could be. It would therefore seem that acute awareness of silence in Zen goes hand in hand with the awareness of language. The voluminous Zen vocabulary concerned with language, and the range of ways in which it enters into discourse, indicates a highly refined sense of language in that tradition. Understood in this way, it is not surprising that the tradition of silent meditation is also East Asia's most interesting and complex literary and rhetorical tradition.

Conclusion: Language in Enlightenment

Having described the role that language might play in various dimensions of Zen experience, it now remains for us to ask: If Zen enlightenment is not literally an unmediated, nonlinguistic awareness of "things as they are" in themselves, then what kind of experience is it? And, if a relation to language is essential to the life and experience of a Zen master, what kind of relation is that, and how does it differ from the language use of the "unenlightened"? This final section aspires only to suggest directions in which promising answers to these questions might be found.

Anyone familiar with descriptions of the character of the great masters in Zen texts will recognize that their most noticeable feature of distinction is the unusual way that language emerges in their lives. Therefore, many of these classic texts consist in "recorded sayings" and in descriptions of the Zen masters' "dialogical encounters" with other great practitioners. Given this fact, it now seems important to recognize that the crucial difference between the enlightened and the unenlightened is a discursive, linguistic difference—a distinction between very different ways in which the enlightened and unenlightened participate in their language. If the experience of awakening is mediated through the symbols, texts, instructions, and linguistically shaped social practices of Zen, then perhaps the outcome of this educative process ought to be conceived as a transformation of how one dwells in the linguistically shaped cultural world that is the practitioner's inheritance. In this case, awakening would consist, among other things, in an awakening *to* rather than *from* language. Focus on this dimension of awakening would help make sense of the ever-present connection made in classical Zen texts between "radical rhetoric" and "awakened vision."

On this model, Zen monastic training would be understood to require a fundamental reorientation of one's sense of language. Initially, this would be experienced by the novice as a transgression upon, and subversion of, everyday language and the common sense that issues from it. Among other things, one's linguistically structured self-understanding would be radically thrown into question. The effects of this process would vary, of course, depending on what background of understanding was being called into question. Any process of disorientation will be dependent in character on a prior orientation. But whatever the background, this desocialization and concurrent resocialization work on practitioners by disturbing their conventional sense of self and their ordinary comportment in language.

This would be, in effect, a contemplative estrangement from ordinary, worldly language games that, in addition to being disrupted, are being replaced through the process of hearing and imitating the Zen master's unusual rhetoric. Far from being a transcendence of language, this process would consist in a fundamental reorientation within language.

A Zen reorientation in language would require training to a level of fluency in distinctive, nonobjectifying, rhetorical practices. Only from within these practices could one come to experience the point of Zen. Moreover, we see that new rhetorical practices gave rise to new rhetorical categories and new ways of talking about discourse. Zen monks became attentive to turning words, words upon which the point of a speech act turned and that were thought to have the power to "turn" the mind of properly trained practitioners. They distinguished between "live words" and "dead words." Dead words were thought to lack the power of transformation because they tend to presuppose, and therefore to encourage, ordinary modes of experience. Live words were a disruptive force. They functioned to break down and to dislodge assumptions that were essential to ordinary, worldly discourse and experience. They did violence to common sense and so, from the perspective of noninitiates, often failed to make sense. But in addition to their deconstructive force, they were constructive, and what they constructed was a transformed relation to language and world.

Therefore, more important than whatever doctrinal content was being taught in Zen discourse was a particular mode of being in and with language. The "means" of Zen teaching was in fact a significant "end," a particular way with words that was being taught. Awakening was characteristically judged by the extent to which a practitioner could participate in this new discursive milieu. "Excellence" in Zen, therefore, was measured primarily in the extent to which one could successfully "do things with words" within the monastic community. What sets enlightened monks off from the others is the power and the relative ease with which they are able to work, perform, and accomplish the emancipatory purposes of the discursive community.

Given larger East Asian cultural contexts, it would not be appropriate to call this discourse of awakening "natural." Acquiring it typically called for a whole life of mental training. Old linguistic habits, and the sense of self and world that accompanied them, had to be systematically dislodged from the mind. While this training did indeed entail a critical rejection of tradition, more importantly, it required an in-depth appropriation of the tradition, including traditional modes of "critical rejection." To enter the monastery was to surrender the mind to a lifetime of reshaping that occurred through Zen language and social practice. Only upon this background was Zen freedom and spontaneous discourse possible.

The effort of this chapter to place language in relation to Zen enlightenment does not imply that Zen enlightenment is in any sense reducible to language. The intention, rather, is to understand the extent to which language is both actively manifest and presupposed in the constitution of this experience. We have found, first, that language is involved in the linguistic stage-setting and shaping of enlightened experience and, second, that the effects of enlightenment are most clearly manifest in their linguistic form. Upon a Zen cultural-linguistic foundation, and often with a discursive impetus, Zen awakening is commonly conceived as a "sudden," "overpowering," "breakthrough" experience. Its power is precisely its otherness, its inability to cohere perfectly with any conventionally established form, linguistic and otherwise. Its most decisive metaphors figure it as an experience of the "void" at the heart of all things, as "emptiness," openness, groundlessness. Moreover, it is not, strictly speaking, a voluntary experience. No one has control over it; it befalls the practitioner; it overwhelms and transforms beyond all subjective intention. The condition of its possibility is receptivity, a kind of openness, however, that is not without the finite form and shape of a particular tradition.

Given the sense of the extraordinary or otherness in the experience, it was commonly claimed to be ineffable. One could not communicate or say exactly what it was about. But this experience of linguistic inadequacy should not deceive us into thinking that the experience has no significant relation to language. The awareness that language is not in direct correspondence to experience is not in fact uncommon and not restricted to religious matters (although the domain of the "wholly other" is certainly its primary area of application). East Asian poets and painters would, drawing on the development of Zen vocabulary, make the same claim for love, suffering, landscape vistas, and the taste of persimmons. No set of metaphors could reproduce an extraordinary experience in the uninitiated. Language is always in some way inadequate to experience.

Two points help us to put this realization in context, however. First, the claim that language cannot fully communicate or describe an experience does not require the additional claim that language had no role in the cultural shaping of that experience. These assertions are distinct, and the position of this chapter is that while the former is common and legitimate, the latter is mistaken. The second point is that there is a close relation between the awareness of the inadequacy of language and the language that structures this particular awareness. In the case of Zen, this would entail that the experience of linguistic inadequacy and its articulation were both shaped and made possible by the extensive and highly nuanced vocabulary of ineffability as it became established and evolved in East Asian culture.

It is also worth observing that the focus in Zen was less on moments of sudden, ineffable breakthrough than on what this breakthrough made possible—the kind of intraworldly freedom that issues forth from it in paradoxical sayings, spontaneous dialogue, and unusual acts. What was of greatest interest was a new kind of correspondence to the world that could be observed in Zen masters' comportment, in their actions and discourse. The thesis of this chapter has been that not only is language present in the enactment of the Zen master's enlightened bearing; it also plays a fundamental role in the origins and development of the monastic world that made a uniquely Zen experience of awakening possible. Realizing this, we find ourselves in a better position, first to appreciate Zen Buddhist experience as one of the monumental achievements of East Asian culture and second to learn what we can from it.

Enlightenment and the Practice
of Meditative Reading

IN THIS CHAPTER we engage in a sustained reflection on the practice of
reading as a form of meditation that was central to the quest for awakening in classical Chinese Chan Buddhism and that continues to be important in contemporary Buddhism globally. Meditative reading in Chan is of
particular interest due to the strongly ironic relation between the antitextual ideology of the tradition, encapsulated in the slogan "no dependence
on language and texts," and the sheer fact of the massive textual tradition
through which that ideological meaning is communicated. Placing this
tradition within the larger context of reading and textuality in Chinese culture, we can begin to see how elements of a sophisticated theory of reading are scattered throughout Chan literature. Given the prominent role
of reading in Chinese culture as a whole, it would appear to be inevitable
that this avant-garde medieval Chinese sect of Buddhism would develop
a set of textual practices that are both extremely complex and oriented
to the particular focus on enlightenment that characterizes this tradition.
The practice of textual, conceptual meaning would inevitably be closely
connected to the experience of enlightenment, and the intention of this
chapter is to show how that is so.

A startling and revealing irony persists in the role that reading has
played within the history of Chinese Chan Buddhism. On the one hand,
this tradition is perhaps most famous for its ridicule of the scholastic tradition in China. Reading and writing were frequently and eloquently dismissed as practices that not only failed to evoke awakening but also that
actually prevented it. Texts were ridiculed by such great masters as Linji
as "dung clods" and "worthless dust," while the tradition defined itself

in terms of a formula mandating "no dependence on texts." Valorizing direct and unmediated experience of what they called the "great matter," Chan masters dismissed all scholarly forms of mediation as obstacles to the Way.

On the other hand, the texts that present this antitextual point of view grew voluminously through the early history of this tradition to the point that, looking back at it today, we can say unequivocally that the Chinese Chan tradition produced by far the largest and most sophisticated textual corpus in East Asian Buddhism. Obviously, therefore, we would expect to find in this canon a very complicated, even convoluted relation between the ideology of the tradition and the texts within which that ideology was honed and communicated. It should also not be surprising, given this long and highly prestigious history, that ideas about the role and the practice of reading rose to a level of sophistication within the Chan tradition that had not been attained before in Chinese culture.

In order to understand and appreciate this irony fully, we will want to develop an understanding of the role that reading played in and among the spiritual practices of Chan Buddhism. In order to show how Chan cultivated the kinds of spiritual reading that it did against the background of its prominent antireading ideology, it will be helpful to consider that specific history within the larger history of reading in China, in this case, obviously, very schematically.

Textual Traditions in China

It is well known that the practices of writing were independently invented without being borrowed or influenced by earlier or outside textual traditions in very few cultures in the world. China is one of these. Isolated from the earlier textualities of Egypt, Mesopotamia, and the Indus Valley on the far eastern side of the Eurasian continent, a Chinese priestly caste began to construct a rudimentary textuality—the famous oracle bones—at least as early as 1500 BCE.

As elsewhere, writing proved to be enormously useful in ever-proliferating spheres of culture even though the mechanism for Chinese textual practice was the more cumbersome pictograph or ideograph form of writing. This system continued even after the idea of alphabetic language had been introduced to China by way of caravan travelers, because China had already by that time become one of the most textually oriented cultures in the world. The prestige of the skills of reading and writing grew along with the power of the scholarly Confucian tradition to the point that no one lacking these skills would hope to attain a position of power, influence, or wealth. Against this background, it is hard to imagine that it was by simple historical accident that printing was first discovered and practiced in China.

This background of cultural sophistication is part of what makes the conversion of China to Buddhism remarkable. It was not the case in China, as it was elsewhere in the Buddhist world, that Buddhism brought sophisticated literary arts into a culture that was lacking them. China had its own well-developed textual and ideological traditions, already diversified into various schools of thought, competition between which enabled further cultural refinement. Nevertheless, Buddhism was eagerly incorporated into Chinese cultural traditions, and this outside or foreign influence had an enormous impact on the ways in which China would develop further in the future.

But the difference in this case is interesting. Those who converted to Buddhism and who would be shaped by its worldview were not at the same time learning the literary practices of reading and writing for the first time. These were already in place such that the availability of translated Buddhist texts was for many people simply the availability of a new canon, a new corpus of texts. These new texts would, to be sure, require the mastery of new vocabulary, a new style of spiritual practice, and a whole new way of looking at the world and were therefore not easily assimilated. But they nevertheless could be comprehended and conceived within the already established textual practices as simply a new canon of writing juxtaposed to others that were already on the Chinese literary agenda.

This new canon of texts was far from meager, however, and the effort to translate, classify, and appropriate their meaning would take centuries. By the time Buddhism was beginning to be accepted into Chinese culture in the fourth and fifth centuries of the Common Era, it was a religion that was approaching a millennium in age. Over this period of time literally thousands of Buddhist texts had been produced in India and central Asia. Although not all Buddhist texts produced in India and central Asia would make their way successfully to China, the most widespread and important ones certainly did. Today, in fact, the Buddhist canon in Chinese is the largest extant in any language.

No doubt the arrival of this huge corpus was perplexing to the Chinese. Hundreds of these texts were sutras and therefore claimed the status of the word of the Buddha himself. These varied in form from one page in length to a thousand, as would have been the case for the *Avatamsaka sūtra,* for example. They also varied in style, teachings, and overall orientation. Other genres of writing complicated the matter even more. There were *vinaya* texts codifying the Buddhist precepts and rules of comportment for monks and nuns. There were philosophical treatises, devotional tracts, ritual manuals, instructions in magic, and much, much more. The cultural output in terms of time and attention that was required in China to sort all this out was enormous.

At the height of the Tang dynasty in the seventh and eighth centuries, the processes of producing Buddhist culture in China were amazingly sophisticated, no doubt one of the most prosperous "industries" in the country. Monastic institutions led the effort, with monks serving in a wide variety of administrative capacities. The most important of these capacities continued to be text based monks capable of reading and handling the Buddhist sacred texts. Some monks specialized in philology and translation and could read earlier Buddhist languages and turn them into a consumable Chinese form. Others were expert in the history and classification of texts, an extremely important function since Buddhism came to China in the form of thousands of texts in a wide variety of editions. Some specialized in interpreting these texts, making their meaning clear in a new cultural context, while others were well versed in comparative studies, showing how the ideas found in one text related to the ideas in another. Others were creative and philosophical writers; they took the meaning of the Buddhist sacred texts as grounds for their own Buddhist thinking. And still others recited and chanted these texts into the culture and minds of everyday Chinese life.

It was common for scholar monks to specialize in one sutra, typically committing it to memory so that it could be recited on ritual occasions. All the while the corpus of Buddhist texts continued to grow: new translations of newly imported texts, improved translations of already translated texts, new classification schemas, and more commentaries on what all of this might mean. The invention of printing right at the height of this extensive cultural activity is not surprising, and while printing made certain textual tasks much easier, it rendered the role of the text all that much more complicated and important.

One symbol of this importance was the occasional literacy exam imposed upon the monastic institution by the Imperial government primarily as a means to counter the power of the Buddhist institutions, especially the tax advantages enjoyed by the monasteries and all of the monks who administered them. Eager to diminish the number of tax-exempt monks residing in Chinese monasteries, the government would occasionally require an exam on sutra literacy to expose and expel all those monastic residents who on cultural literary grounds were considered to have failed to master the skills required to practice and disseminate the dharma. In the mid-ninth century, for example, a compulsory exam was administered throughout China, a monumental undertaking. Monks and nuns were to be examined on their mastery of sutra literature, either through recitation of three hundred sutra pages from memory or reading five hundred pages of text. Monks or nuns found unable to accomplish one of these feats were expelled and returned to the laity as tax-liable citizens.[1]

Our point here, however, is that text-based skills were assumed to be the basis of monastic life. We can certainly imagine other plausible criteria: adherence to the code of monastic life, skills in meditation, knowledge of ritual, and so on. But by that point in Chinese history and at that point in the history of Chinese Buddhism, literacy went unchallenged as the criterion of authentic participation in Buddhist life. Inability to perform these textual practices meant ineligibility for participation in monastic Buddhism. Textual meaning had come to be established as the very foundation of Chinese Buddhism.

The Chan Critique of Reading

All of this background in the textuality of Chinese Buddhism sets the context within which reading would function as a spiritual practice in the Chan school in the critical and sophisticated way that it did. Chan began to emerge as a new style of Buddhist practice in the eighth century and took as one of its defining principles the importance of meditation. Although early emphasis had been placed on the practice of meditation, this did not function to the exclusion of the textual practices that had defined Buddhism up to that point. Indeed, as in other forms of Chinese Buddhism, meditation was taken to include reading practices. A monk or nun reading a sutra either in communal ritual or privately on his or her own was considered to be engaged in a meditative spiritual practice. Nevertheless, as the tradition developed, critique of scholarly Buddhist practices became a rallying point of Chan identity. As a Buddhist practice aimed at the experience of awakening, reading became suspect.

What particular textual practices would have been subject to the Chan critique? Ritual use of texts for the purpose of merit procurement was one natural focus of criticism, since this form of reading proceeded without regard for the meaning of the text. A certain number of Chinese monks had made a vocation out of public sutra recital. This practice was based on the Indian idea of spiritual merit, and the propagation of sacred texts was considered one of the most lucrative practices available. One practice named the "turning of texts" was considered particularly efficacious because a monk could chant the entire corpus of sutras by intoning only the first line of each text. Turning texts guaranteed that no sutra would be left out of circulation no matter how irrelevant its meaning may have become in the tradition.

Other monks dedicated themselves to the career goal of reading through the entire corpus of sacred texts, a practice that often took a decade or more of daily activity. Sutras could also be "turned" or "read" mechanically by being placed on a revolving bookshelf, which, like prayer wheels, could be ritually activated regardless of literacy. Magical conceptions of sacred texts are found in all Buddhist cultures as they are in many non-Buddhist cultures throughout the world, and, given the illiteracy of the majority of Chinese Buddhists at that time, the sacred texts and the practices of reading maintained an exalted aura.

These practices, although widespread in popular culture throughout Chinese Buddhism, were not the focus of the Chan critique. These deficiencies were already obvious to many practitioners whether literate or not. The Chan critique was aimed instead at scholarly reading practices, the practices of the dominant and most prestigious Buddhists in Tang dynasty China. Their reading practices were not susceptible to magical conceptions and not so easily criticized. Indeed, the criticism had less to do with the lack of sophistication than the presence of it. What the Chan critique focused on was the goal or point of reading. What was the point of scholarly reading?

Since China had inherited Buddhism primarily in the form of sacred texts, the task of accomplishing an authentic transmission of Buddhism to China depended upon accurate knowledge of this voluminous literary canon. And because sutras were understood to be the words of the Buddha, knowledge of the contents of these sacred texts was thought to be the noblest of aspirations, the highest goal of study conceivable as a Buddhist. Monastic scholars, therefore, applied themselves to a full explication of the sutras, including such dimensions as the origins of the sutras, their setting and narrative, the primary concepts, and their overall position on Buddhist issues. The sutras became objects of knowledge about

which much could be profitably known. The Chan critique of these scholarly practices focuses on the limitations of "objectification," and on "sutra
knowledge" as an end in itself. Treating the sutras as objects of knowledge
came to be an obvious and admirable occupation. Those who knew the
most about the origins and teachings of the sutras were rewarded with
prestige and honor. But from an evolving Chan point of view, knowing
what the sacred texts had to say about awakening was not the same as
awakening, and the difference was the dividing point for Chan monks
between authentic use of the texts and uses that, from their point of view,
were more obscurantist than enlightening.

We can see the force of this critique in the remark of Zongmi, the
eighth- to ninth-century Chan scholar who wrote that "the important thing
is to get the idea and not to value specialization in the texts."[2] The "specialization" he has in mind here is the scholarly goal of knowing "about" the
sutras, in contrast to an effort to "get the idea" or to come to understand
the point of the sacred text. Specialization takes the text as an end in itself
and values mastery over all else.

It is interesting that the Chan critique focuses on Chinese words for
study that were prominent in the Confucian tradition. This is appropriate
because it was natural for the scholarly monks in earlier Buddhist monasteries to adopt Confucian language to conceive of their own Buddhist
practices of study and commentary on primary texts. That was the most
impressive model available. But when Chan Buddhism emerged, the
Confucian relation to texts characterized by *zhi* (knowledge) and *xue*
(learning) were set in contrast to a series of Daoist-inspired Chan words
for intuitive perception and immediate vision. At that point Confucian-
style knowledge and learning came to be seen as the reason that Chinese
Buddhist leaders were great scholars who were nevertheless "unawak-
ened" to "the Great Matter," the depth dimension of enlightenment.

A parallel exists between this critique of sutra study and the critique of
Buddhist images. Chan monks tended to be iconoclastic in both domains.
Sutras, they thought, were being objectified or externalized in the same
way that statutes of Buddhist deities had been. Reifying the words of the
sutra was thought to have the same detrimental effect as reifying the
Buddha. Both practices seemed to prevent the possibility of awakening
rather than enabling it. Guided by this thought, irreverent behavior and
iconoclastic acts in relation to both sacred texts and sacred images began
to appear in Chan, not so much in daily practice but rather as the focal
point of radical, inspiring narrative. Stories of Chan monks ripping the

sutras or burning sacred items are found throughout the "transmission" stories in Chan literature. Among the best-known stories of sutra defilement are Deshan ripping up the *Diamond Sutra* and all of his scholarly commentaries on it following his awakening experience and the account of antitextuality in Linji who, after having "made a wide study of the sutras and shastras," "threw them all away."[3]

A less famous story, but one in which the larger Buddhist point is clear, can be found in the Muzhou Daozong fascicle of the *Transmission of the Lamp*. The story reads as follows:

> When the master (Muzhou) was reading the sutras, the Minister Zhenzao asked him, "Master, what sutra are you reading?" The master said, "The *Diamond Sutra!*" The Minister said, "The *Diamond Sutra* was translated in the Sixth Dynasty; which edition are you using?" The master lifted up the book and said, "All things produced by causation are simply an elusive dream and the shadow of a bubble."[4]

The importance of this story is that it gives greater focus to the Chan critique. The target of criticism is not reading itself, or texts. We know that because the hero of the story, Master Muzhou, is himself reading a text. Instead it focuses on a certain *unenlightened* kind of reading, one that gives its attention to something other than the central issue in the text. The minister, a well-educated scholar-official, is interested in the particular edition of the *Diamond Sutra* that the master is reading. Muzhou refuses to discuss the matter and shows his disdain for the minister's interest in that question by shifting attention in an odd way to something else, to what he might have referred to as the heart of the text. Quoting the sutra, he says that "All things produced by causation are simply an elusive dream and the shadow of a bubble."

As a response to a relatively straightforward question about which edition of the text is being read, this is a startling retort. But its meaning is clear. The *Diamond Sutra* offers a collection of metaphors for how anything, including texts, ought to be conceived. Three of these are "dreams," "shadows," and "bubbles." These three entities in the world of experience are remarkably ephemeral; they are fleeting, caused by other things that somehow seem more real than their effects. But they are not unreal; they are really there, even if momentarily and only in relation to other things that temporarily bring them into existence. Muzhou directs the minister not to the unreality of texts but rather to the particular character of their reality.

Texts, like dreams, bubbles, and shadows, are impermanent, provisional, dependent, and thus, in Buddhist philosophical terms, "empty" of inherent existence. For Muzhou, to discuss the *Diamond Sutra* is to enter deeply into its central point—the "empty" qualities of mind and reality—and to apply that insight to the issues closest at hand. To focus their attention on which edition is being read is to miss the sutra's primary point and to fail, therefore, in applying that point to the reality of the conversation in which they are currently engaged. When Muzhou reads the sutra, his concern is not with the text itself—which edition? who cares!—but rather with the truths to which it can point when properly read. He applies the teaching of the text to the act of reading as a spiritual practice and, beyond that, to the transformation in his own experience that it makes available.

Reorienting the Practice of Reading in Chan

What appears to have emerged in Chan texts from the ninth century on through the Sung dynasty, therefore, is not so much a rejection of reading as its redefinition, a rethinking of how the practice of reading should be conducted and what its goal should be. Another metaphor for reading, drawn from the *Essentials of Mind Transmission (Chuanxin fayao)*, shows this transformation clearly. This text draws upon digestive metaphors to show the insufficiency of scholarly reading practice and to suggest that the consumption of textual discourse is analogous to the consumption of food. The passage reads as follows:

> Currently people seem to desire a great deal of knowledge and learning; pursuing literary sophistication, they call this the cultivation of practice. What they don't know is that so much knowledge and learning has the opposite effect of blockage and obstruction. Seeking only knowledge and learning is like a child who, stuffing himself with curds, gets indigestion. ... When knowledge and learning are not digested they become poisons.[5]

The target of this critique is clearly the Confucian-inspired scholar-monks who, through decades of sutra study, accumulated an enormous appetite for

knowledge about these texts. The text imagines that those who pride themselves on such knowledge of the sutras are unknowingly following the paths
of "craving and gluttony." They fail to recognize how this form of practice
obstructs or misses the point of the sutras that they study—the overcoming
of just such craving and egocentric pride. Their insatiable desire to consume
the sacred texts eventuates in nothing but indigestion. Inappropriately consumed, even good things have devastating consequences. Accumulating in
one's mind and body, knowledge fails in its transformative task. It is prevented from becoming an active part of the reader's life, except as excess
weight, which restricts vision rather than opening it.

Although it would be true that the overarching context for reading practice in the Buddhist tradition would be meditation, this would be especially
the case in Chan, whose very name means meditation. What in Indian
Buddhism is known as *vipassanā*, or insight meditation, is in Chinese
called *guan*, which is best translated as contemplation. One of the primary
categories of meditation, contemplation is a thoughtful practice in which
Buddhist doctrinal teachings are commonly the point of mental focus. In
early Buddhism the sutras were frequently the inspiration for this kind of
meditation, and reciting them or later reading them was included in the
category of insight meditation. In East Asian Buddhism this continued to
be a widespread practice such that sutra reading was both spiritual reading
and the practice of meditation.

We can tell from early Chan texts that this tradition was still in effect
there. By the end of the ninth century, however, critique of reading practices of this sort began to undermine the use of sutras as focal points in
meditation because these practices were so susceptible to reification and
other spiritual failures. We can see in the "discourse records" of the great
Chan masters from Mazu to Linji that highly rhetorical critiques of traditional reading practices were beginning to transform the role that this
practice played.

It would not be long, however, before something had the potency to
take its place. Gradually, with the rise in prestige of the Chan sect, the sayings of the great masters attained the same level of status that the words
of the Buddha had played. Although there were strong prohibitions on
this inauthentic, "unenlightened" practice, it was common for monks to
write down in secret the sayings of the master of the monastery. Eager for
spiritual sustenance—eager, in fact, for reading—monks would turn to
their secret notes whenever possible. As the decades rolled by and many
of the great masters died, their sayings began to be gathered from these

secret notes that were apparently widespread. The *yulu* (recorded sayings) genre of Chan literature was born from these notes and over time accumulated into an extensive corpus of sacred texts. Both in their primitive note form and in their more highly evolved literary form, these recorded sayings became the focal point of contemplative meditation and ironically the new reading materials of choice.

Since these new texts were read in monasteries and then later among the laity for many centuries, and remain today the primary genre of Chan literature, we can imagine the variety of ways in which they must have been used for spiritual purposes over this millennium-long span. Reading practices continued to diversify and to change as the religious setting for them changed, and, as a consequence, there is no simple way to characterize the remaining history as a single form of practice. There is, however, one schematic or structural feature that might help us to classify these practices and that might even be useful beyond the boundaries of the Buddhist tradition. How people read and how they conceive of this practice depends in large part on their conception of the text they are reading and on the way in which they understand their own role in the process. The "sacredness" of the text and the extent to which it is conceived as presenting divine wisdom rather than human understanding has a great deal to do with the way in which it will be read. Correspondingly, the role that the religious practitioner attributes to him- or herself as an agent of spiritual development as opposed to the role played by spiritual forces beyond the human is also crucial.

For the purposes of making this distinction clear, let us borrow the classification of religious practices made famous by Pure Land Buddhists, the convenient distinction between practices whose power is thought to reside within the practitioner him- or herself (self-power) and practices whose transformative force is thought to derive from a larger, more comprehensive, transhuman source (other-power). Pure Land Buddhists realized quite insightfully that there are two polar positions, between which there are of course many hybrid options in terms of which to understand what exactly happens in prayer, or ritual, or spiritual reading. We can understand our prayer or our contemplative reading as our own spiritual exercise, just as we might understand our practice of swimming as our own physical exercise. We benefit from it to the extent that we are focused, sincere, and successful in carrying it through.

Practice takes us just as far as our own powers enable it to go; in contemporary terms we get out of it exactly what we put into it; it is self-empowered. At the other polar extreme is a conception of religious practice—prayer or reading—that emphasizes the extent to which human powers are limited and a fully authentic spiritual vocation is beyond our capacity. In order to bridge the chasm figured by these images, powers beyond the human are summoned into the setting of religious practice. Practice, therefore, when successful, is conceived as empowered by what is other than the human. In this case, spiritual exercises are thought to be initiated and generated not by the practitioners but by a transformative source beyond their understanding and control. Pure Land Buddhists called it "other-power practice" and understood this to be an occasion of grace, an awakening that is not self-caused.

When the practice in question is reading, the text itself is brought to the center of our attention. How is the text conceived by those who read it? Is it a human spiritual product intended by an author to assist others in human self-cultivation, or is its existence conceived as a disclosure from a source of power beyond the human sphere? And, correspondingly, on which side of the reading relation does the power of religious transformation lie—in the sacred text itself, or in the quality of the reader's textual practice? Or, much more commonly, because not at one pole or the other, in what combination of these two? Does the ideal spiritual outcome reside in the ideality of the text, in the intentional discipline of the practice of the text, or dispersed between the two? Using this schematic division, it is not difficult to find a wide array of conceptions and practices in the history of Chinese Buddhism. Indeed, I think that both extremes and a range of middle positions can be found in Chan Buddhism itself.

"Self-power" reading would be written into the structure of meditation practice. If reading is meditation and meditation is one's own spiritual work, then the outcome of the practice would be fully dependent on the way one goes about it. If, on the other hand, the text is the real source of transformation, and the practitioner is responsible only to attain the appropriate quality of receptivity, then the power of religious change resides in "the other," the text or the power behind that text that issues its work on the practitioner as a form of grace that is either undeserved or unexpected. Notice that these options are also applicable beyond the religious sphere. If we are captivated or enthralled by this novel or film but not at all by some other one, we understand the difference to reside primarily in the objects themselves and not in our own efforts. On the other hand, when two readers or viewers encounter the same novel or film, and one is transformed by the experience and the other is not, we would very likely attribute the difference to their different capacities for reading or viewing or to the perspective or point of orientation to the cultural object.[6]

It seems likely that the spiritual practice of even a single practitioner would move back and forth between these postures, at one time mostly self-empowered and at another time receptive to the power of the text as agent. We can see in Chan texts interesting combinations of these. One form that this combination has taken is the idea that one's own initial effort in Chan contemplation and meditation is crucial but that a substantial part of this effort is directed at letting go of oneself, the ability to turn oneself over to the work of the text. The mental agency of all forms of meditation includes at least some degree of relinquishment of the will and intentional exposure to the force of the text (including, of course, the "text" of the master's verbal instructions). It should be clear enough how the receptivity dimension of contemplation aligns with Buddhist critiques of the substantiality of the self and its agency. To say that subjectivity is "empty," or that there is "no-self," is to say, among several things, that the readers come to be who they are dependent upon the qualities of language—the texts, the narrative—that have been incorporated into their identities and that individual selves are never the sole agents of that transformation.

One place in Chan spiritual practice where this can be seen clearly is *kōan* meditation. *Kōans* were cryptic, puzzling sayings of famous Chan masters employed as focal points in meditation. *Kōans* would initially be read from a text or given orally as a "text" of the master's instructions and then "read" over and over in one's mind until their deepest meaning penetrated the practitioner. To read a *kōan* successfully would be to share the role of agency or actor with the *kōan* itself. This is based on the realization that although initially one's willful effort is essential to the process of awakening, much of this effort would be directed to the possibility of relinquishing one's own will and desires, in this way empowering the *kōan* as textual agent to perform its work on the reader. Authentic awakening in Chan was in some sense judged by the extent to which a reversal of subjectivity had occurred, when what the practitioner took to be his or her object of study—the words of the *kōan*—takes on the transformative powers of subjectivity subjecting the reader to its power of transformation. For the reader or practitioner to become the "object" of this reversal amounted to a form of awakening from the illusory assumption that he or she is fully in control of the enlightening process.

Beyond this point in practice, contemplative reading ceases to be an act of will, an act of grasping or taking possession of the text or its meaning.

Instead, meditative reading becomes a process of opening up or out beyond the scope of the reader's own will to whatever it is that the text may disclose and beyond that to whatever transformation in the reader that this disclosure may bring about. Nothing magical need be intended here. It is always the case that when we read a text, analyze it, and work on it, simultaneously the text may be performing its work on us in a way that is not entirely within our control. It may do something to us that we never intended and could not have imagined. But in Chan contemplative reading, both sides of this process are accentuated, and the transformative point of the whole exercise is brought to the forefront.

Perhaps *kōans* are the culminating apex of this development and the point at which the division of powers between reader and text is most fully realized. Originally enlightened sayings from the minds of Chan masters, *kōans* became potent clues that would allow a practitioner to trace his or her own lines of access back to the awakened state of mind from which the *kōan* originally emerged. The *kōan* text was itself regarded as possessing transformative power, but only for the practitioner who had cultivated the quality of open receptivity required by the occasion of awakening.

Our thesis has been that behind literal antitextuality in Chan Buddhism can be found a sophisticated theory of reading that developed in a culture—China—that was more than any other in the world at that time oriented around a wide range of textual and literary practices. That reading and Chan meditation were linked together shows us something very interesting about the way textual practice was conceived, located, and structured in Chinese Chan Buddhism. The crucial question that remains, of course, is what to make of these insights. How might a glimpse into this very different and very sophisticated textual culture provide us with a critique of our own practices of reading and suggestions for how to extend them?

It is difficult to judge whether the practice of reading was more important in medieval Chan Buddhism or in the global Buddhism of our time. But one noticeable difference may be that we are less likely to regard our reading practices as a form of meditation. That difference in framing may affect how we engage in reading, and one thing that we can learn from Chan is to engage in this practice with the same spiritual seriousness that we call up when we sit in meditation. Obstacles to this shift are substantial. A millennium ago, at the height of Chan Buddhism, a substantial percentage of texts available would have been religious texts. That is certainly not the case today anywhere in the world. Reading is what we do in almost every sphere of our lives and at all times, which would make any serious reorientation difficult. Nevertheless, it would be worth our while to ask how our practices of reading would change if we began to think of them as meditative practice. And if we made that shift of framing in our minds, what elements of meditation practice could we extend into the domain of meditative reading?

IO

From the Thought of Enlightenment
to the Event of Awakening

ONE OF THE crucial issues that has emerged throughout the history of
Buddhism concerns whether practitioners who advance in their practice should expect to find a discernable and predictable pattern of stages
along the path toward enlightenment. Are there linear stages that can be
described in advance of any quest for enlightenment, sequential stages of
development through which any practitioner would expect to progress?
Some sutras and commentarial texts claim that there are necessary stages
of this sort and set out to describe them. The *Daśabhūmika sūtra*, a text
now set within the larger *Avatamsaka* or *Huayan sūtra* describing the ten
stages of the bodhisattva, is among the most famous of them.

Other Buddhist texts, however, argue against any set sequence of
stages, maintaining that enlightenment is a potential within all human
beings that can emerge at any time through a wide variety of means and
in any number of ways. One of the most interesting places in the history
of Buddhist thought where this issue was debated occurs within Chinese
Huayan Buddhism. Huayan Buddhism, the preeminent philosophical
form of Buddhism in the early Tang dynasty, was instrumental in lay-
ing the conceptual foundations for virtually all subsequent forms of East
Asian Buddhism. This Huayan legacy includes all lineages of Chan, Son,
and Zen and all forms of Pure Land, the nonphilosophical, predominantly
devotional form of Buddhism that came to dominance in the centuries
to follow. In this sense, Fazang, the third patriarch and foremost philosopher of Huayan, can be considered one of the forefathers of East Asian
Buddhism today.[1] By focusing on one element in Fazang's thought, this
chapter attempts to articulate the overall character of Huayan thought on

the issue of stages to enlightenment and, in the process, shed light on its connection to other dimensions of the Buddhist tradition.

In Fazang's monumental *Treatise on the Five Teachings*,[2] the mental image of a house is taken to model the *Dharmakāya* universe as a whole. On Fazang's account, since any one part of the house—his example is a rafter—is a condition for the house as a whole, that one part through its complex relations with other parts encompasses the whole house and is therefore able to reveal it comprehensively. What he calls the "one flavor" of the *Dharmakāya* can be fully tasted in any one part. Adopting Fazang's systematic principle and taking the concept of *bodhicitta* (the thought of enlightenment) as the focal point of the study, this chapter attempts to show the "one flavor" of Fazang's Buddhist thought through the innovative treatment he gives to this traditional Indian Buddhist concept of the beginning of the quest for enlightenment.

The Thought of Enlightenment

The concept of *bodhicitta* comes up frequently in Fazang's voluminous writings. That, however, would not make it exceptional since, like Vasubandhu, his Indian Buddhist model, Fazang works with the full historical repertoire of Buddhist concepts. And although *bodhicitta* warrants an entire text named in its honor—*The Huayan Bodhicitta Treatise*—one would still be overstating the case to claim that this is a central concept for Fazang. Nevertheless, as promised by Fazang, no matter which part, even down to a speck of dust in the entire universe, the character of the whole can be seen clearly in this *bodhicitta* component.

There is no question but that the most important claim that Fazang makes about *bodhicitta* is that in the moment when the first thought or aspiration to *bodhi* or awakening arises, complete and perfect enlightenment has already been attained. For example, Fazang writes: "In practicing the virtues, when one is perfected, all are perfected . . . and when one first arouses the 'thought of enlightenment' one also becomes perfectly enlightened."[3] This claim is unusual, of course, and counterintuitive because it overturns our expectations about all attainments of excellence—that they come after long and hard work, certainly not in the first serious thought or aspiration. So on what basis has Fazang made this claim about *bodhicitta*, and what does it mean?

Perhaps the best way to understand Fazang's point here is to resort back to his conceptual model of the house mentioned earlier. *Bodhicitta* would, in this analysis, belong to the entire quest for enlightenment as one of its many essential parts. Unless we have an idea of enlightenment and come to consider it worth our aspiration and pursuit, we will be very unlikely to ever attain it. The relevant claim for Fazang is that all parts are identical in that they are all both *empty* (i.e., empty of its own self-nature because dependent on something else) and serve as conditions for the whole being what it is. A rafter, Fazang tells us, is like any part of the house in that (a) it becomes a rafter only in relation to other parts of the house and to the house as a whole and (b) without it, the house could not be what it is. This fact entails several further claims relevant to our concern for *bodhicitta*: that, as an essential condition for the house, the rafter possesses the power to "create" the entire house in the sense of making it exactly what it is and that therefore the one rafter stands in a relation of identity to the house as a whole.

Rather than examine Fazang's logic on these points, let us consider their extension to the concept of *bodhicitta*. The "thought of enlightenment" is indeed a condition of possibility for the enlightenment quest. Without this initial step, without an idea of what one is after and an earnest intention to seek it, there clearly would be no such outcome. But in what sense would the reverse be true? How would the first thought of enlightenment depend on its eventual attainment? How can something occurring now depend on something not yet in existence? The answer is that the former can depend on the later only *when* the later has come into being. *When* it has come into being, then both depend on each other to be exactly what they are in the specific sense that they are defined in relation to each other.

The temporal element in this sentence indicated by the word "when" is the key to Fazang's understanding of *bodhicitta*. Notice that the model of the house, and virtually all of Fazang's conceptual models, are static in structure; that is, time is not a component or a variable in the model. Fazang has us examine the house and its components from the perspective of its completion, not in the stages of its construction. This is an important factor in understanding Huayan metaphysics. Fazang responds to every narrative sequence such as the stages leading up to enlightenment by asking how it would appear from the perspective of the end of time. A piece of lumber becomes a rafter only when it is a part of a completed house; the part is made a part by the subsequently completed whole. Analogously, enlightenment is fully present in the initial thought of enlightenment but only from the perspective of the completion of the journey.

The understanding of temporality that sets the stage for Fazang's *bodhicitta* doctrine is based on his understanding of the "emptiness of time," to which we now turn. Fazang lays the dimensions of time out in the same way that he does the parts of a house. Like the parts of any whole, a segment of time, for Fazang, depends on all others, shapes all others, and, through their complex interpenetration, contains the whole of time within it. Therefore, he writes: "Because an instant has no essence, it penetrates the eternal, and because the lengthy epochs have no essence, they are fully contained in a single instant. ... Therefore, in an instant of thought all elements of the three periods of time—past, present, and future—are fully revealed."[4] Taking the perspective of the end of time, Fazang can operate the principle of "dependent arising" both forward and backward in time. Not only is the end dependent on the beginning, but the beginning is dependent on the end. Both beginning and end mutually define and contain each other. It is not just that the outcome of enlightenment depends on an initial thought of enlightenment but also that the first moment of *bodhicitta* depends on the completion of the quest. Therefore, from this Huayan point of view, because perfect enlightenment is a cause or condition for the initial thought of enlightenment, that cause or condition is contained within it.

One reason the logic of these arguments is frustrating is that Fazang does not distinguish between the various senses of dependency. Wherever dependence, or any form of relation, is present Fazang evokes all the linguistic and logical traditions of emptiness and moves the argument forward from there. We can see the insightfulness in recognizing that something earlier really does depend on something later: for example, the meaning of the assassination of Archduke Ferdinand is overwhelmingly determined by the fact that it led to a world war, just as the answer to "Who was the Buddha?" is determined less by what happened in Northeast India in the fifth century BCE than by what happened all over Asia in the centuries to follow. But it seems crucial for us to recognize that the nature of this dependence is fundamentally different from the dependence of linear causation.

The foundation of the house is a condition for the rafter in a sense that the rafter is not a condition for the foundation. Whereas we cannot have a rafter without a foundation to hold it up, we can have a foundation without a rafter, as in the case of a house that is framed but not yet roofed, or a house that never gets finished, or a house whose carpenter decides on a rafterless roof. Moreover, the hammer, the lumber, the architectural plans, the carpenter, and the farm that grows food for these agents are all conditions for the rafter but each in different senses. So to declare them identical by virtue of their mutual dependence depends on two related moves: first on conflating the various senses of dependency and second on understanding all components and all possible conditions as simultaneously present, that is, taking the perspective of final completion or the end of time.

So whereas in its traditional meaning *bodhicitta* entails a Buddhist theory of *marga*, the complexities of a gradual, sequential path toward enlightenment, Fazang accepts that common-sense meaning and then moves far beyond it. The thought of enlightenment is extended to symbolize, in the trope of irony, the sudden total presence of the completion of enlightenment even though in its initial point of departure. Precisely because the earlier tradition had conceived of *bodhicitta* as the true beginning of the path to enlightenment, Fazang is able to use that concept to make a startling, counterintuitive claim about the presence of enlightenment within, thereby directing our attention away from linear stage theory toward a new understanding of what *bodhi* or enlightenment is.

The Evolution of Enlightenment

One way to imagine the history of Buddhist thought up to and through the career of Fazang is to consider it a constant, impressive unfolding and enlargement of the concept of enlightenment. With every passing century, "enlightenment" in its various linguistic forms received a substantial upgrade—new dimensions and further refinement added to the ideal over time. It is as though this history could be considered an application of something like Anselm's ontological argument to the concept of enlightenment.[5] A renowned medieval monk and archbishop, Anselm constructed a measure for thinking the concept of divinity by defining God as "that than which no greater could be thought." Applied to the history of Buddhist enlightenment and the historical unfolding of ever-new dimensions to that ideal, enlightenment seems to have functioned as that transcendent mode of being "than which no greater could be thought." Any new Buddhist who, standing on the shoulders of his or her predecessors, could conceive of enlightenment in some greater and more cogent way, would have in effect extended and transformed the ideal. Enlightenment would have been extended beyond its previous articulations, regardless of the inventors' efforts to attribute their innovations to a prior sutra or text.

Although it takes a long time for cultures to notice this development as an ongoing process, from our historical point of view, this is what cultural ideals are: they are the most compelling image or conception that can be imagined at any given point in time and are therefore continually pushed along by historical impermanence.

In India this development took an unusual form, or an unusually creative and exalted form, owing to the indigenous concept of rebirth. Idealizations in India did not need to conform to enlargements of human capacity imaginable in a single person's current lifetime. Indeed, they could be projected far ahead of the present life by thousands or tens of thousands of evolutionary lives. While from a Chinese point of view this elevation of temporal perspective had a negative effect on the practical applicability of Indian ideals, it did serve as a catalyst for their imaginative character and for the extension of metaphysical and ethical thinking into previously unencountered realms of reflection. This is certainly no place to attempt to trace the history of this development, but just imagine for a moment the movement of the concept of nirvana from a state of an individual's curtailed emotional suffering due to the conquest of desires and the emptying of self-interest to a state pictured, for example, in the *Gandhavyuha* portion of the *Avatamsaka* or *Huayan sūtra*, where the ideal now includes grand visions of enormously complex and interpenetrating realms, other world systems imagined in vivid depth and detail, compassionate concern for all sentient beings, even to the point of vowing to lead these virtually innumerable beings into this enlightened state of exaltation.

Or consider vast sections of the *Huayan sūtra* where important elements of the bodhisattva identity are explored—"The Ten Abodes," "The Ten Practices," "The Ten Dedications," "The Ten Concentrations," "The Ten Stages," and so on. Although these lists of ten each contain practices and attainments that we can imagine in some sense, almost none of them are imaginable as accomplishments of an actual human being. The point of the sutra is to elevate vision to the very limits of conceivability but not to offer practical advice about how to get there for those of us in a human state of existence. The chapter on the ten stages, for example, begins stage one at a level that no human being has even come close to attaining, a level of transcendence that inspires the reach of imagination rather than offering concrete advice or instruction on how we human beings might come to transcend our state. This monumental transformation in goal occurred in just over a half a millennium of Buddhist history!

When, in the seventh century, Fazang was in position to survey this magnificent ideal of enlightenment, the distance that must have been felt between any existing practitioner, no matter how advanced in Buddhist practice, and the way the goal was then conceptualized must have been overwhelming. Fazang, therefore, faced a daunting challenge as a Buddhist philosopher, especially in the highly creative atmosphere of the early Tang dynasty. In order to gather the Buddhist tradition together into its most exalted form, he had to ask himself what Anselm asked: What is the conception of enlightenment "than which no greater could be thought"? Here is Fazang's answer in a nutshell: enlightenment includes every admirable attribute of human awakening, no matter how transcendent, that had accumulated in the Buddhist tradition up to that point, *and* all of this is realizable right now, in this moment of this life, not thousands of lifetimes from now. Here is where we can see most clearly Fazang's motive for handling the *bodhicitta* teaching as he did. The serious thought of and aspiration for enlightenment is not simply a first step on an arduous path whose terminus we should not expect to glimpse for eons. Instead, Fazang's *bodhicitta* is a moment of liberating insight in which the end, and all the future leading up to it, is fully revealed.

Buddhist Philosophical Foundations

Of the many Buddhist ideas that Fazang drew up into his new system of Buddhist thought, three are especially germane to understanding how *bodhicitta* comes to receive the treatment that it does. First, Fazang is well known for the eagerness with which he received the teaching of *tathāgatagarbha*, the Indian and central Asian concept of the "womb of the Buddha," or the embryo of enlightenment resident within all sentient beings. Although this innate womb of enlightenment might be thought not to fit convincingly with Fazang's focus on emptiness, he nevertheless finds in this conception a perfect image to assist in bringing enlightenment nearer to the practitioner. Different texts, of course, stake out different conceptions of this teaching, based on different metaphors and different visual images. They cover a range from an image of enlightenment as an innate seed that would, if properly cultivated, eventuate in a fully mature, awakened bodhisattva, to an image of enlightenment not in the form of potential but rather in a state of full accomplishment.

Positioned as he was in Chinese Buddhist history, Fazang leans toward the latter of these images, where enlightenment is the diamond discovered when the dust that obscures it is wiped away; it is eternally the same, does not need to grow and mature, and is radiantly present the moment even a section of it comes to light. At this point it is easy to see why Fazang's way of classifying all of the Buddhist teachings in a hierarchy according to level of enlightenment that they express places the doctrine and texts of *tathāgatagarbha* on top of those articulating other Mahayana themes like emptiness and "consciousness only." Assuming, as Fazang did, the applicability of emptiness to all things and the primary role of consciousness in the construction of human experience, he is simply more interested at that historical moment in how it is that all these exalted realizations can be expected to come to fruition in the life of an actual here-and-now human being. They do so, he came to conclude, because all of these elements of enlightenment constitute the innate structure of the "Buddha within" and come to fruition in the natural unfolding of this depth structure.

This is also why Fazang takes an interest in the early Buddhist idea of "irreversibility," the idea that at some point along the path the journey's completion is assured. Characteristically, Fazang placed this moment shockingly early in the process, earlier than Abhidharma masters might have thought useful for the purposes of incentive to practice. For Fazang, *bodhicitta*, the incipient thought of enlightenment, is the moment when the *tathāgatagarbha*, the Buddha nature, shows itself, the moment when the diamond first comes to light and from which point on there is certainty of irreversible destiny.[6] *Bodhicitta* therefore arises dependent on nothing but the inner inevitable motion of the Buddha within all things.

The second of three factors that would have helped Fazang shape the concept of *bodhicitta* as he did was the increasingly prevalent tendency in Chinese Buddhism to redescribe the enlightenment experience as a sudden breakthrough rather than as a slow, gradual transformation through practice. Since the sudden/gradual debate and its later development in the Chan school are so well known, we do not dwell on it here except to show how Fazang weighs in on the issue and how it affects his placement of the thought of enlightenment. Suffice it to say that although Fazang's doctrine of sudden awakening was not and could not have been as well developed conceptually and practically as it came to be several generations later with Huayan masters like Guifeng Zongmi, or with the emergence in the eighth and ninth centuries of the Chan school, it is nevertheless essential to the way Fazang conceives the character of enlightenment. But as an early instance of this later spiritual theme, the forms of philosophical reasoning behind it are evident in a way that they are not later in the Chan tradition where this background is simply presupposed.

Words denoting an abrupt and sudden experiential transformation can be found throughout Fazang's treatises. And, beyond his Chinese predecessors, there was ample precedent in the Indian and central Asian Buddhist tradition for the expectation of sudden awakening. No doubt foremost among Fazang's inspirations would have been segments in the *Avatamsaka sūtra*, the final *Gandavyuha* chapter in particular, where sudden insight typified the experience of the *bodhisatta* Sudhana in his journey through increasingly profound levels of realization. In classifying and ranking all Buddhist teachings, Fazang would reserve the second-highest level for those articulating doctrines of sudden breakthrough.

The third and last conceptual factor that set the stage for Fazang's treatment of *bodhicitta* is the dichotomy that began to develop in Fazang, and came to fruition in later Hua-yen and Chan, between *yuanqi* or "dependent arising" and *xingqi* or "nature arising." While Fazang's historical reputation as a philosopher of dependent arising is well deserved given the ubiquity and sophistication of dependent arising in his writings, the ultimate trajectory of Fazang's thought is away from the gradualism implied in linear dependency and toward the nonlinear abruptness of his concept of Buddha nature. The Chinese character *xing* or "nature" is as central and as important a concept as we can find in the history of Chinese thought from Mencius' propositions about human nature to the early and fateful translation of the Sanskrit *svabhāva* into *zixing*, or "self-nature," and beyond. Fazang's treatment of the concept *xing* is merely a part in a much larger cultural whole. While Fazang would continue throughout his career to teach the emptiness of self-nature, he would simultaneously elevate the overarching vision of emptiness as the "true nature" wherein *xing* would attain identification with concepts of *Tathāgata, Dharmakāya*, and other symbols of non-empty ultimacy.

Therefore, we see in Fazang an important reversal of images. Dependent arising had encouraged Buddhist practitioners in the earlier tradition to visualize Buddhahood as the end product of an extended series of linear transformations. What Fazang had begun to imagine, from the nonlinear perspective of temporal interpenetration, was the explosive power within that drives this process from the outset. In this view *bodhicitta* is the "Buddha nature" making itself known in the form of inevitability and irreversibility, something pushing out from within rather than something eventually coming into actuality through causation. Rather than a result of mature practice and cultivation, Buddhahood is its cause, the ultimate source from which all realities have emerged. The Daoist images that came to be so potent in later Chan discourse were already functioning in the philosophical writings of Fazang.

While later Hua-yen and Chan thinkers would set dependent arising and nature arising in contrast to each other, Fazang did not do so both because in his time the impetus to metaphysical doctrines of suddenness was not as severe as it would be later and because his interest was in the "non-obstruction" between these two Buddhist conceptions. Nature arising, for Fazang, could encompass dependent arising without obstructing it. While all individual things arise dependent on others, from a more lofty perspective, this whole process of impermanent coming to be and passing away is the arising of just one thing—Buddha nature.[7] Therefore, he writes: "All arisings are simply the arising of the *Tathāgata*."[8] "There is nothing that does not arise from the *dharmakāya* and there is nothing that does not return to and become enlightened in the *dharmakāya*."[9]

Practice and Enlightenment

For Fazang these two apparently contradictory processes—dependent arising and nature arising—are simultaneously true and non-obstructing because they operate at very different levels of intelligibility and can be experienced from different points of view. "When the *dharmakaya* circulates in the five destinies," writes Fazang, "it is experienced as sentient beings. When sentient beings are seen, the *dharmakāya* does not appear."[10] The world of dependent arising, in all its everyday complexity, is for Fazang set within another all-encompassing narrative that gives the story a moral. This narrative—nature arising, the seed of awakening, *tathāgatagarbha*— explains how the endless movement of complex, dependent particulars is all directed to the end of global insight, full and complete enlightenment. It is the story of the Buddha's own continual circulation through ignorance and enlightenment. For Fazang, however, both levels of insight appear simultaneously, and their simultaneity, as we have seen, is predicated upon the extent to which he can picture himself both in time and standing outside of it. It is only on this basis that *bodhicitta* can be both an initial stage on the path to enlightenment and its complete and final accomplishment. Asserting non-obstruction between them, he writes: "The stages are not disturbed, yet they are mutually identified. Identity is not disturbed, yet there always remains a sequence. Therefore these two concepts are mutually inclusive and non-obstructing."[11]

Therefore, if we ask Fazang: "Does enlightenment arise dependent on the particularities of Buddhist practice?," we get a complex answer. Yes, says Fazang, from one point of view insight is based on practice, and from the moment of *bodhicitta* on the practitioner moves steadily through a sequence of dependent stages toward an ultimate end. On the other hand, Fazang and much of the East Asian tradition after him were inclined to answer the question in the negative: no, enlightenment does not arise dependent on practice since practice is simply the unfolding and out-pouring of preexistent enlightenment. Moreover, these two truths do not obstruct one another. It is not that dependent arising and nature arising constitute separate or dual realities; it is rather that one reality and one view encompasses the other.

From Fazang's perspective, both the "small vehicle" view of *bodhicitta* as the beginning of a linear journey and the "great vehicle" view of *bodhicitta* as a complete and final experience of enlightenment are simultaneously true, the latter encompassing and upstaging the former. However, when Fazang says that "there is no contradiction between simultaneity and sequence,"[12] it is important to recognize that the point of view from which he can say that can only be higher order simultaneity, the perspective from which past, present, and future are completely present. It is the character and status of this atemporal perspective that makes Fazang's *bodhicitta* doctrine, and his thought as a whole, both spiritually powerful, and for us at this point in time, philosophically perplexing.

Among the many reasons Chinese Huayan philosophy was so compelling throughout the subsequent history of Buddhism in East Asia was the capacity of Fazang and other Huayan masters to draw deep inspiration from Chinese Daoist sources while simultaneously showing complex mastery of the subtleties of the Indian tradition that had become so readily available in that era. The character of Buddhist enlightenment could be both indescribably exalted beyond all human capacity—as the *Avatamsaka* or *Huayan sūtra* imagined it—and fully present even in the very first thought of enlightenment. That sudden enlightenment emerged from these juxtapositions of ideas and experiences as the most Chinese of all teachings should not be surprising given the lineage of cultural development that gave rise to it.

Throughout the subsequent intellectual/experiential history of Buddhism, we can witness a pendulum swing back and forth between two poles—one emphasizing the importance of the discipline of gradual practice and another emphasizing ecstatic, sudden breakthrough. We can easily see one such swing of emphasis even in the short history of Western Buddhism. Although it was the sudden, ecstatic emphasis of Japanese Rinzai Zen that initially captured the imaginations of early Buddhist enthusiasts in the West from Beat Zen to early Zen publications, by the late 1970s the opposite emphasis was clearly emerging and today dominates Western Buddhism—interest in the discipline of seated meditation, the introduction of Tibetan forms of Buddhism, Southeast Asian Vipassana "insight" meditation, and mindfulness training that presents Buddhist techniques in a way that can be practiced in and applicable to all areas of ordinary life. And now, after the turn of the millennium, neuroscience has taught us how to conceive of the gradual path in terms of "experience-dependent neuroplasticity," the gradual transformation of the brain through intentional sculpting of the experiences available to it.[13] All of these historical developments currently help provide us with reasons to prefer the "gradual" side of Buddhist thought and practice.

It is highly unlikely, however, that we have seen the end of this story, since the freedom of disciplined choice in gradual practice is always susceptible to being upstaged by the greater freedom of ecstatic abandon. Perhaps this reemergence of interest in sudden awakening will occur in China where the fascination with capitalism will at some point run its course and deep Daoist intuitions will once again surge forth. But as the great Huayan philosopher Fazang has taught us, both history and the ultimate ground of history are simultaneously present, even if in our finitude we can only be enthralled by one of these at a time.

Conclusion

TEN THESES ON CONTEMPORARY ENLIGHTENMENT

Thesis One: That neither Buddhist philosophy nor contemporary standards of thinking would justify Buddhists today continuing to assume, as many traditional Buddhists have, that enlightenment is a preexistent human ideal that is fixed and unchanging for all human beings in all times. Even though Buddhism was founded on the profound realization that all things are impermanent and interdependent, faith in a fixed and independent human nature and corresponding to that nature an unchanging enlightened ideal for life have been maintained throughout much of the Buddhist tradition. We can certainly understand and admire the extent to which the tradition took the image of the Buddha's enlightenment as the standard against which all others would be measured and on which all forms of human excellence would be modeled. But that timeless conception of enlightenment can no longer be underwritten for us either by traditional Buddhist narratives or by a static conception of human nature. As human practices, capacities, needs, and interests change, so will the images of human excellence that we come to admire and pursue in our lives.

The greater the insights that contemporary Buddhists have on this matter, the less the tradition will feel inclined to suppress variation and innovation and the more open and flexible Buddhist teachings and practices can become. Although all of us readily divinize and eternalize aspects of our own heritage—in spite of unrelenting impermanence—the unfortunate effects of this instinct can be seen throughout human history. In this light, even something as brilliant as the Buddhist quest for enlightenment can take on an oppressive character when the contextually specific views and cultural practices of one era are passed down as requirements and obligations for descendants. There are traditions that we choose to continue for good reasons and those that we continue even when what were once good reasons have altered or expired.

Although insight into the open, impermanent, and historical character of enlightenment may be experienced as unsettling and destabilizing, it is important to recognize its liberating effect. The emergence of new possibilities for human life and of previously unimaginable forms of human insight energize and motivate human beings now just as they have in the past. Although largely hidden from view by static assumptions about enlightenment, the history of Buddhism is a history of lineages of successive insights and a history of the unfolding of new possibilities for what true excellence in human life might entail.

There have been moments in Buddhist history when the open and diverse character of enlightenment was acknowledged and appreciated. The Zen claim, for example, that to measure up to the spiritual depth of the master a student of Zen would need to "go beyond" the teacher's enlightenment is one such recognition of the variability and particularity of enlightenment. Each emerging Zen master would achieve a form of enlightenment that would be unprecedented and unique in some way. With this image of enlightened variability in mind, we can learn to see the different traditions of Buddhism as vital lineages of innovation and renewal. Although traditions are authentic bases of coherence and unity, they are also internal debates, in-house arguments and contestations through which new and more refined forms of human culture and experience are brought into being. In every healthy tradition, these debates will on occasion yield significant change, change that in effect reformulates the understanding, the practice, and the experience of enlightenment.

Thesis Two: That attunement to the language in which we understand and practice Buddhism helps deepen and bring to maturity our encounter with this tradition and that meditation on the European word "enlightenment" is one important point of departure for this attunement. The metaphor of enlightenment has long been the central symbol of our Western engagement with Buddhist ideals. Although "enlightenment" was never an important name for the highest ideal in earlier Buddhist languages, it certainly is now, due to its invention in nineteenth-century Europe and subsequent dissemination throughout the world.[1] When the word "enlightenment" was injected into Buddhist vocabulary in the 1850s, it was not as a translation of Asian language into Western language so much as it was the result of a search for a word in European vocabularies that carried the cultural profundity and weight necessary to represent the central concern of Buddhism. Although this may be sufficient reason now for academic historians to reject the word "enlightenment" in reference to premodern Asian Buddhism, that reasoning does not hold for other current purposes. Contemporary global Buddhists should focus their primary attention not on accurate representation of an "original" Buddhism but rather on extensions of the tradition that have the potential to deepen our encounter with life and the primary challenges of our time.

When we ask ourselves why the word "enlightenment" was chosen for this exalted purpose, we need look no further than the life of Max Müller, who appears to be the inventor of this now longstanding cultural and linguistic custom. The life of F. Max Müller (1823–1900) exemplifies the spirit of the Age of Enlightenment in its later stages as it carries over into the Age of Romanticism. Born into a culturally prominent Eastern German family whose network of friends included the Mendelssohns, the Webers, and Goethe, Müller was immersed in the cosmopolitan spirit of nineteenth-century Germany. His career would take him to the center of German culture in Berlin where he would begin cultivating his passion for Indian philosophy along with his teacher, F.W.J. Schelling, and then beyond Berlin to Paris, London, and finally to Oxford where he spent most of his career teaching and writing in English. By the middle of the nineteenth century, the advantage of residing in England for anyone studying the religion and culture of the East was—to put it indelicately—that the British were more successful imperialists and therefore had greater, more direct access to the materials of Asian cultures both past and present. Ships from India and China arrived almost weekly into the leading ports of England bearing not just fashionable silks and porcelains but also artifacts, ideas, and texts. Although important scholarship about what was then called "the Orient" did appear in other European languages, especially German and French, anyone hoping to keep up with the new translations and commentaries had to maintain the practice of reading in English.

Müller's education was grounded in German philosophy, especially Immanuel Kant, the paradigm of enlightenment thinking, whose influence helped Müller formulate his own critical assessment of world religion and mythology. Although Müller was the English translator of Kant's *Critique of Pure Reason*—the text that more than any other defines modernity and the Enlightenment era—most of Müller's own work was post-Kantian in its emphasis on history and the necessity of world historical reflection to understand human life. His writings on comparative mythology and linguistics are extensive, culminating in the massive *Sacred Books of the East* in forty-nine volumes, which offered translations into English of the primary sacred texts of China, India, Persia, and the Arabic/Islamic world. One of Müller's primary intellectual claims was that human language was the key to understanding the origins of humanity and the early emergence of religion in human culture. Müller had a longstanding friendship and debate with Charles Darwin and maintained ongoing conversation and correspondence with him on the question of linguistic evolution and its role in the human species. That the word "enlightenment" would come to Müller's mind in contemplating the dominant religion of Asia is not at all surprising given this historical background.

Müller's choice of the word "enlightenment" to name the point of the Buddhist tradition could not have been more auspicious. On the one hand, enlightenment carried with it enormous prestige, the prestige that accompanied the thinking behind science and technology, democratic political reform, and the emerging market economies. On the other hand, it tended to associate Buddhism with forms of culture in the West that were not tied to the religious establishment. That meant that the cultural avant-garde, the romantics in the second half of the nineteenth century, could not help but take an interest in Buddhism, and the list of European luminaries who engaged in sustained inquiry into Buddhist enlightenment is astonishing—Nietzsche, Schopenhauer, Weber, Wagner, to just begin the list of Germans, all the way to Anglo-American counterparts like Emerson and Thoreau.

By the time Sir Edwin Arnold published *The Light of Asia*, an enormously influential 1887 book on Buddhism, the direction of interpretations of Buddhism had already turned a decisive corner. By then, Arnold could refer to the Buddha's "enlightenment" without hesitation, assuming quite freely that the Europeans who were willing to think and to experiment cross-culturally would know what to make of the connection between enlightenment and this newly discovered Asian religion. Today, more than a century and a half beyond the initial association of Buddhism with enlightenment, the link between these two is so strong that in popular discourse the Buddhist meaning, taken in a broad sense, is what the word "enlightenment" means. It would appear that in at least this one instance a reversal of imperialism has occurred through which Buddhist meanings have occupied an important Western concept.

Although still the most widely used term for the goal of Buddhism, in recent writing "enlightenment" is sometimes replaced by another, quite similar metaphor: "awakening," a far better translation of the Sanskrit, *bodhi*. These similarities can be seen in the metaphoric relation between "the dawning of light" and "waking up," both of which enable clarity of vision. But whereas "enlightenment" carries heavy overtones of modern science and politics, "awakening" has a different set of resonances, some to modern psychology and others to the evangelical emotions of the Great Awakening in American religious history. Both metaphors have extensive references in Western culture, and these undercurrents have now been absorbed into the emerging tradition of global Buddhism. That we now say the word "enlightenment" with some degree of tongue-in-cheek irony is also significant, perhaps mirroring the critical irony in which radical Zen Buddhists held their most important words. Attunement to the evolving language in which we understand and practice Buddhism and its effects on us should become increasingly important in contemporary Buddhism.

Thesis Three: That the most admirable and effective conceptions of enlightenment in contemporary Buddhism will avoid the subtle temptations of transcendent otherworldliness to which traditional forms of Buddhism sometimes succumbed. Otherworldliness here includes all interpretations of enlightenment as omniscient certainty—a comprehensive experience of things as they really are apart from any shaping influence of the finite perspectives we have on them. In these images, the enlightened no longer face ambiguity and uncertainty, since the finite conditions of human life have been altogether transcended. Many traditional accounts of enlightenment in Buddhism picture imperturbable saints who are immune to disruptions, who are no longer subject to the instabilities of change, contradiction, and human perplexity. Although we have become accustomed to these traditional religious images, if we attend to them mindfully, they pose important questions to us: Are these transcendent representations of enlightenment helpful as ideals for actual human beings engaged in transformative practice, or do they instead elevate the "enlightened" so far above our lives that we can no longer recognize ourselves in their light?

Moreover, can otherworldly images of excellence be reconciled with some of the human values that we admire most—for example, the human emotional vulnerability of compassion and profound love; experiences joy and laughter; practical concern for the welfare of others; the creativity, ingenuity, and boundless energy that seeks to accomplish something significant in life and that maintains purpose and thoughtful intention? Or do some of these images of transcendent equanimity preclude the values and ideals that we cannot avoid admiring and seeking in our own lives?

Does acknowledging and accepting the Buddhist teachings of impermanence and contingency mean that even the most enlightened lives face ambiguity, uncertainty, risk, need, and many other human forms of limitation? If so, then we acknowledge that transhuman and superhuman images of enlightenment in Buddhism and elsewhere are in some very basic sense "inhuman." They are images of divine power that are simply not applicable to us as effective models for practical aspiration in our lives. They orient us to awe and worship rather than to the disciplined work on our communities and ourselves that constitutes both our current responsibility and our most important image of human achievement.

Disillusioned by transcendental and magical accounts of enlightenment, we would be profoundly mistaken to respond by surrendering the quest for enlightenment altogether rather than opening our minds to explore what enlightenment might mean in our time. If unmediated omniscience and transcendental equanimity are inappropriate for us as images of human excellence, then what directions for human aspiration remain—quests for more mature contact with the world, for more open, comprehensive vision, for more inclusive, insightful, and imaginative dealings with the world, with greater levels of care and compassion in more and more expansive communities? Part of our task in picturing contemporary versions of enlightenment will thus entail recognizing the extent to which ancient, medieval, monastic images of greatness may no longer provide the most helpful orientation for our lives of practice and engagement.

Aspects of the initial critical task can be gleaned from Nietzsche's critiques of Christian otherworldliness. His often overblown tirades about the degradation of Western culture include the valuable insight that our traditional values have been steeped in a devaluation of *this* world in preference for an imagined world of purity that transcends our own. The consequence of this devaluation is that we implicitly condemn finite human life and imagine instead a life that transcends the inevitably frustrating limitations of our bodies, intentions, and purposes. In its most detrimental form, this "ascetic ideal," as Nietzsche calls it, can become a form of living death, a life that rejects everything that makes us human in deferral to a realm beyond this one and a future far beyond the present.

Although Nietzsche could not carry it through without resentment, he recognized something else that we should strive to embody in our own culture of enlightenment: that simply denouncing the ascetic and otherworldly ideals of classical and medieval religion misses an essential point—that their teachings and practices established the foundations that have made our current images of enlightenment and our critical moves beyond medieval culture possible. The values that Buddhism and Christianity introduced were in sharp conflict with the warrior values that had previously dominated humanity everywhere, the values extolled in the *Iliad*, the *Mahabharata*, and elsewhere. The Buddhist and Christian claim was that a penitent, self-effacing, meditative life transcended lives of conquest, violence, and acquisition. Lives of contemplative prayer, medita- tion, philosophy, and the arts began to make previous warrior images of greatness look childish and immature. As a result, whole new, previously unimaginable cultural possibilities were opened. We still accept these claims and receive the historical benefit of their insights, even if we can now recognize that the withdrawal of the sages into inner contemplative spaces and their implicit rejection of life in this world often went too far.

If early monastic asceticism went too far in throwing the baby of engaged, worldly living out with the bathwater of conquest and violence, the task for us is to think clearly about all of the options that lie between these extremes. Between Homer's heroic warriors and the Christian saints of the desert, or between the battle-loving heroes of the *Mahabharata* and Arjuna's final renunciation of everything, are many possibilities that we can now explore. Those of us who are tempted to conclude that Mahayana Buddhism managed just such a renunciation of total renunciation should recognize the extent to which neither the classic texts nor the Buddhists who were inspired by them followed through on this momentous insight. Although concern for others and for the world in which we live were sanc- tified in principle, these concerns were rarely developed beyond the initial insight that they ought to be important for bodhisattvas who dedicate their lives to compassionate involvement in the world. We see very few images of lives embodying this abstract concern in practice; few proposals for institutions or sociopolitical orders that really do care for the poor, under- privileged, and those who are suffering; and very little evidence that the emphasis on individualized spiritual greatness was diminished. Although Mahayana images of nirvana were crafted to discourage thinking of the ultimate goal as the extinction of finite life, for the most part Mahayana monks continued to practice as though it was.

If we are honest with ourselves, however, we will acknowledge that there are similar temptations of transcendence that continue to affect our lives whether we are "religious" in any traditional sense or not. These are individual daydream narratives that we actively entertain on a regular basis. In our typical patterns of daydreaming, we imagine our own lives under conditions in which we lack nothing and in which our awkward uncertainty is gone. We daydream ourselves into situations where we always know precisely what to say and do, where our brilliance, charm, and resources are unlimited. Indeed, most of us spend some part of every day imagining ourselves living our lives without some of the constraints of human finitude. For this very important reason, it would be dishonest and arrogant of us to boast that our own Buddhism or our lives are beyond traditional escapism and otherworldliness. They are not. But that does not mean that we cannot or should not recognize the escapist tendencies that we too practice and begin to contemplate our way out from under their negative, life-denying impact.

Thesis Four: That enlightenment in our time will become more communal, collective, and intersubjectively shared than in any earlier epoch. This point may seem entirely counterintuitive given the strength of modern individualism in contrast to the strong communal sensibilities of earlier traditions. Reasons for asserting it and evidence in support of it are plentiful, however. The extraordinarily high level of global awareness that we now share with others all around the world, the undeniable economic and political interconnectedness that we all feel, the recent realization that we all share one planet and that the human-created ecological disaster we will all face together are unprecedented developments in human self-awareness. These realizations link us together more coherently than ever before possible in human history. The invention of socialism at the height of the emergence of modern individualism and capitalism, and the emergence from that invention of social democracies structured to make basic human services available to all citizens, is yet another sign of our growing collective awareness.

Perhaps even more important is the moral recognition common to many people today that our past traditions of exclusion and otherness are incompatible with a deeper sense of our shared humanity. Increasingly we find discrimination on the bases of class, caste, ethnicity, race, gender, sexuality, religion, and a growing number of other differences to be morally unacceptable in ways that it has never been in human history. And now that we recognize our shared ancestry in evolutionary terms, we can no longer avoid the conclusion that we are all in this together. All of these substantial historical developments make the additional factor of global connectivity through our communication technologies look like a mere afterthought.

When we look closely at what was occurring in the overall history of Indian religion at the time of the emergence of Buddhism, we discover the extraordinary degree to which earlier collective traditions of religion in India were becoming radically individualized. Following this breakthrough period of the *Upanisads* and early Buddhist *sutras*, Brahmanical/Hindu and Buddhist spiritualties became the most highly individualized on the planet. The doctrine of karma, which governs the important moral sphere of culture, left no doubt in anyone's mind that the drama of human life is ultimately individual. Each person's actions were understood to create karmic paths having an effect on that individual's subsequent life rather than on the family or larger community as had typically been true of earlier traditions there and elsewhere. Only faint hints of collective karma—the ancient and contemporary sense that the character of our society is shaped by our past communal acts—can be found in the entire history of Buddhism. In so individualized a spiritual tradition, the more ancient tribal and communal orientation had no significant foothold, even though it was clearly present in India in the early Vedas and pre-Vedic traditions, just as it was and continued to be in the other major Ur religion—Judaism.

Reinforcing this individualist understanding of human life was the prevalence of meditation as the most highly revered spiritual practice in the Indian and Buddhist cultural worlds. Since meditation is what we do in the privatized depths of our own minds, and since the karma that it generates or disposes is individually understood, an extraordinarily wide divergence between the spiritual standing of high-achieving sadhus and ordinary people naturally arose as a widespread cultural assumption. Even the traces of collective understanding that emerged in the early Mahayana concern for compassion and the deferral of nirvana could not reverse this overwhelming tendency to think of spiritual matters in strictly personal terms. The most exciting, most compelling religious and cultural developments at the time of the emergence of Buddhism were overwhelmingly individual in orientation, and their historic contribution to human cultural evolution cannot be overestimated. In fact, there are good reasons to suspect that this highly sophisticated individualism of Indian religion is precisely the reason that it appealed so strongly to modern Western converts. It fit perfectly with the individualized tendencies that already defined modernity in the West.

In consequence, and in some degree of irony, it may be that a greater sense of collectivity and community could be one contribution that contemporary Buddhists are in a good position to add to the evolution of

Buddhism. In the wake of important developments such as modern historical consciousness and evolutionary theory, we understand more than any early sage could the extent to which the achievement of enlightenment in one person is just as much the achievement of a family, a community, a society, and a particular history. We understand that greatness never appears in a vacuum and that human excellence is always cultivated in conjunction with others rather than in spite of them. Enlightenment in our time includes the sense that societies establish the conditions for individual achievement and that all possibilities for personal accomplishment are shaped in advance by historical and social forces. The individual self has been effectively decentered in the philosophy of our time, and this emerging understanding is already refashioning what we consider "enlightenment" to be.

The extent to which both individual self-creation and the cultivation of community are already woven into the fabric of contemporary Western Buddhism as interrelated tasks is abundantly clear in the interaction between thriving traditions of meditation and the widespread activism of Buddhists on issues of environmental and social justice. Personal fulfillment and communal responsibility in our time cannot be as clearly separated as they have been in past cultures. We understand how focusing exclusively on our own individual states of enlightenment in fact reduces the scope of who we are. A quest for self-actualization that ignores one's responsibility for the larger whole is seriously deficient. Focusing narrowly on the project of self-transformation robs us of a fundamental facet of enlightenment—the sympathies and openness that interpersonal connection and solidarity produce. Increasingly, our moment in cultural history encourages us to make a developmental move from seeking enlightenment as a personal benefit to seeking enlightenment as the shared maturation and flourishing of humanity.

All of these reasons press upon us the new requirement that we go beyond the modern individualistic understanding of ourselves and of human life. In this sense our task is to reincorporate the ancient sense of collectivity that we can still see in older communal religions, a reverence for what is larger and greater than ourselves but now enlarged far beyond the family and our own ethnic and religious group. As a consequence of these realizations, enlightenment will increasingly entail participation in collective work to create a global society of equal opportunity and shared responsibility.

One final point is important: that the community sensibility that we will cultivate in ourselves cannot be taken, as it was in traditional societies, to be in opposition to and in exclusion of individual uniqueness. Traditional communities, as we can see clearly in historical studies, required the suppression of individuality, an intentional, security-motivated demand for conformity. By contrast, enlightened collectivity will now need to incorporate the widest possible range of human diversity. This is our democratic vision of a global society that can encompass the radical pluralism of significantly different quests for enlightened self-creation without feeling the compulsive need to suppress otherness and difference. As Buddhist oppression of Hindus in Sri Lanka and Muslims in Myanmar shows, a wider tolerance for other conceptions of spiritual life and other human interests needs to be cultivated. This is our challenge, the emergence of an enlightenment that expands indefinitely to open the scope of what it means to be a human being and what it could mean among human beings to achieve some unique form of distinction or excellence.

Thesis Five: That contemporary Buddhists are in an excellent position to develop and extend the dimension of enlightenment that we experience as "freedom" in greater breadth and depth. There is a profound sense of freedom or liberation entailed in both traditional Buddhism and in the European Age of Enlightenment. But these are obviously not the same. Our word "freedom," for which there is no traditional Buddhist counterpart, encompasses a range of liberating meanings and effects. The most basic meaning of freedom available to us is what has come to be called "negative freedom," the liberty of individuals and communities to make choices and to act as they choose without unnecessary restraint. Freedom from constraint is deeply inscribed in modern political thinking and in the founding covenants of modern societies.

Almost nothing is said about this form of freedom in the massive canon of Buddhist texts. It would be a mistake, however, to conclude from this that negative freedom is not a legitimate Buddhist concern. Modern Buddhist communities all over the world have had to determine how to incorporate concern for democratic rights and liberties into their organizational structures, and this is an important work in progress. How to carry out the politics of local community is not the only issue, however. The larger question of how Buddhist teachings can best be brought into relation to global political concerns remains to be addressed, and if Buddhists are to make substantial contributions to the important contemporary issues of human suffering, global justice, environmental ethics, and more, then questions about freedom as political liberty will need to be addressed. On this issue Buddhists of all nationalities have already learned a great deal from non-Buddhist sources of wisdom.

The Buddhist contribution to the development of the meaning of freedom has taken us in an entirely different direction. Buddhist inclinations reorient the discussion significantly by addressing an even more fundamental concern than the issue of individual rights. This basic sense of freedom entails a recognition that what we have naively assumed to be our own free choices and behaviors are in truth controlled by habits, desires, emotions, opinions, and ideologies that we have neither chosen, nor even considered, but that nonetheless rule our lives.

This liberating dimension of enlightenment has been discovered in some form in other religious and cultural traditions at the point in history when introspective aspirants realized that they were not so much possessed by evil spirits as they were by their own deep-seated habits and desires. Although a great deal was made of this realization over two millennia ago at the origins of Buddhism, it is no less relevant for us today. Recovering it and extending it further is one of the most important tasks of our time. Enlightenment encompasses emancipation from previously unexamined compulsions that have shaped our lives and will continue to do so until the human innovations of self-knowledge, self-rule, and self-change begin to provide some degree of freedom. Enlightenment in this sense entails a transition, cultivated through intentional practice, from passively living our lives to actively leading them.

Enlightenment at this elemental level is grounded in the realization that for it to really be *your* life, you would need to engage in practices that assess your inner states and actively choose among the elements that shape your existence. By taking responsibility for the content of your mind and actions, you begin to take responsibility for your character—your particular way of being in the world. Moreover, new forms of freedom beyond these await our discovery and realization. To the extent that enlightenment liberates, contemporary Buddhists will be motivated to cultivate and to extend our understanding and experience of freedom.

Thesis Six: That practices of meditation constitute both the greatest traditional resource and the greatest future opportunity for contemporary Buddhism. Although contemplative practices like these are not unique to Buddhism among the world's spiritual traditions, nowhere else have they been developed to the height of sophistication that they have in the long history of Buddhism. It is now becoming clear that this contribution to world culture is extraordinarily valuable and that incorporating these practices into individual lives and communities yields profound life-enhancing effects. Recognizing this, it will be important for both Buddhists and non-Buddhists to realize that the primary question for us now is not what meditation was in the past but what it *could* be now and in the future as a cultural resource for the development of human consciousness.

What can we make of this profound inheritance of meditation, and how can it be extended and reshaped beyond traditional models so that it aligns with current global circumstances in order to do the most enlightening and transformative work possible today? To begin to answer that question, it is important to recognize the broad range of practices that already operate under the overall rubric of meditation. These range from contemplative practices that encourage us to withdraw consciousness temporarily from the world in order to develop deep focus and concentration to visualization practices that are broadly imaginative or meditation techniques that open our minds to aspects of the world and our own experience that we have never consciously encountered.

They also range from mindfulness practices that are fully unselfconscious, because they are entirely focused outwardly on what we encounter in the world, to alternative mindfulness practices that entail direct, introspective self-examination of the emotions and interpretations we bring to experience. Going further, meditation encompasses mental exercises that are philosophically sophisticated and that cultivate the powers of human thought while also including practices that curtail thinking altogether in order to prevent us from deluding ourselves or clouding our minds in the anxieties of mindless, compulsive thinking. In each case, however, no matter how different the orientation of practice, meditation aims to elevate and open consciousness, to lift us up out of our ordinary habits of mind. Through spiritual exercises that open new vision, enhance perception, deepen understanding, and stabilize emotion, we can raise the maturity level of our actions and lives in the world.

One area of contemplative practice that has an open and promising future in global Buddhism is the link between meditative practice and the articulation of an effective philosophy of life. The pursuit of philosophical insight in Buddhism was once regarded as an essential meditative practice, one that provides overall orientation and direction to other practices and to life as a whole. Because the exchange of ideas and counter-ideas, and open debate and argument are not always encouraged or permitted in more recent forms of Buddhism, this dimension of practice has not been as thoroughly cultivated as others.

The historical moment is excellent, however, to reinvigorate this dimension of Buddhist contemplative practice. There is an eagerness and a need for a concrete philosophy of life that is now being felt by many within global Buddhism and in other traditions. Modern Western philosophy has failed to provide these models for deliberative life practice as it became more technical, more academic, and further removed from the lives that people really do live. But that is now beginning to change. One sign of this, among a number of others, is the revival of interest in the various schools of Roman thought where philosophy was practiced as a form of transformative exercise. Pierre Hadot's suggestion that philosophy be practiced as a "way of life"[2] has reminded philosophers of the spiritual dimension of their discipline in which learning and wisdom are the goals, not the enclosure that we have come to call "knowing." As philosopher Martha Nussbaum reminds us, in skillful deliberation, "what counts is flexibility, responsiveness, and openness to the external; to rely on an algorithm here is not only insufficient, it is a sign of immaturity and weakness."[3] Although Buddhist philosophical practice has recently tended to be somewhat "algorithmic," now is an excellent time to reopen the important practices of reflection and contemplation that launched Buddhism in the first place.

Even more important for our times, however, are forms of Buddhist meditation that operate at a deeper level of consciousness and that function effectively to open us to a wider range of human experience. A mind distracted and unconcentrated will be ill prepared to think with clarity and maturity and unable to stay focused on what really matters. The wide range of meditation styles, all grounded in the cultivation of breathing, are enormously effective in diminishing the distortions deriving from self-absorption and lack of mental clarity. The deep concentration and poise of equanimity that arise from the steady practice of all nonreflective forms of meditation provide the foundations for life in all of its dimensions. There are human comportments or mental bearings that tend to yield insight and depth, and the cultivation of these enabling conditions occurs in meditation. If we can now imagine that meditation as we have inherited it is still in rudimentary stages of development, we will begin to sense its virtually unlimited potential for growth and expansion.

Thesis Seven: That contemporary Buddhists are in an excellent position to appropriate insights from neuroscience and learning theory concerning the role of habituation in the construction of our characters. These insights are becoming the theoretical cornerstone of "practice" in all of its various forms. The reason that Buddhists find themselves in this excellent position is that the realizations that are now coming to our attention by way of contemporary neuroscience were already implicitly understood and put into practice throughout the early disciplines of Buddhist meditation. Now what was once a brilliant assumption is rapidly becoming a set of scientifically explicated principles applicable to disciplines from athletics to educational theory and beyond. The central point is this: every action shapes the mind and body of the actor, and this effect compounds exponentially when patterns of action become engrained habit. We become what we do, think, feel, and experience, and this realization, once put into intentional practice, constitutes the basis of enlightened self-sculpting. As the understanding of experience-dependent neuroplasticity matures, our capacity to direct the gradual construction of our lives and societies will substantially deepen.[4]

This principle of psychophysical self-cultivation is universal. Every human being is engaged in practice if by "practice" we mean the performance of repetitious behaviors that have retroactive effects on the actors. Although we are all engaged in these exercises of training and habituation even when we are not at all aware that our acts have this dramatic effect, there is an enormous difference between implicit and explicit practice, that is, between involuntarily acquired habits and habits that result from a disciplined resolution to exert an influence on conditioning processes by means of consciously chosen patterns of action.

Meditation is, of course, the quintessential example of consciously chosen, explicit practice performed with the intention of shaping the mind in specific, enlightening ways. Physical training from yoga to athletics is an equally strong example of this same principle in its effects on the body. The romantic image of the spontaneous, amateur athlete or ingenious inventor who performs acts of brilliance quite naturally without prior training has been exposed as an exaggeration of the scope of natural, genetic gifts, if not simply a falsification that disguises the crucial role played by experience and practice.

Meditation uses the processes of mental habituation to negate the effects that unchosen habits have already inculcated by overlaying new and intentionally selected patterns of mindful behavior upon older unconstructive or destructive habits of mindlessness. The difference is the recognition that we can take control of this self-formative process and that we can acquire the disciplined will to actually carry that out. This entails a shift from passive to active practice, from finding ourselves under the control of unchosen compulsions to greater and greater degrees of autonomy.

Once this process is rendered visible and explicit, everyone from athlete to meditator understands how to begin taking an active role in the formation of his or her future.

It is worth recognizing that the difference between implicit and explicit practice is not just the freedom of choosing, the act of intention that is exerted in the latter case and not at all in the former. A further difference concerns the kinds of reasons for which an explicit exercise is chosen and carried out. Not all practices are chosen for good reasons, and as a consequence not all deliberate practices work similarly to the benefit of the practitioner. Ideally, practices are motivated in relation to a person's "thought of enlightenment" so that these higher ideals help shape our activities all the way down. Our personal answer to the question "What is enlightenment?" is thus not at all an abstract ideal that lacks effective power; it is a motivating force that helps determine the direction and extent of our self-sculpting practices.

This realization leads to the recognition that repetitive learning or habituation and intuitive spontaneity are neither mutually exclusive nor necessarily opposed to each other. Once a practice-cultivated second nature *has become* our nature, simplicity and naturalness return, but on new grounds. The famous spontaneity of Zen masters is a highly refined achievement resulting from years or decades of meditative self-sculpting in which mindfulness and openness replace former patterns of destructive reactivity. Highly cultivated Zen masters can respond spontaneously and without thinking in some areas of life when the disciplines of intentional practice have rendered their instinctual responses reliably wise and compassionate.

This is also what is at stake in the difference between sudden and gradual enlightenment in Zen. Gradual enlightenment is the overall pattern of growth and evolution through practice, and sudden enlightenment is an occasional glimpse into the depth dimension of our world and ourselves. Ecstatic moments of sudden breakthrough or insight are grounded in the gradual self-change of meditative practice. The deepening of mindfulness can enable unpredictable moments of sudden insight. But the obverse is important as well. The motivation to undertake a discipline of intentional self-transformation and carry it through derives from the inspiration of unexplained moments of enlarged vision and insight. When a genuinely transformative moment of insight occurs, the discipline of further effort is inspired and empowered. Gradual practice enables sudden insight, and moments of sudden insight motivate gradual practice.

Thesis Eight: That one very fruitful image of contemporary enlightenment is the expansion of horizons, an enlargement of "vision" in any and
every sphere of human life. In these terms, an experience of enlightenment is an expansion of the reach of consciousness, an event of enlarged
comprehension through which we see more or further than we could
before. An experience of this kind is liberating; it sets us free of some previous constriction or limitation and generates enlightening consequences
felt both immediately and from that point forward. Any dimension of
human life can be expanded or enlarged in this way. Among many possibilities, two examples that are pertinent to contemporary Buddhism are
the enlargement of responsibility and the expansion of possibility.

The scope of responsibility that human beings feel can differ widely
among people. Although adults tend to be held accountable for their
behavior, for providing for themselves and for fulfilling their basic
social obligations, not all people manage this. Beyond that minimal
level, many mature adults take responsibility for the safety, shelter, and
nourishment of their families, sometimes including their aging parents, occasionally adult siblings or other relatives. Among these responsible adults, those with even greater maturity also feel some degree of
responsibility for their places of work, their neighborhoods, and their
communities. As the boundaries of responsibility enlarge from the
individual to family to local community to larger and more expansive
spheres of society and world, the extent to which we might be tempted
to regard their views and actions as "enlightened" will grow. Breaking
through typical boundaries of self-enclosure, they reach further and
further out beyond themselves. Some may become global activists in
the international political order or take responsibility for just distribution of assistance in times of disaster. Some may take responsibility for
the environment, the well-being of all forms of life, and ultimately the
entire planet on which we live. While it feels natural to most of us to
take responsibility for ourselves or our families, we can see from examples of what we take to be enlightened human beings that a cultivated
sense of responsibility can extend far beyond these limitations.

The Mahayana Buddhist image of the compassionate bodhisattva is
just such an expansion in which selflessness is manifest not so much as
the absence of anything than as an enlargement of what human beings
are capable of including within their spheres of responsible concern. To
care as much about the well-being and the enlightenment of others as we
do about our own is to have expanded the normal boundaries of concern

to the point that much more is encompassed. For the ideal bodhisattva conceived in Mahayana sutras, this enlargement means that the ordinary distinction between self-concern and concern for others has dissolved in some significant way. Such a bodhisattva's conception of who he or she is, his or her purposes, priorities, and desires, has been rearranged through ongoing practices of enlargement. For this person, enlightenment, universally conceived, has become the primary object of desire, a human aspiration that has been expanded and enriched to become much more comprehensive in scope.

Enlightenment can also be imagined in terms of an expansion and enlargement of the range of possibility, either for an individual or for a community. Processes of cultural evolution that are always underway will open up possibilities for human beings in the future that are beyond what we can currently imagine. But even on an individual scale, we all experience moments in which a greater range of possibility dawns on us. We all experience minor or momentous insights that break through specific boundaries that were previously unrecognized as barriers. In that experience, the field of what seems possible expands.

Waking up to present possibilities can occur in various forms throughout life; when these events occur, they recreate who we are. Expanding boundaries, however, is an image of enlightenment that stands in tension with another valuable image, that of finding one's center or purifying one's life practice down to a single point of focus. Although they are opposites, these emphases are both fundamental to human life and important for Buddhist practice. A life of practice may alternate back and forth between these poles, at certain times opening up to expand horizons and at other times deepening focus and concentration. We dwell on the image of enlargement here. Its importance to Buddhism is substantial on both individual and communal scales because this image enables the adaptation of Buddhism to contemporary circumstances and prevents the ossification of traditions. Diversity and growth are positive, enlightening attributes that complement their opposites, unity and concentrated focus.

Thesis Nine: That in contrast to images of unemotional saints whose profound equanimity removes them from participation in ordinary human life, contemporary images of enlightenment will envision a full range of emotions remaining fundamental to life. An affective enlightenment practice would explore the deepest caverns and outer edges of felt experience. This point is important because lives lived without laughter, sadness, longing, and joy strike us as impoverished in some important way; they seem less than human at least as much as they strike us as beyond the human realm.

One fact about emotions, however, might seem to remove them from the sphere of discipline, practice, and attained freedom. Emotions are involuntary; we do not control them. They come upon us, enter our minds and hearts, and take possession of us. Perhaps that is one of the reasons that many images of enlightened greatness in Buddhism and elsewhere imagine a profoundly peaceful state beyond the disruptive reach of emotion—deep, unmoved equanimity. Although it is true that each instance of emotion just happens to us without our choosing it, emotions can be shaped in advance of their occurrence. Some forms of meditation are emotionally therapeutic in that they work to develop the conditions within us that will make enlightening emotional responses more readily available in response to predictable kinds of provocation. That is the function of "premeditation," a kind of emotional advanced planning in which we study our own inner emotional life, anticipate situations that may give rise to particular affects, and deliberately choose which emotional reactions might be cultivated in greater depth as our newly acquired second nature.

We do shape our emotions in relation to ongoing feedback from ourselves and others without necessarily being aware of it, because when emotional impulses are altogether unregulated, they lead to patterns of recurring suffering. Beyond the ordinary level of adult stability that most people manage to attain, however, are far deeper recesses of emotional life that can also be cultivated through meditative and contemplative practice, feelings of profound peace, joy, gratitude, and compassion. Those who follow this more advanced path become the agents of their emotional lives. They attain high levels of emotional intelligence, and their understanding and experience of the domain of feelings goes far beyond that of ordinary lives. Such an enlightenment of the "heart" has consequences as far reaching as the awakening of mind.

Because our normal social obligation is to curtail our passions and unruly emotions, many traditions of philosophy and religion extend that line of thinking about maturity by maintaining that to act in a virtuous and enlightened way is to act against inner inclination. These traditions imagine lives of greatness resulting from constant, diligent repression of unwanted inner urges. But this way of understanding the development of emotional intelligence assumes that the outcome of cultivated self-control is a kind of puritanical resistance to emotion, an enlightenment of grim determination and clenched teeth that has developed the strength to diminish the impact of emotions in life. Rather than characterize enlightenment as acting *against* inner inclinations, there are good reasons to pursue instead a life in which feelings have been shaped and deepened as a result of meditative development. An enlightened life of this kind doesn't feel one way while acting another way in resistance to feeling. Instead, emotions mature along with thinking and intention so that they arise in concurrence. An enlightened life in that affective sense has not suppressed emotion. On the contrary, it maintains and cultivates a full range of emotions—hope, fear, pride, shame, regret, excitement, boredom, contentment, frustration, and more—but does so in a way that demonstrates the development of deep emotional intelligence.

In opposition to images of enlightenment characterized by stern self-control, one element of enlightened brilliance worthy of our cultivation is the lightness of humor. Wherever disciplined seriousness undermines and renounces laughter, a rigid posture of willful self-importance prevails. While seriousness is essential to any admirable life, taking oneself too seriously is a form of self-deception that prevents open, gentle generosity. The humorless inability to relax and release an anxious grip is a painful form of self-enclosure. In laughter we experience an ecstatic loss of self-absorption, an opening of emotion-laden insight. Overtaken by laughter, our illusory sense of separation from others dissolves emotionally. Celebratory, humbling, and unifying, laughter opens a deep sense of belonging and ease that, even if momentary, has long-lasting effects.

Every aspect of our emotional lives includes similar complexities, extremes, and dangers. Pursuing emotional enlightenment, we learn both to enjoy and to suffer intelligently. The domain of human suffering is the most challenging test case. When we suffer wisely we release clenched fists and resentful opposition to what is and to what will be regardless of our efforts and desires. Allowing suffering to have its inevitable place in our life just like all other lives, it is possible to feel undertones of serenity in the midst of anguish and pain. Is it also possible to experience a trace of joy even in suffering? I think so. When we listen to segments of Mozart or classical Indian ragas in which the depths of human suffering are openly explored, we hear and experience a serene elevation of spirit in the midst of the hard anguish of life. Listening mindfully, we can feel suffering carry over into joy and, in exalted moments, experience a hint of the religious astonishment that there is anything at all rather than just nothing. In great music perhaps more than anywhere else, awe and gratitude surface even in the face of human suffering. On these and other grounds, it is clear that emotional enlightenment will become a significant area of development in contemporary Buddhism.

Thesis Ten: That the discipline of constructing a personal, existential response to the question "What is enlightenment?" is more like improvisation in music or dance than it is a calculative skill. The goal itself, although as real as anything in our lives, is structurally elusive, and the skills required to move in its direction—skills such as openness, mindfulness, responsiveness, resilience, and flexibility—all require rhythmic extemporizing as much as analytical precision.

Consider first the goal of the quest. In spite of all the reasons given throughout this book for the necessity of a well-honed conception of enlightenment, no enlightenment will ever be achieved by maintaining direct aim at such a goal. The focal point of daily practice will mostly be elsewhere. Sometimes that focus will be far from one's aspirations or ideals—on work, family, current problems, frustrations, anger, or happiness. Focus may be on art, politics, the environment, the economy, the small object in front of us, or the task at hand. When we concentrate our energies on any of the innumerable aspects of our experience, we do not aim our intentions directly at enlightenment but nevertheless move toward or away from it by virtue of those other intentions. The thought of enlightenment grounds and gives direction to all of these aims or pursuits but cannot itself become the primary focal point of our attention. Although it provides guiding light that illuminates every dimension of our lives, too much time spent gazing directly into that light is counterproductive—it blurs vision rather than accentuating it. Even the memory of a profoundly moving experience or intuition of enlightenment will be misleading as the focal point of our quest, because when we attach our minds to the memory or feeling of such an experience, we fail to attend to the conditions that gave rise to that experience in the first place, and in so doing we obscure the path. As Zen master Dogen says so brilliantly, "Enlightenment disappears in the practice of letting go."[5]

If, as we have seen throughout this book, the quest for enlightenment cannot assume a fixed and unchanging goal, then there is no steady threshold that we can strive to cross, no finish line that could be marked out in advance as the clear aim of our enterprise. There is no universal blueprint for enlightenment, no binding rules for everyone to follow. In place of these illusory aims—the "mirages" named in Mahayana sutras—we find only the maintenance of an ongoing discipline of mindfulness, compassion, and integrity forming the background from which personally improvised life can arise.

Like dance or musical improvisation, those on a contemporary Buddhist path will, through training, aspire toward a highly evolved capacity to release conscious control and let the self disappear into the fluid movements and interactions of life. Like dancers and musicians, we train and train and train some more while directing this strenuous discipline toward the capacity to just be ourselves spontaneously. The tension and opposition between the discipline of training and the freedom of improvisation is real, as is the difficulty of holding them in balance throughout life. Discipline and training express the laudable will to get hold of ourselves, to take charge of our lives, to be in control, to attain some degree of freedom. But as Buddhist images of "clinging" and "release" show, grasping arises from our insufficiencies—from our needs and desires. Our training is itself an act of grasping, even when its ultimate goal is the freedom of nongrasping. The will to control, to be in possession of oneself, follows from our wanting something in life, especially freedom, which we do and should want. But, like a roller coaster ride, the more we grip tight to secure ourselves, the more our entire body freezes up in rigid resistance. We won't even feel the ride much less enjoy it until we release our death grip.

That irony in the midst of our situation in life is startling to contemplate. At some point along the path of training we find ourselves fully in the grip of our own effort and grasping, ensnared by our own purposes, controlled by our own will to control. The firmer our grip, the further our fall into the suffering of anxious resistance. That is why, at this point, watching the dancers and studying the musicians is enlightening. Grounded in the most rigorous discipline and training imaginable, they release control and let themselves be taken over by the shape of the moment. They glide through the movements of sound and motion with a lightness of touch and resilient flexibility that from our perspective looks like ecstatic freedom. In the midst of our disciplines of practice we can learn from these improvisers how to relax our grip and let selfless improvisation get underway.

That crucial relationship between discipline and release is one clue to the *kōan* with which we began this book. Recall that when Subhuti asked the Buddha, "How, then, is enlightenment attained?" the Buddha replied that "Enlightenment is attained neither through a path nor through a nonpath." While the path of practice is rigorous and disciplined, the nonpath of improvisation allows unplanned pilgrimages off the beaten path and onto a unique way in life that is ours and ours alone. That "way," once we find ourselves in its groove, has no preordained destination that awaits our arrival. The goal, in fact, is just being there, on our way through life in meditative openness, worldly wisdom, and graceful compassion. Therefore the Buddha concludes his *kōan*-like instructions to us by conflating path and goal, the awkward separation between "means" and "ends." With a faint smile of ironic brilliance, *he finally tells us what enlightenment is:* "Just enlightenment is the path, just the path is enlightenment."[6]

Notes

INTRODUCTION

1. In December of 1783, the *Berlinische Monatsschrift* published an article that gave rise to this important debate in Germany and then the rest of Europe. Theologian Johann Friedrich Zöllner, writing in opposition to civil as opposed to church marriage ceremonies, wrote in a footnote, "What is enlightenment?" on the thought that this new movement stood on vague and insufficient intellectual grounds. Answers to his question began pouring into the publisher and continued for years. Among many important responses, some from famous intellectuals, Immanuel Kant's is by far the most decisive. "Beantwortung der Frage: Was ist Aufklärung?" *Berlinishche Monatsschrift* 4 (1784), 481–494.

2. See the Conclusion, Thesis Two, for further reflection on the choice of the European word "enlightenment" to name the central concern of Buddhism and its larger implications.

3. Edward Conze, trans., *The Large Sutra on Perfect Wisdom* (Berkeley: University of California Press, 1975), 617.

CHAPTER 1

1. Thich Nhat Hanh, "We Are the Beaters; We Are the Beaten," *Los Angeles Times*, April 15, 1991.

2. Ibid.

3. Ibid.

4. Robert Thurman, trans., *The Holy Teaching of Vimalakīrti* (University Park: Pennsylvania State University Press, 1976) , 21.

5. Ibid., 20.

6. Ibid., 79.

7. Ibid., 66.

8. Ibid., 73.
9. Ibid., 21.
10. Ibid., 57.
11. Ibid., 39.
12. Ibid., 57.
13. Dalai Lama, *Ethics for the New Millennium* (New York: Riverhead, 1999) , 61.
14. Ibid., 55.
15. Thurman, trans., *The Holy Teaching of Vimalakīrti,* 58.

CHAPTER 2

1. Most of what I have learned about the artist Im Kwon-taek, the film *Mandala,* and, even more important, how to watch a film, I learned from David E. James. On Im Kwon-taek, see David E. James and Kyung Hyun Kim, *Im Kwon-Taek: The Making of a Korean National Cinema* (Detroit: Wayne State University Press, 2002). On the film *Mandala,* see David E. James, "Im Kwon-Taek: Korean National Cinema and Buddhism," in ibid. Both of these are the point of departure for my own thinking on *Mandala.*

2. In the process of telling its story, *Mandala* presents what in my judgment is the best excursion into a Buddhist world in modern film. Set in the Son or Zen monasteries of the Korean mountains, the film provides a rare glimpse into a Buddhist world by way of everything from art and architecture, sermons and rituals, to debates and asceticism. Whether the film *Mandala* is itself Buddhist or rather simply about Buddhism is an open question, regardless of claims or the explicit identities of the filmmaker. Ways to begin to ponder the difference are provided by David James in "Im Kwon-Taek: Korean National Cinema and Buddhism" and in a fine essay by Francisca Cho, "Imagining Nothingness and Imaging Otherness in Buddhist Film," in S. Brent Plate and David Jasper (Eds.), *Imag(in)ing Otherness: Filmic Visions of Living Together* (Atlanta, GA: Scholars Press, 1999).

3. On the question of freedom in East Asian Buddhism, see Dale S. Wright, *Philosophical Meditations on Zen Buddhism* (Cambridge, UK: Cambridge University Press, 1998), chapters 7 and 8.

4. James and Hyun Kim, *Im Kwon-Taek,* 259–260.

5. See James, "Im Kwon-Taek," 64.

6. The "otherness" featured here is different from that so well articulated by Cho in "Imagining Nothing and Imaging Otherness in Buddhist Film," where otherness is the vision of "nothingness" to which Zen monks aspire, a transcendent otherness. The otherness discussed here is simply the human other, which for participants in a monastery becomes exacerbated by the remoteness of their lives and the stark difference between their aspirations and those of others in the society.

7. A weakness in the development of the film's theme can be seen here, as David James claims, in that our only access as viewers to Jisan's courageous and self-less act is through the second-hand narration of Sugwan. Although we take the rumor to be true, its power is diminished by indirection, and it cannot play the central role that the theme of the film would otherwise require. See James, "Im Kwon-Taek," 66.

8. Paul Riceour, *Oneself As Another* (Chicago: University of Chicago Press, 1992), 170.

9. James and Hyun Kim, *Im Kwon-Taek*, 265.

10. Ibid.

11. On the issue of a socially responsible cinema in Im Kwon-taek, see James, "Im Kwon-Taek," especially 71. This essay goes on to describe how Im Kwon-taek worked on the same theme in his other explicitly "Buddhist" film *Come, Come, Come Upward.*

CHAPTER 3

1. Stephen Batchelor, *Confession of a Buddhist Atheist* (New York: Spiegel and Grau, 2010).

2. Stephen Batchelor, *After Buddhism: Rethinking the Dharma for a Secular Age* (New Haven, CT: Yale University Press, 2015) , 21.

3. Ibid., 307.

4. Ibid., 24–25.

5. Ibid., 25.

6. Ibid., 148.

7. Ibid., 231.

8. Ibid., 234.

9. Ibid., 145.

10. Ibid., 255.

11. Ibid., 17

12. Ibid., 15.

13. Ibid., 21.

14. Ibid., 15.

15. Ibid., 15.

16. Ibid., 15.

17. Ibid., 15.

18. Ibid., 16.

19. Ibid., 28.

20. Ibid., 316.

21. Ibid., 316.

22. Ibid., 315.

23. Ibid., 134.

24. Paul Tillich, *The Dynamics of Faith* (New York: Harper, 1957).

25. Stephen Batchelor, "A Secular Buddhist," London Insight Meditation. www.londoninsight.org/images/uploads/A_Secular_Buddhist_(2).pdf.

26. Batchelor, *Confession*, 181.

27. Stephen Batchelor, *Buddhism Without Beliefs* (New York: Riverhead Books, 1998).

28. Batchelor, *After Buddhism*, 207.

29. Ibid., 207.

30. Ibid., 207.

31. Ibid., 24.

32. Ibid., 24.

33. Ibid., 24.

34. Ibid., 24.

35. Ibid., 24.

36. Ibid., 239.

37. Ibid., 239.

38. Ibid., 239.

39. Ibid., 239.

40. Ibid., 239.

41. Immanuel Kant, "What is Enlightenment?" Originally published as "Beantwortung der Frage: Was ist Aufklarung?" *Berlinishche Monatsschrift* 4 (1784): 481–494.

42. Friedrich Nietzsche, *The Gay Science*, edited by Bernard Williams (Cambridge, UK: Cambridge University Press, 2001), section 125.

CHAPTER 4

1. *Anguttara Nikaya:* iv, 77.

2. See Susan Neiman, *Evil in Modern Thought* (Princeton, NJ: Princeton University Press, 2002).

3. Richard Gombrich and Gananath Obeyesekere, among them.

4. Although not a historian of early Indian culture, I suspect that the ethicization of the concept of karma was occurring not just in Buddhist monastic circles but more widely in other avant-garde segments of Indian culture at the same time.

5. Alaisdair MacIntyre, *After Virtue* (Notre Dame: University of Notre Dame Press, 1981), 188.

6. The first thing that accrues from an act of this sort is that someone is helped, something good has been done to the world out beyond the practitioner. But my focus here is on the rewards that come to the agent.

7. MacIntyre, *After Virtue*, 191.

8. Dalai Lama, *The Way to Freedom: Core Teachings of Tibetan Buddhism* (San Francisco, CA: Harper, 1994), 100.

9. Rick Hanson, *Hardwiring Happiness: The New Brain Science of Contentment, Calm, and Confidence* (New York: Harmony Books, 2013), 10.

10. See William Waldron, *The Buddhist Unconscious* (London: Routledge/Curzon, 2003), 160–169.

11. It is often argued that *without* a belief in individual immortality, that is, some theory of the soul, a fully ethical life is not possible. While respecting the motivation and sincerity of those who do consider the idea of rebirth to be essential both to Buddhism and to enlightened life, I disagree with the arguments provided and find adherence to contemporary standards of critical thinking the more compelling consideration. For the best of these arguments, see Robert Thurman, *Infinite Life: Seven Virtues for Living Well* (New York: Riverhead Books, 2004).

12. Winston L. King explores the question of the separability of karma and rebirth, concluding that "a doctrine of karmic rebirth is not essential to a viable and authentic Buddhist ethic in the West." "A Buddhist Ethic Without Karmic Rebirth," *Journal of Buddhist Ethics* 1 (1994): 33–44.

13. The question of what to do about people who can *only* be motivated by promises of external rewards is an important social question but not one within the scope of a philosophical effort to reflect on the truth of the matter or on what the rest of us should believe for motivational purposes.

14. For the connection between meditation and Buddhist ethics, see Georges Dreyfus, "Meditation as Ethical Activity," *Journal of Buddhist Ethics* 2 (1995): 28–54.

CHAPTER 5

1. Brian Victoria, *Zen War Stories* (New York: RoutledgeCurzon, 2003), 67.
2. Ibid., 12.
3. Ibid., 169.
4. Although there were never historical occasions that drew attention to it, this "moral blindness" that we see so clearly in Japanese Zen can also be found in the original Chinese tradition and in its Korean variants. Victoria, *Zen War Stories*, 15.
5. Another common "explanation" for Japanese war atrocities alludes to the relative isolation of Japan and the international inexperience that was certainly common in that country. This is taken to mean that the "otherness" of other people was experienced in a more extreme way than it would be for people who have regular contact with "outsiders." But it is worth noting that in its invasions of China and Korea, Japan was reversing a longstanding reverence for mainland culture and the esteem in which these cultures were held as the source of many of Japan's own values, including Buddhism and Confucianism. But this kind of explanation still leaves our question unanswered: What is the relation between Zen enlightenment and morality, and how should we expect enlightenment to manifest in the moral sphere?
6. By "morality" here I assume a distinction between a form of morality that consists in following social custom and norms and a form of morality as "social

ethics" that includes a concept of justice above and beyond social custom, as well as the capacity to give critical assessment to prevailing norms.

7. An important exception to this claim would be instruction in and meditation on the precepts and rules of comportment relevant to life in a Zen monastery. This focus, however, was largely on the meaning of the precepts for the cultivation of one's own spirituality, rather than on concern for those beyond the walls of the monastery.

8. It is also important to recognize how social structure conditions moral/political participation in any society. Zen, like other forms of Buddhism, was fully dependent on the larger society and on the government for its resources. We have learned that it is excessively naïve to ignore the question of who is footing the bill for any institution. Realizing this, it is important to ask: What kinds of reciprocal exchange and agreement are included in the unwritten contract between Zen monastic institutions and the political power structures of East Asian societies? Still, providing social, political, and economic explanations for why Zen enlightenment might not encompass morality fails to attribute to Zen masters the capacity to recognize these social, political, and economic deficits and the freedom to consider doing something about them. An explanation beyond the sociological is still required.

9. Cited in Brian Victoria, *Zen at War* (Lanham, MD: Rowan and Littlefield, 2005), 148.

10. Ibid., 148–149.

11. Ibid., 149.

12. Ibid., 76.

13. Ibid., 87.

14. The contemporary Chan tradition may be one notable exception to this. Although not necessarily responding to Neo-Confucian critiques at this point, many Chan masters broadened their teachings considerably to re-envelope Chan concerns and practices within the tradition of Mahayana Buddhism. This allows the image of the enlightened Chan master to meld with the image of the bodhisattva, bringing depth of moral concern more forcefully back into Chan than the earlier tradition had allowed.

15. Cited in Victoria, *Zen at War*, 148.

16. It is certainly true that religious leaders in all nations at all times have tended to something like this same compliance. But that historical fact does not alter our contemporary sense that a higher form of enlightenment would include the ability to raise critical and moral questions about wartime activities.

17. Cited in Victoria, *Zen War Stories*, 145.

CHAPTER 6

1. http://www.whiteplum.org/Maezumi%20Biography.htm.

2. Peter Mattheissen, *Nine-Headed Dragon River: Zen Journals 1969–1982* (Boston: Shambhala, 1998), 239.

3. James Ishmael Ford, *Zen Master Who? A Guide to the People and Stories of Zen* (Boston: Wisdom, 2006), 168.

4. Mattheissen, *Nine-Headed Dragon River*, 237.

5. Nora Jones, "White Plums and Lizard Tails: The Story of Maezumi Roshi and his American Lineage," *Shambhala Sun* (March 2004): 2.

6. Mattheissen, *Nine-Headed Dragon River*, 238.

7. http://www.whiteplum.org/Maezumi%20Biography.htm.

8. David L. Preston, *The Social Organization of Zen Practice: Constructing Transcultural Reality* (Cambridge, UK: Cambridge University Press, 1988), 32.

9. Jones, "White Plums and Lizard Tails," 1.

10. Ibid.

11. Helen Tworkov, *Zen in America: Five Teachers and the Search for American Buddhism* (New York: Kodansha, 1994), 8.

12. Mattheissen, *Nine-Headed Dragon River*, 239.

13. Philip Kapleau, *The Three Pillars of Zen: Teaching, Practice, and Enlightenment* (New York: Anchor Books, 1989).

14. David Chadwick, *Crooked Cucumber: The Life and Teachings of Shunryo Suzuki* (New York: Broadway Press, 2000), chapter 10.

15. Mattheissen, *Nine-Headed Dragon River*, 238.

16. Ford, *Zen Master Who?*, 164; Jones, "White Plums and Lizard Tails," 2.

17. Rick Fields, *How the Swans Came to the Lake: A Narrative History of Buddhism in America* (Boson: Shambhala, 1992), 244.

18. Mattheissen, *Nine-Headed Dragon River*, 123.

19. Fields, *How the Swans Came to the Lake*, 244.

20. Ibid., 261.

21. Jones, "White Plums and Lizard Tails," 3.

22. http://www.whiteplum.org/Maezumi%20Biography.htm.

23. Ford, *Zen Master Who?*, 164.

24. Interview with Wendy Egyoku Nakao, Occidental College, April 4, 2008.

25. Jones, "White Plums and Lizard Tails," 4.

26. Ibid., 4.

27. Interview with Wendy Egyoku Nakao, Occidental College, April 4, 2008.

28. Ibid.

29. Ibid.

30. Interview with Jan Chozen Bays, Occidental College, March 7, 2008.

31. Mattheissen, *Nine-Headed Dragon River*.

32. Philomene Long, *American Zen Bones: Maezumi Roshi Stories* (Los Angeles: Beyond Baroque Books, 1999).

33. Ford, *Zen Master Who?*

34. Interviews with Jan Chozen Bays and Charles Tenshin Fletcher.

35. Long, *American Zen Bones*, 3–4.

36. Interview with Charles Tenshin Fletcher, Occidental College, March 26, 2008.

37. Sean Murphy, *One Bird, One Stone* (New York: Renaissance Books, 2002), 73.
38. Interview with Charles Tenshin Fletcher, Occidental College, March 26, 2008.
39. Mattheissen, *Nine-Headed Dragon River*, p. 128.
40. Interview with Wendy Egyoku Nakao, Occidental College, April 4, 2008.
41. Interview with Jan Chozen Bays, Occidental College, March 7, 2008.
42. Long, *American Zen Bones*, 73.
43. http://www.urbandharma.org/udharma3/womlib.html.
44. Interview with Wendy Egyoku Nakao, Occidental College, April 4, 2008.
45. Jones, "White Plums and Lizard Tails," 4.
46. Anne Cushman, "Under the Lens: An American Zen Community in Crisis," *Tricycle: The Buddhist Review* (Fall, 2003): 42–47.
47. http://www.cuke.com/Cucumber%20Project/interviews/maezumi.html.
48. Mattheissen, *Nine-Headed Dragon River*, 240.
49. Interview with Jan Chozen Bays, Occidental College, March 7, 2008.
50. http://www.cuke.com/Cucumber%20Project/interviews/maezumi.html.
51. Anne Cushman, *Zen Center: Portrait of an American Zen Community* (Miracle Productions, 1987).
52. Ibid.
53. Ibid.
54. Interview with Wendy Egyoku Nakao, Occidental College, March 4, 2008.
55. Interview with Dennis Genpo Merzel, Occidental College, February 11, 2008.
56. Ibid.
57. Tracy Cochran, "Into the West," *Parabola* (Winter 2007), quoting Bernie Glassman.

CHAPTER 7

1. Romans 7:19.
2. My references to Paul in this chapter are not intended to make text-based historical claims about the original intentions of Pauline theology but rather to use the familiar categories and distinctions provided by these traditions for the theoretical purposes of this chapter. I state this qualification because I am aware that interest in the Pauline epistles and debate over how they should be interpreted have been particularly lively over the past two decades, such that the traditional readings that I simply assume in this chapter may at this point be out of accord with scholarly opinion. What is at stake here is the issue of the will itself, not the particular history of claims made about it.
3. Saint Anselm (1033–1109) was the archbishop of Canterbury Cathedral in England and one of the greatest theologians in Christian history. In a text called the *Proslogion*, he developed what came to be called the ontological argument for the existence of God. This argument, which has been more influential in Christian theology as a rule for thinking the concept God than it has been as a proof, defines God as "that than which no greater can be thought."

4. Matthew 5:17–48.

5. It is important to recognize, of course, that change in a tradition can also be understood as a "fall" or as a degradation, and virtually all reformers within a tradition draw upon that possibility in order to justify the changes that they propose. And, of course, there are times when cultures or traditions do deteriorate, times when new practices or new ways of thinking lead a society in a direction that they later look back upon with regret. Currently, Steven Batchelor's articulation of a "secular Buddhism" is just such a reform proposal. Interpreting the history of Buddhism as a continued forgetfulness of the early, noninstitutional, nonreligious dharma, Batchelor's inspired reading of the early texts offers both a new look at the teachings of the Pali canon and a version of Buddhism meant to align with our modern, secular condition.

6. This form of religious thought arises most prominently in Pure Land Buddhism, especially in the thought of Shinran.

7. Shantideva, *Bodhicaryavatara*, chapter 6, verse 10.

8. Friedrich Schleiermacher, *The Christian Faith*, translated by H.R. Mackintosh, edited by J.S. Stewart (Edinburgh, UK: T&T Clark, 1999).

9. Paul Ricoeur, *Oneself as Another* (Chicago: University of Chicago Press, 1992), 189.

10. Alasdair MacIntyre, *After Virtue* (Notre Dame: University of Notre Dame Press, 1981), 204.

11. See David E. Klemm and William Schweiker, *Religion and the Human Future: An Essay on Theological Humanism* (Oxford: Blackwell, 2007).

CHAPTER 8

1. Erich Fromm, D.T. Suzuki, and Richard DeMartino, *Zen Buddhism and Psychoanalysis* (New York: Harper & Row, 1960).

2. Ibid., 94.

3. Ibid., 98.

4. Ibid., 128–129.

5. Ibid., 127.

6. Ibid., 98.

7. For an excellent discussion of the instrumental theory of language and a full critique, see Hans-Georg Gadamer, *Truth and Method* (New York: Seabury Press, 1975).

8. Fromm et al., *Zen Buddhism*, 94.

9. Ibid., 109.

10. Ibid., 110.

11. Ibid., 118.

12. Ibid., 98.

13. Ibid., 105.

14. Ibid., 106.

15. Ibid., 141.

16. Alasdair MacIntyre, *Whose Justice? Which Rationality?* (Notre Dame: University of Notre Dame Press, 1988), 334.

17. T.P. Kasulis, *Zen Action: Zen Person* (Honolulu: University of Hawaii Press, 1981).

18. Ibid., 113.

19. Ibid., 56.

20. Ibid., 134.

21. Ibid., 134.

22. Ibid., 134. Emphasis mine.

23. Ibid., 61.

24. Ibid., 61.

25. Ibid., 61.

26. For a critique of this possibility see Gadamer, *Truth and Method*, 405; and Richard Rorty, "Pragmatism and Philosophy," in Kenneth Baynes et al., *After Philosophy* (Cambridge, MA: MIT Press, 1987), 26–66.

27. Kasulis, *Zen Action*, 23.

28. Ibid., 22.

29. Ibid., 23.

30. Ibid., 23.

31. Fromm et al., *Zen Buddhism*, 110.

32. Where by "poststructuralist" I mean no more than the view that we begin our reflection within the realization that the structures we discover to be true are historical and contingent. Note that this position does not imply that there are no structures or that there is no truth but rather that the structures and truths that govern our experience are open both to transformation and to being seen otherwise.

33. Fromm et al., *Zen Buddhism*, 105.

34. Kasulis, *Zen Action*, 138.

35. Ibid., 134.

36. Ibid., 141.

37. Ibid., 141.

38. This "myth" is first named and criticized by Wilfrid Sellars in *Science, Perception and Reality* (New York: Humanities Press, 1963).

39. For the most influential articulations of this position, in the analytic tradition, see the works of Davidson, Kuhn, MacIntyre, Sellars, and Wittgenstein; among American pragmatists, see the works of Fish, Rorty, and Stout; and in continental thought, see the works of Derrida, Heidegger, Gadamer, and Ricoeur.

40. Martin Heidegger, *Being and Time*, translated by John Macquarrie and Edward Robinson (New York: Harper & Row, 1962).

41. Robert Gimello has in two earlier essays argued similarly about the relation between mystical experience and the Buddhist cultural tradition. See "Mysticism

and Meditation," in Steven T. Katz (Ed.), *Mysticism and Philosophical Analysis* (Oxford: Oxford University Press, 1978), 170–199.

42. See *Being and Time*, section 34.

43. Wittgenstein first introduces the idea of the "language game" in the *Blue Book* (p. 17) and develops it further in the *Brown Book* and in *Philosophical Investigations*.

44. Harold Bloom, *The Anxiety of Influence* (Oxford: Oxford University Press, 1973).

45. MacIntyre develops the theme of "acquiring a conception of the good" throughout *Whose Justice? Which Rationality?*

46. In addition to *Truth and Method*, see H.G. Gadamer, *Philosophical Hermeneutics* (Berkeley: University of California Press, 1976), and *Reason in the Age of Science* (Cambridge, MA: MIT Press, 1981), as well as Joel C. Weinsheimer, *Gadamer's Hermeneutics: A Reading of Truth and Method* (New Haven, CT: Yale University Press, 1985), and Georgia Warnke, *Gadamer: Hermeneutics, Tradition and Reason* (Stanford, CA: Stanford University Press, 1987).

47. James Boyd White, *When Words Lose Their Meaning: Constitutions and Reconstitutions of Language, Character, and Community* (Chicago: University of Chicago Press, 1984), 20.

48. It is also true that the centrality of discursive practice in the overall scheme of classical Zen practice can be seen in the centrality of the dharma hall within the monastic institution. The dharma hall is figured in classical Zen texts as the most common setting for the dialogical encounter between Zen masters and Zen monks as well as for the experience of awakening. See Martin Collcutt, *Five Mountains: The Rinzai Zen Monastic Institution in Medieval Japan*, Harvard East Asian Monographs 85 (Cambridge, MA: Harvard University Press, 1981), 194.

49. Ruth Fuller Sasaki, trans., *The Record of Lin-chi* (Kyoto: Institute for Zen Studies, 1975) , 51 (*Taisho shinshu daizkyo* 47 [1985]: 504c).

50. Ibid., 56 (505c).

51. Ibid., 40 (503a).

52. Ibid., 60 (506b).

53. This slogan appears in numerous classical Zen texts from Sung dynasty Chinese texts on into later publications. By the mid-Sung it seems to have taken on central significance as the phrase most definitive of the self-understanding of Zen.

54. *Taisho shinshu daizkyo* 48.2012A (1924): 382a. Iriya Yoshitaka takes this line from the *Ch'uan-hsin fa-yao* to be traceable to the *Diamond sutra* in *Denshin hoyo* (*Zen no goroku* 8 [1969]: 54).

55. See especially the works of Yanagida Seizan, Philip Yampolsky, John McRae, Carl Bielefeldt, and T. Griffith Foulk.

56. Due in part to its encounter with Western thought, the modern Japanese Zen tradition does, in fact, have a great deal to say on this issue.

57. Kasulis, *Zen Action*, 134.

CHAPTER 9

1. See Stanley Weinstein, *Buddhism Under the T'ang* (Cambridge, UK: Cambridge University Press, 1987), 111–112.
2. Jeffry Broughton, *Kuei-feng Tsung-mi: The Convergence of Ch'an and the Teachings* (Ann Arbor, MI: University Microfilms, 1975), 107.
3. *Taisho shinshu daizokyo*, 85 vols. (Tokyo: Taisho Issaikyo Kankokai, 1924–1933), Vol. 47, 502c. Also see Yanagida Seizan, "The Life of Lin-chi I-hsuan," *The Eastern Buddhist* 5.2 (1972).
4. *Taisho*, Vol. 51, 291; See Chung-yuan Chang, *The Original Teachings of Ch'an Buddhism* (New York: Vintage Press, 1969), 111.
5. *Taisho*, Vol. 48, 382c.
6. For further reflections on this dimension of the practice of reading, see Dale S. Wright, *Philosophical Meditations on Zen Buddhism* (Cambridge, UK: Cambridge University Press, 1998), chapter 2.

CHAPTER 10

1. Fazang (643–712), although the third patriarch in the Huayan lineage, was the first philosopher focused on the Huayan sutra to bring that text to prominence in China. He served as National Teacher under Empress Wu, a position from which his fame and influence spread.
2. *The Treatise on the Five Teachings* is Fazang's effort to survey the vast collection of Buddhist texts and ideas in order to place them into an understandable order. His "classification of the teachings" (*panjiao*) shows extraordinary sophistication and wide-ranging knowledge of the history of Buddhism and attempts to demonstrate at that time which parts of this overwhelming tradition were most worthy of study and meditation.
3. *Wujiao zhang, Taisho Shinshu daizokyo*, 85 vols. (Tokyo: Taisho Issaikyo Kankokai, 1924–1933), Vol. 45, 507c.
4. *Huayan jing yihai baimen*, (Tokyo: Taisho Issaikyo Kankokai, 1924–1933), Vol. 45, 630c.
5. Saint Anselm (1033–1109) was the archbishop of Canterbury Cathedral in England and one of the greatest theologians in Christian history. In a text called the *Proslogion*, he developed what came to be called the ontological argument for the existence of God. This argument, which has been more influential in Christian theology as a rule for thinking the concept God than it has been as a proof, defines God as "that than which no greater can be thought."
6. *Wujiao zhang*, Vol. 45, 489b.
7. *Huayan jing wenda*, Vol. 45, 610b.
8. *Wujiao zhang*, Vol. 45, 497a
9. *Wujiao zhang*, Vol. 45, 497a, quoting the *Mahayanasamgraha*, Vol. 31, 249.

10. *Huayan budixin zhang*, (Tokyo: Taisho Issaikyo Kankokai, 1924–1933), Vol. 45, 653b.

11. *Wujiao zhang*, Vol. 45, 490a.

12. *Wujiao zhang*, Vol. 45, 482c.

13. Rick Hanson and Richard Mendius, *The Buddha's Brain* (Oakland, CA: New Harbinger, 2009).

CONCLUSION

1. Some of the ideas in this section originated as a paper, "When Nirvana Became Enlightenment: Meditations on the Language of Buddhism" presented to the Graduate Program in Religious Studies at the University of Iowa.

2. Pierre Hadot, *Philosophy as a Way of Life: Spiritual Exercises from Socrates to Foucault* (Oxford: Wiley-Blackwell, 1995).

3. Martha Nussbaum, *Love's Knowledge: Essays in Philosophy and Literature* (Oxford: Oxford University Press, 1992), 75.

4. Rick Hanson, *The Buddha's Brain: The Practical Neuroscience of Happiness, Love, and Wisdom* (Oakland, CA: New Harbinger, 2009).

5. Kazuaki Tanahashi and Peter Levitt, *The Essential Dogen: Writings of the Great Zen Master* (Boston: Shambhala, 2013), 124.

6. Edward Conze, trans., *The Large Sutra on Perfect Wisdom* (Berkeley: University of California Press, 1975), 617.

Bibliography

Almond, Philip. *The British Discovery of Buddhism*. Cambridge, UK: Cambridge University Press, 1988.

Anderson, Carol S. *Pain and Its Ending: The Four Noble Truths in the Theravada Buddhist Canon*. Richmond, UK: Curzon, 1999.

Annas, Julia. *The Morality of Happiness*. New York: Oxford University Press, 1993.

Antonaccio, Maria, and William Schweiker. *Iris Murdock and the Search for Human Goodness*. Chicago: University of Chicago Press, 1996.

Arendt, Hannah. *Essays in Understanding*. New York: Schocken Books, 2003.

Aristotle. *Nicomachean Ethics*. Trans. Terence Irwin. Indianapolis: Hackett, 1985.

Arnold, Dan. *Buddhists, Brahmins, and Belief: Epistemology in South Asian Philosophy of Religion*. New York: Columbia University Press, 2005.

———. *Brains, Buddhas, and Believing: The Problem of Intentionality in Classical Buddhist and Cognitive-Scientific Philosophy of Mind*. New York: Columbia University Press, 2014.

Batchelor, Stephen. *Buddhism Without Beliefs: A Contemporary Guide to Awakening*. New York: Riverhead Books, 1998.

———. *Confession of a Buddhist Atheist*. New York: Spiegal and Grau, 2011.

———. *After Buddhism: Rethinking the Dharma for a Secular Age*. New Haven, CT: Yale University Press, 2015.

Becker, Lawrence C. *Reciprocity*. London: Routledge, 1986.

Beckwith, Christopher I. *Greek Buddha: Pyrrho's Encounter with Early Buddhism in Central Asia*. Princeton, NJ: Princeton University Press, 2015.

Bellah, Robert. *Beyond Belief: Essays on Religion in a Post-Traditional World*. Berkeley: University of California Press, 1991 (original work published in 1970).

Berlin, Isaiah. *Four Essays on Liberty*. Oxford: Oxford University Press, 1969.

———. *The Sense of Reality: Studies in the Ideas and Their History*. New York: Farrar, Strauss and Giroux, 1996.

Berofsky, Bernard. *Liberation from Self*. New York: Cambridge University Press, 1995.

Bloom, Harold. *The Anxiety of Influence*. Oxford: Oxford University Press, 1973.

Brandom, Robert. *Articulating Reasons: An Introduction to Inferentialism.* Cambridge, MA: Harvard University Press, 2001.

Broughton, Jeffrey, Trans. *The Chan Whip Anthology: A Companion to Zen Practice.* Oxford: Oxford University Press, 2014.

Bruns, Gerald. *Hermeneutics: Ancient and Modern.* New Haven, CT: Yale University Press, 1995.

———. *On Ceasing to be Human.* Stanford, CA: Stanford University Press, 2010.

Buddhaghosa, Bhadantācariya. *The Path of Purification.* Trans. Bhikkhu Nanamoli. Seattle: Buddhist Publication Society Pariyatti Editions, 1999.

Buswell, Robert E.Jr., and Robert M. Gimello, Eds. *Paths to Liberation: The Marga and Its Transformations in Buddhist Thought.* Honolulu: University of Hawaii Press, 1992.

Buswell, Robert E. Jr., and Donald S. Lopez. *The Princeton Dictionary of Buddhism.* Princeton, NJ: Princeton University Press, 2013.

Butler, Judith. *Antigone's Claim: Kinship Between Life and Death.* New York: Columbia University Press, 2000.

———. *Giving an Account of Oneself.* New York: Fordham University Press, 2005.

Cabezón, Jośe Ignacio. *A Dose of Emptiness.* Albany: State University of New York Press, 1992.

———. *Buddhism and Language: A Study of Indo-Tibetan Scholasticism.* Albany: State University of New York Press, 1994.

Chadwick, David. *Crooked Cucumber: The Life and Teachings of Shunryo Suzuki.* New York: Broadway Press, 2000.

Chodron, Pema. *No Time to Lose: A Timely Guide to the Way of the Bodhisattva.* Boston: Shambhala, 2007.

Clarke, J.J. *Oriental Enlightenment: The Encounter Between Asian and Western Thought.* London: Routledge, 1997.

Clayton, John. *Religions, Reasons, and Gods.* Cambridge, UK: Cambridge University Press, 2006.

Collins, Steven. *Selfless Persons: Imagery and Thought in Theravāda Buddhism.* Cambridge, UK: Cambridge University Press, 1982.

Conze, Edward. *The Perfection of Wisdom in Eight Thousand Lines and Its Verse Summary.* Bolinas, CA: Four Seasons Foundation, 1973.

———. *The Large Sutra on Perfect Wisdom.* Berkeley: University of California Press, 1975.

Crane, Tim. *The Objects of Thought.* Oxford: Oxford University Press, 2013.

Crosby, Kate, and Andrew Skilton. *Śāntideva: The Bodhicaryāvatara.* Oxford: Oxford University Press, 1996.

Dalai Lama. *The Way to Freedom: Core Teachings of Tibetan Buddhism.* New York: Harper, 1991.

———. *Ethics for the New Millennium.* New York: Riverhead, 1999.

Damasio, Antonio R. *Descartes' Error: Emotion, Reason, and the Human Brain.* London: Penguin Books, 1994.

———. *The Feeling of What Happens: Body and Emotion in the Making of Consciousness.* New York: Harcourt, 1999.

Davidson, Donald. *Inquiries into Truth and Interpretation.* Oxford: Oxford University Press, 1984.

Davis, Bret W. *Japanese and Continental Philosophy: Conversations with the Kyoto School.* Bloomington: Indiana University Press, 2011.

Dayal, Har. *The Bodhisattva Doctrine in Buddhist Sanskrit Literature.* London: Kegan Paul, Trench, Trübner & Co, 1932.

Dennett, Daniel C. *Darwin's Dangerous Idea: Evolution and the Meanings of Life.* New York: Simon & Schuster, 1995.

Dharmasiri, Gunapala. *The Fundamentals of Buddhist Ethics.* Antioch, CA: Golden Leaves, 1989.

Dreyfus, Georges B. J. *Recognizing Reality: Dharmakirti's Philosophy and Its Tibetan Interpretations.* Delhi: Sri Satguru, 1997.

Dunne, John. *Foundations of Dharmakirti's Philosophy.* Boston: Wisdom, 2004.

Eckel, Malcolm, David. *To See the Buddha: A Philosopher's Quest for the Meaning of Emptiness.* Princeton, NJ: Princeton University Press, 1992.

Epstein, Mark. *The Trauma of Everyday Life.* New York: Penguin Books, 2014.

Faure, Bernard. *Chan Insights and Oversights: An Epistemological Critique of the Chan Tradition.* Princeton, NJ: Princeton University Press, 1993.

Fields, Rick. *How the Swans Came to the Lake: A Narrative History of Buddhism in America.* Boulder, CO: Shambhala, 1992.

Flanagan, Owen. *The Problem of the Soul: Two Visions of Mind and How to Reconcile Them.* New York: Basic Books, 2002.

———. *The Bodhisattva's Brain: Buddhism Naturalized.* Cambridge, MA: MIT Press, 2011.

Ford, James Ishmael. *Zen Master Who? A Guide to the People and Stories of Zen.* Boston: Wisdom, 2006.

Foucault, Michel. *The Care of the Self: History of Sexuality,* Vol. 3. New York: Random House, 1986.

Frankfurt, Harry G. *The Importance of What We Care About.* Cambridge, UK: Cambridge University Press, 1988.

———. *The Reasons of Love.* Princeton, NJ: Princeton University Press, 2004.

Fromm, Erich, and D.T. Suzuki. *Zen Buddhism and Psychoanalysis.* New York: Harper & Row, 1960.

Fronsdal, Gil. *The Issue at Hand: Essays on Buddhist Mindfulness Practice.* Markham, ON: BookLand Press, 2008.

Gadamer, Hans-Georg. *Philosophical Hermeneutics.* Berkeley: University of California Press, 1976.

———. *Truth and Method.* Trans. Joel Weinsheimer and Donald G. Marshall. New York: Crossroad, 1989.

Garfield, Jay L. *The Fundamental Wisdom of the Middle Way: Nāgarjunā's Mūlamadhyamakrārikā.* New York: Oxford University Press, 1995.

————. *Empty Words: Buddhist Philosophy and Cross-Cultural Interpretation.* New York: Oxford University Press, 2002.

————. *Engaging Buddhism: Why It Matters to Philosophy.* New York: Oxford University Press, 2015.

Gethen, Rupert. *The Foundations of Buddhism.* Oxford: Oxford University Press, 1998.

Goleman, Daniel, Ed. *Healing Emotions: Conversations with the Dalai Lama on Mindfulness, Emotions, and Health.* Boston: Shambhala, 1997.

————. *Destructive Emotions: How Can We Overcome Them? A Scientific Dialogue with the Dalai Lama.* New York: Bantam Books, 2003.

Gombrich, Richard. *How Buddhism Began: The Conditioned Genesis of the Early Teachings.* Atlantic Highlands, NJ: Athlone Press, 1996.

Gregory, Peter N. *Traditions of Meditation in Chinese Buddhism.* Honolulu: University of Hawaii Press, 1987.

Griffiths, Paul J. *On Being Mindless: Buddhist Meditation and the Mind-Body Problem.* La Salle, IL: Open Court, 1986.

————. *On Being Buddha: The Classical Doctrine of Buddhahood.* Albany: State University of New York, 1994.

Gyatso, Janet, Ed. *In the Mirror of Memory: Reflections on Mindfulness and Remembrance in Indian and Tibetan Buddhism.* Albany: State University of New York Press, 1992.

————. *Being Human in a Buddhist World: An Intellectual History of Modern Tibetan Medicine.* New York: Columbia University Press, 2015.

Hacking, Ian. *The Social Construction of What?* Cambridge, MA: Harvard University Press, 1999.

Hadot, Pierre. *Philosophy as a Way of Life.* Ed. Arnold I. Davidson. Trans. Michael Chase. Oxford: Blackwell, 1995.

Hahn, Thich Nhat. *Being Peace.* Berkeley, CA: Parallax Press, 1987.

————. *The Diamond That Cuts Through Illusion: Commentaries on the Prajnaparamita Diamond Sutra.* Berkeley, CA: Parallax Press, 1992.

————. *Miracle of Mindfulness.* Boston: Beacon Press, 1999.

Hampshire, Stuart. *Innocence and Experience.* Cambridge, MA: Harvard University Press, 1989.

Hanson, Rick, and Richard Mendius. *The Buddha's Brain: The Practical Neuroscience of Happiness, Love, and Wisdom.* Oakland, CA: New Harbingers, 2009.

Hanson, Rick. *Hardwiring Happiness: The New Brain Science of Contentment, Calm, and Confidence.* New York: Harmony Books, 2013.

Harvey, Peter. *The Selfless Mind: Personality, Consciousness and Nirvana in Early Buddhism.* London: Curzon, 1987.

————. *An Introduction to Buddhist Ethics.* Cambridge, UK: Cambridge University Press, 2000.

Heidegger, Martin. *Basic Writings.* New York: Harper Collins, 1993.

————. *Mindfulness.* New York: Continuum, 2006.

Heine, Steven. *Opening a Mountain: Kōans of the Zen Masters*. New York: Oxford University Press, 2002.

———, and Dale S. Wright, Eds. *The Kōan: Texts and Contexts in Zen Buddhism*. New York: Oxford University Press, 2000.

———. *Zen Masters*. New York: Oxford University Press, 2010.

———. *Like Cats and Dogs: Contesting the Mu Kōan in Zen Buddhism*. New York: Oxford University Press, 2013.

Heisig, James W. *Philosophers of Nothingness: An Essay on the Kyoto School*. Honolulu: University of Hawaii Press, 2002.

Heisig, James W., and John C. Maraldo. *Rude Awakenings: Zen, the Kyoto School and the Question of Nationalism*. Honolulu: University of Hawaii Press, 1995.

Herman, Barbara. *Moral Literacy*. Cambridge, MA: Harvard University Press, 2008.

Hirakawa, Akira. *A History of Indiana Buddhism from Śākyamuni to Early Mahāyāna*. Honolulu: University of Hawaii Press, 1990.

Hori, Victor. *Zen Sand: The Book of Capping Phrases for Kōan Practice*. Honolulu: University of Hawaii Press, 2010.

Ives, Christopher. *Zen Awakening and Society*. Honolulu: University of Hawaii Press, 1992.

James, David E., and Kyung Hyun Kim. *Im Kwon-Taek: The Making of a Korean National Cinema*. Detroit: Wayne State University Press, 2002.

Jasper, David, and Dale S. Wright, Eds. *Theological Reflection and the Pursuit of Ideals*. London: Ashgate, 2013.

Kabat-Zinn, Jon. *Wherever You Go There You Are: Mindfulness Meditation in Everyday Life*. New York: Hyperion, 1994.

Kapstein, Matthew. *Reason's Traces: Identity and Interpretation in Indian and Buddhist Thought*. Somerville, MA: Wisdom, 2001.

Kasulis, T.P. *Zen Action: Zen Person*. Honolulu: University of Hawaii Press, 1989.

Katz, Nathan. *Buddhist Images of Human Perfection: The Arahant of the Sutta Piṭaka Compared with the Bodhisattva and Mahāsiddha*. Delhi: Motilal Banarsidass, 1982.

Kaza, Stephanie, and Kenneth Kraft, Kenneth, Eds. *Dharma Rain: Sources of Buddhist Environmentalism*. Boulder, CO: Shambhala, 2000.

Kekes, John. *Moral Wisdom and Good Lives*. Ithaca, NY: Cornell University Press, 1995.

———. *The Art of Life*. Ithaca, NY: Cornell University Press, 2002.

Keown, Damien. *The Nature of Buddhist Ethics*. Basingstoke, UK: Macmillan, 1992.

Kierkegaard, Soren. *The Concept of Irony, with Continual Reference to Socrates*. Trans. H.V. Hong and E.H. Hong. Princeton, NJ: Princeton University Press, 1992.

King, Karen L. *What Is Gnosticism?* Cambridge, MA: Harvard University Press, 2003.

King, Richard. *Indian Philosophy: An Introduction to Hindu and Buddhist Thought*. Washington, DC: Georgetown University Press, 1999.

Klein, Anne C. *Path to the Middle: Oral Madhyamika Philosophy in Tibet*. Albany: State University of New York Press, 1994.

Klemm, David E. *The Hermeneutical Theory of Paul Ricoeur*. Lewisburg, PA: Bucknell University Press, 1983.

———. *Hermeneutical Inquiry*. 2 vols. Atlanta: Scholars Press, 1986.

Klemm, David E., and William Schweiker. *Religion and the Human Future: An Essay on Theological Humanism*. London: Wiley-Blackwell, 2008.

Kopf, Gereon. *Beyond Personal Identity: Dogen, Nishida, and a Phenomenology of No-Self*. New York: Routledge, 2001.

Kraft, Kenneth, Ed. *Inner Peace, World Peace: Essays on Buddhism and Nonviolence*. Albany: State University of New York Press, 1992.

Kuhn, Thomas S. *The Structure of Scientific Revolutions*. 2d ed. Chicago: University of Chicago Press, 1970.

Kupperman, Joel J. *Character*. New York: Oxford University Press, 1991.

———. *Learning From Asian Philosophy*. New York: Oxford University Press, 1999.

———. *Value. . . and What Follows*. New York: Oxford University Press, 1999.

Lakoff, G., and M. Johnson. *Philosophy in the Flesh: The Embodied Mind and Its Challenge to Western Thought*. New York: Basic Books, 1999.

Lamotte, Etienne. *Śūramagamasamādhi sūtra*. Delhi: Motilal Banarsidas, 2003.

Lamrimpa, Gen. *Realizing Emptiness: Madhyamaka Insight Meditation*. Trans. B. Alan Wallace. Ithaca, NY: Snow Lion, 2002.

Little, David, and S.B. Twiss. *Comparative Religious Ethics: A New Method*. New York: Harper & Row, 1978.

Lopez, Donald S. Jr. *Heart Sutra Explained*. Albany: State University of New York Press, 1987.

———. *Elaborations on Emptiness: Uses of the Heart Sūtra*. Princeton, NJ: Princeton University Press, 1996.

Loy, David. *The Great Awakening: A Buddhist Social Theory*. Somerville, MA: Wisdom, 2003.

———. *The New Buddhist Path: Enlightenment, Evolution, and Ethics in the Modern World*. Somerville, MA: Wisdom, 2015.

MacIntyre, Alasdair. *After Virtue*. Notre Dame, IN: University of Notre Dame Press, 1983.

———. *Whose Justice? What Rationality?* Notre Dame, IN: University of Notre Dame Press, 1988.

———. *Three Rival Versions of the Moral Enquiry*. Notre Dame, IN: University of Notre Dame Press, 1990.

Makransky, John J. *Buddhahood Embodied: Sources of Controversy in India and Tibet*. Albany: State University of New York Press, 1997.

Marion, Jean-Luc. *Being Given: Toward a Phenomenology of Givenness*. Trans. Jeffrey L. Kosky. Stanford, CA: Stanford University Press, 2002.

Mattheissen, Peter. *Nine-Headed Dragon River: Zen Journal 1969–1982*. Boulder, CO: Shambhala, 1998.

McDowell, John. *Mind and Reality*. Cambridge, MA: Harvard University Press, 1996.

McGinn, Collin. *The Mysterious Flame: Conscious Minds in a Material World.* New York: Basic Books, 1999.

McMahan, David L. *The Making of Buddhist Modernism.* New York: Oxford University Press, 2008.

McRae, John R. *Seeing Through Zen: Encounter, Transformation and Genealogy in Chinese Chan Buddhism.* Berkeley: University of California Press, 2003.

Misra, G.S.P. *Development of Buddhist Ethics.* New Delhi: Munshiram Manoharlal, 1984.

Mohanty, Jitendra Nath. *Classical Indian Philosophy.* Lanham, MD: Rowman & Littlefield, 2000.

Murdoch, Iris. *The Sovereignty of Good.* London: Routledge, 1970.

Murphy, Sean. *One Bird, One Stone: 108 American Zen Stories.* New York: Renaissance Books, 2002.

Nagel, Thomas. *The View From Nowhere.* New York: Oxford University Press, 1986.

Nakasone, R.Y. *Ethics of Enlightenment: Essays and Sermons in Search of a Buddhist Ethic.* Fremont, CA: Dharma Cloud Publishers, 1990.

Nattier, Jan. *Once Upon a Future Time: Studies in a Buddhist Prophecy of Decline.* Berkeley, CA: Asian Humanities Press, 1991.

———. *A Few Good Men: The Bodhisattva Path According to the Inquiry of Ugra.* Honolulu: University of Hawaii Press, 2003.

Nehamas, Alexander. *The Art of Living.* Berkeley: University of California Press, 1998.

Neiman, Susan. *Evil in Modern Thought: An Alternative History of Philosophy.* Princeton, NJ: Princeton University Press, 2004.

Nietzsche, Friedrich. *On the Genealogy of Morality.* Trans. M. Clark and A. Swensen. Indianapolis: Hackett, 1998.

———. *The Gay Science.* Ed. Bernard Williams. Cambridge, UK: Cambridge University Press, 2001.

Nishitani, Keiji. *Religion and Nothingness.* Berkeley: University of California Press, 1992.

Nussbaum, Martha C. *The Fragility of Goodness.* Cambridge, UK: Cambridge University Press, 1986.

———. *The Therapy of Desire.* Princeton, NJ: Princeton University Press, 1986.

———. *Love's Knowledge: Essays in Philosophy and Literature.* Oxford: Oxford University Press, 1992.

Oakeshott, Michael. *On Human Conduct.* Oxford: Clarendon Press, 1975.

Obeyesekere, Gananath. *Imagining Karma: Ethical Transformation in Amerindian, Buddhist and Greek Rebirth.* Berkeley: University of California Press, 2002.

O'Flaherty, Wendy Doniger, Ed. *Karma and Rebirth in Classical Indian Traditions.* Delhi: Motilal Banarsidass, 1983.

Pagel, Ulrich. *The Bodhisattvapitaka: Its Doctrines, Practices and Their Position in Mahayana Literature.* Tring, UK: Institute of Buddhist Studies, 1995.

Parks, Graham, Ed. *Heidegger and Asian Thought.* Honolulu: University of Hawaii Press, 1987.

Powers, John. *Wisdom of Buddha: The Samdhinirmochana Sutra.* Cazadero, CA: Dharma Publishing, 1995.

Preston, David L. *The Social Organization of Zen Practice: Constructing Transcultural Reality.* Cambridge, UK: Cambridge University Press, 1988.

Pye, Michael. *Skilful Means: A Concept in Mahayana Buddhism.* London: Duckworth, 1978.

Queen, C.S., and S.B. King, Eds. *Engaged Buddhism: Buddhist Liberation Movements in Asia.* Albany: State University of New York Press, 1996.

Rawls, John. *Theory of Justice.* Cambridge, MA: Harvard University Press, 1971.

Ray, Reginald A. *Buddhist Saints in India: A Study in Buddhist Values & Orientations.* New York: Oxford University Press, 1994.

Ricard, Matthieu. *Happiness: A Guide to Developing Life's Most Important Skill.* New York: Little, Brown, 2006.

Ricoeur, Paul. *Oneself as Another.* Trans. Kathleen Blamey. Chicago: University of Chicago Press, 1992.

———. *The Just.* Chicago: University of Chicago Press, 2000.

———. *Memory, History, Forgetting.* Trans. Kathleen Blamey and David Pellauer. Chicago: University of Chicago Press, 2004.

Rorty, Richard. *Philosophy and the Mirror of Nature.* Princeton, NJ: Princeton University Press, 1979.

———. *Philosophy and Social Hope.* New York: Penguin, 1999.

Rothberg, Donald. *The Engaged Spiritual Life: A Buddhist Approach to Transforming Ourselves and the World.* Boston: Beacon, 2006.

Saddhatissa, H. *Buddhist Ethics: Essence of Buddhism.* London: George Allen & Unwin, 1970.

Schweiker, William. *Theological Ethics and Global Dynamics: In the Time of Many Worlds.* London: Wiley-Blackwell, 2004.

Sellars, Wilfred. *Science, Perception, and Reality.* New York: Humanities Press, 1963.

Sharf, Robert. *Coming to Terms With Chinese Buddhism.* Honolulu: University of Hawaii Press, 2003.

Shklar, Judith N. *Ordinary Vices.* Cambridge, MA: Belknap Press, 1984.

Shusterman, Richard. *Practicing Philosophy.* New York: Routledge, 1997.

Siderits, Mark. *Personal Identity and Buddhist Philosophy: Empty Persons.* Aldershot, UK: Ashgate, 2003.

Siderits, Mark, Evan Thompson, and Dan Zahavi, Eds. *Self, No Self? Perspectives From Analytical, Phenomenological, and Indian Traditions.* Oxford: Oxford University Press, 2013.

Singer, Peter. *Writings on an Ethical Life.* New York: HarperCollins, 2000.

Slingerland, Edward. *Effortless Action: Wu Wei as Conceptual Metaphor and Spiritual Ideal in Early China.* New York: Oxford University Press, 2003.

Sloterdijk, Peter. *You Must Change Your Life.* Malden, MA: Polity Books, 2014.

Stout, Jeffrey. *Ethics After Babel.* Boston: Beacon Press, 1988.

————. *Democracy and Tradition*. Princeton, NJ: Princeton University Press, 2004.

Tatz, Mark. *Asaṅga's Chapter on Ethics, With the Commentary of Tsong-Kha-Pa: The Basic Path to Awakening, the Complete Boddhisattva*. Lewiston, PA: Edwin Mellen Press, 1986.

Taylor, Charles. *Sources of Self: The Making of the Modern Identity*. Cambridge, MA: Harvard University Press, 1985.

————. *The Ethics of Authenticity*. Cambridge, MA: Harvard University Press, 1991.

Thannissaro, Bhikkhu. *The Buddhist Monastic Code*. Valley Centre, CA: Metta Forest Monastery, 1994.

Thera, Nyanaponika. *The Heart of Buddhist Meditation*. New York: Samuel Weiser, 1973.

Thurman, Robert A.F. *The Holy Teaching of Vimalarkīrti: A Mahāyāna Scripture*. University Park: Pennsylvania State University Press, 1976.

Tillemans, Tom. *Scripture, Logic, Language: Essays on Dharmakirti and His Tibetan Successors*. Boston: Wisdom, 1999.

Trungpa, Chogyam. *Cutting Through Spiritual Materialism*. Boulder, CO: Shambhala, 2002.

Tworkov, Helen. *Zen in America: Five Teachers and the Search for American Buddhism*. Tokyo: Kodansha, 1994.

Victoria, Brian. *Zen War Stories*. London: Routledge/Curzon, 2003.

————. *Zen at War*. New York: Rowan & Littlefield, 2005.

Waldron, William. *The Buddhist Unconscious: The Alaya-vijnana in the Context of Indian Buddhist Thought*. London: Routledge/Curzon, 2003.

Wallace, B. Alan. *The Taboo of Subjectivity: Toward a New Science of Consciousness*. New York: Oxford University Press, 2000.

————. *Balancing the Mind: A Tibetan Buddhist Approach to Refining Attention*. Ithaca, NY: Snow Lion, 2005.

Walzer, Michael. *On Toleration*. New Haven, CT: Yale University Press, 1997.

Wayman, Alex. *Lion's Roar of Queen Srimala*. Delhi: Motilal Benarsidas, 1974.

Weinsheimer, Joel C. *Gadamer's Hermeneutics: A Reading of Truth of Method*. New Haven, CT: Yale University Press, 1985.

Weinstein, Stanley. *Buddhism Under the T'ang*. Cambridge, UK: Cambridge University Press, 1987.

White, James Boyd. *When Words Lose Their Meaning: Constitutions and Reconstitutions of Language, Character, and Community*. Chicago: University of Chicago Press, 1984.

Williams, Bernard. *Moral Luck*. Cambridge, UK: Cambridge University Press, 1981.

————. *Ethics and the Limits of Philosophy*. London: Collins, 1985.

Williams, Paul. *Mahāyāna Buddhism: The Doctrinal Foundations*. London: Routledge, 1989.

————. *Altruism and Reality: Studies in the Philosophy of the Bodhicaryāvatāra*. Richmond, UK: Curzon, 1998.

————. *The Reflexive Nature of Awareness: A Tibetan Madhyamaka Defense.* Abingdon, UK: Curzon, 1998.

Willis, Janice Dean. *On Knowing Reality: The Tattvārtha Chapter of Asaṅga's Bodhisattvabhūmi.* New York: Columbia University Press, 1979.

Winfield, Pamela D. *Icons and Iconoclasm in Japanese Buddhism: Kukai and Dogen on the Art of Enlightenment.* Oxford: Oxford University Press, 2013.

Wright, Dale S. *Philosophical Meditations on Zen Buddhism.* Cambridge, UK: Cambridge University Press, 1998.

————. *The Six Perfections: Buddhism and the Cultivation of Character.* New York: Oxford University Press, 2009.

Ziporyn, Brook. *Ironies of Oneness and Difference: Coherence in Early Chinese Thought.* Albany: State University of New York Press, 2013.